CARTOON
SUPERSTARS

S0-AII-445

By John Cawley and Jim Korkis

Pioneer Books, Inc.   Las Vegas, Nevada

Designed and Edited by Hal Schuster

Library of Congress Cataloging-in-Publication Data
John Cawley and Jim Korkis—
    The Encyclopedia of Cartoon Superstars

    1.   The Encyclopedia of Cartoon Superstars (animation)
I. Title

Published by Pioneer Books, Inc., 5715 N. Balsam Rd., Las Vegas, NV, 89130.

First Printing, 1990

Dedicated to our parents,
John & Kathryn Cawley / John & Barbara Korkis

ACKNOWLEDGEMENTS...

We did a large amount of new research for this volume. However, we would be remiss if we didn't mention a number of people who directly, or indirectly, assisted in this book. These names include those we talked to directly, and those who have assisted in a general way by paving the way for the animation historian.

Joe Adamson, APATOONS, Sarah Baisley (Hanna-Barbera), Mike Barrier, Jerry Beck, Kevin Bricklin (Harvey Entertainment), Cartoon Quarterly, Daws Butler, Bob Clampett, Will Friedwald, Get Animated!, Jack Hannah, Chuck Jones, Mike Kadlec (Hanna-Barbera), Mark Kausler (who has assisted with almost every major book ever done on the subject of animation), Jeff Lenburg, Dave Mruz, Bill Scott, Scott Shaw!, David R. Smith (The Walt Disney Archives), Karl Toerge, Sylvia Vartanian (Bagdasarian Productions), George S. Woolery, and sadly some we've most likely forgotten, but whose contributions were still appreciated.

JOHN CAWLEY has worked in the animation industry for over a decade doing development, writing and studio management for such studios as Film Roman, Warner Brothers, Don Bluth Productions, Hanna-Barbera, Celebrity Home Video, Sullivan Studios and Walt Disney Productions. His screen credits include AN AMERICAN TAIL and GARFIELD'S BABES AND BULLETS, an Emmy winner. His Get Animated! publications including GET ANIMATED!'S ANIMATION DIRECTORY (listing all studios and related industries), GET ANIMATED! UPDATE (a newsletter) and GET ANIMATED! REVIEW (a publication of reviews) are among the most respected in the animation industry. He also writes on animation for a variety of publications including ANIMATION MAGAZINE (of which he is a former editor), ANIMATOR (published in England), ANIMATO and CARTOON QUARTERLY.

JIM KORKIS has been a key animation historian for over a decade. He has interviewed some of animation's top talents including Bill Scott (voice artist, writer and co-creator of Rocky & Bullwinkle), Jack Hannah (Disney's key Donald Duck director and Oscar nominee) and Bob Clampett (creator of Warner's Tweety and TV's Beany & Cecil). His articles on animation history have appeared in just about every magazine dealing with animation including ANIMATION MAGAZINE, ANIMATO, APATOONS, ANIMANIA and CARTOON QUARTERLY. He has also written for the prestigious Carl Barks' Library from Another Rainbow. His "Animation Anecdotes" column, featuring odd historical bits, has been appearing regularly in various publications for years. As an educator he has been teaching theater, literature and cartooning for over a decade.

Jointly Korkis and Cawley have acted as editors for Gladstone Publications' CARTOON QUARTERLY, columnists for Fantagraphics' AMAZING HEROES and columnists for Krause Publications' COMIC BUYER'S GUIDE.

Cover design by Get Animated!
Layout by Cliff Voorhees
Background Painting by Rolando Oliva
Shadows by Mitch Schauer
Airbrush by Bonnie Callahan
Color Assist from Phyllis Craig

Publicity still from CASPER'S FIRST CHRISTMAS

© Hanna-Barbera

FOREWORD

When I was a kid and got hooked on cartoons, I went to my local library to learn more about them. There wasn't a lot to learn.

Walt Disney was the only person about whom anything had been written, and while I was grateful for that, I was frustrated in not being able to find more. Who made those Warner Bros. cartoons I watched every day? Why did Bugs Bunny look different in some of them? Who provided all those funny voices?

Most importantly, which one was Heckle and which one was Jeckle?

Eventually, as I grew older, I started doing my own research and wound up writing a book myself. In the years since then, an impressive number of animation volumes have emerged to fill in various gaps in our collective knowledge of the medium.

But now, John Cawley and Jim Korkis have decided it's time for the great cartoon stars to have a book of their own... a book that transcends linear animation history and focuses on the characters as much as their creators. I salute their efforts, and applaud their work. I just wish this book had been around when I was young.

One problem, though: I still can't tell Heckle from Jeckle.

—Leonard Maltin

Leonard Maltin is a respected film historian and author who appears on ENTERTAINMENT TONIGHT. His books include some of the key works about animation including OF MICE AND MAGIC and THE DISNEY FILMS

**Humphrey the Bear and Donald in BEARLY
ASLEEP.**

© *Walt Disney Productions*

FURTHER FOREWORD

Why did actors like Clark Gable or John Wayne become stars? It was not necessarily their great acting. Would someone who was just as good looking as Clark Gable become another Clark Gable? No, it was their personality that made the difference.

Good cartoon characters are like that as well. Donald Duck had a great personality and the audience had a lot of fun with him. However, Donald Duck was an accident. Just like in real life, someone comes on as an extra and then "BOOM!" Most of the popular animated characters were accidents. They just seemed to work for an audience.

But what elements does an audience want? On the surface, there seems to be nothing in common between a Donald Duck and a Bugs Bunny and a Woody Woodpecker. To me, it means that the audience likes more than just one type of personality. Some like a sweeter, gentler character. Others like a rougher one. The audience would sometimes surprise us about which characters they really accepted.

These characters took on a life of their own. Even though some of these characters haven't appeared in years, people are still interested in them.

I like cartoons. For me they bring back happy memories and I'm happy I was able to be a part of all of it.

—Jack Hannah

Jack Hannah is an animation legend. He spent almost 30 years at the Disney studio as animator, storyman and director. He is best remembered for his outstanding work on the Donald Duck cartoons.

CARTOON SUPERSTARS

INTRODUCTION

This is the first book to ever take a detailed look at such a wide cross-section of the most popular cartoon characters ever created. These are the Cartoon Superstars.

Over 75 years of animation history, dozens of animation studios and cartoon creators are discussed in these pages. New research provided never before published information that appears in each chapter.

Some readers may feel their favorite character has been slighted. No offense is meant by their exclusion from this volume. We chose characters who have become as much a part of modern culture as any live action celebrity. Their names and images are instantly recognizable. Many of these characters have survived the test of time while other, newer ones have only recently captured the hearts and minds of audiences. There are stars from a variety of studios. In the process, we have shown the many different ways Cartoon Superstars are created and how they develop over the years. These are not necessarily our favorite characters, but they are the stars that still make watching animated cartoons one of our favorite pasttimes. We hope this book will encourage you to relive some of your favorite moments of animation magic, and perhaps discover some new ones.

—John Cawley - Jim Korkis,
June 1990

A word about errors...

No book is ever 100% error free. Not even this one. The history of animation is a particularly tangled web. However, for this book, we went back to many of the original sources, and viewed many of the original cartoons. We discovered that previous books on animation had made mistakes in information, description, judgment, or typography. The facts and stories presented in this book may not always agree with other published accounts. Please don't misconstrue that as an error on our part. When we couldn't confirm information, we omitted it.

If you find any errors or have any comments on this book, please feel free to write us. An SASE (self-addressed-stamped-envelope) will guarantee some form of reply.

Write us at PO Box 1458, Burbank, California 91507

Superstar Summary

THE STARS: Alvin and the Chipmunks

YEAR OF DEBUT: 1958 ("The Chipmunk Song)/1961 (THE ALVIN SHOW)

STUDIO OF DEBUT: Format Films for Bagdasarian Films

SIGNATURE: "Aalll-vinnnn!"

KEY CREW BEHIND THE STARS: Ross Bagdasarian, Sr (creator/voices)

CAREER HIGH: THE ALVIN SHOW (1961) — The recording stars become prime time animated TV stars.

lvin and the Chipmunks are among the few animated characters to begin their long career as recording stars. The Chipmunk music albums of the Fifties were so popular that by the time the Chipmunks reached animation in the Sixties, they were already well loved and known characters.

It was their transfer to animation, though, that established distinctive personalities and appearances for the characters that are still loved today. Alvin was always the star of the group. Simon was the tallest, and smartest. Theodore was the short, fat, good natured one. David Seville, a human, was their guardian and manager. However, they have had two different looks: the Sixties Chipmunks and the Eighties Chipmunks.

As mentioned, Alvin was always the lead singer of the group. He wore a long red turtleneck sweater that reached all the way down to his shoes. The sweater sported a huge yellow letter "A" that made him stand out from his two brothers. He wore a red baseball cap. The huge letter and the bright red attire were a physical representation of Alvin's egotism and self-centeredness. Even in the Chipmunks debut, "The Chipmunk Song," Alvin's desires override all other concerns.

The mischievous Alvin really never meant any harm by his actions. Clever and inventive, he was also aggressive and fool hardy. More so than his brothers, he was girl crazy. Alvin played the harmonica, one of his prize possessions, quite well. More stubborn than disobedient, he obviously loved and respected his surrogate father, David Seville. However, that never prevented him from doing what he wanted when he wanted.

Simon was usually attired in a long blue turtleneck sweater that reached his shoes. He wore large round rimmed glasses and was the smartest of the chipmunks when it came to factual information. Although he didn't have the cleverness of Alvin, he got the best grades, knew the right answers and was the most studious. He offered the voice of reason but was continually overpowered by the outgoing Alvin.

Theodore usually distinguishes himself from his brothers by wearing a long green turtleneck sweater that reaches his feet. Especially in the beginning, Theodore loved eating. In today's more health conscious society, that aspect has been downplayed. He was the least bright of the Chipmunks. It seemed to take him longer to grasp ideas and he was very easily led by Alvin. He was shy and hid from the spotlight. One of his distinctive qualities was his frequent giggle, either through embarrassment or as an unselfconscious reaction to an outside event. Like many simple characters, he had a very good heart and seemed to be especially in tune with nature and animals.

The Sixties Chipmunks seemed to be about elementary school age. David Seville was their guardian and manager. The Eighties Chipmunks seem to be in the last year or so of Junior High and David Seville is now identified as their father. The Chipmunks even use the Seville last name.

David Seville was a caricature of Bagdasarian himself and, in fact, it was Bagdasarian's stage name. Unlike Bagdasarian, Seville was a bachelor and never seemed concerned about getting married. However, like Bagdasarian, Seville was a reasonably successful songwriter with three children. Seville was a gentle character and definitely more patient than most. He cared about music and he cared about the Chipmunks. He dressed simply, often in just a short sleeve white shirt with black pants. In the Sixties, he lived in a fairly average suburban house. The Eighties series has upgraded his standard of living.

The original animated trio.

© *Ross Bagdasarian*

WITCH DOCTORS AND CHIPMUNKS

Ross Bagdasarian was a first generation Armenian-American. He came from Fresno, California where his family was associated with the wine business. He became a songwriter and wrote the popular song "Come On-a My House" which was a hit for singer Rosemary Clooney.

By 1956, he had adopted the stage name David Seville. However, in late 1957, the 39 year old Bagdasarian and his family, which now included three children, were almost broke. Bagdasarian used their last $190 to buy a tape recorder. He hoped to use the device to come up with a new song hit.

One day, while fooling around with the recorder, he sang into the machine while it was running at half speed, and played it back at full speed. The high, funny sounding voice that resulted was an inspiration. Bagdasarian composed a song entitled "The Witch Doctor."

In the song, David Seville asks his friend the Witch Doctor for advice on how to win his true love. The Witch Doctor "told him what to say" and "told him what to do" using nonsense words. That advice not only worked for the narrator of the song, but it catapulted the record to a hit, selling 1.5 million copies. Bagdasarian provided the voices for Seville and the pygmy Witch Doctor by using the speeded up voice gimmick for the native Doctor.

Bagdasarian tried to make lightning strike twice by using the same "speeded up" voice in another song, "The Bird on My Head." This time it was a bird who had the high funny voice but the record buying audience wasn't impressed. He then developed a technique where he could record three speeded up voices and play them back at the same time.

HERE COME THE CHIPMUNKS

He debated about the type of animals to make these voices and seriously considered butterflies. Supposedly, while driving in Yosemite National Park, Bagdasarian was impressed by the behavior of a chipmunk in the road that showed an audacious spirit. In actuality, he played the voices for his three children and they labeled the sound as chipmunks. It has been suggested that they may have been influenced by Disney's Chip 'n' Dale, who also spoke in high, speeded up voices.

As an inside joke, Bagdasarian named the Chipmunks after three executives at Liberty records. Alvin was for Al Bennett, Liberty Records, president. Simon was for Si Waronker, vice-chairman of the label. Theodore was for Ted Keep, Liberty's chief recording engineer. Bagdasarian performed all the voices himself.

He recorded "The Chipmunk Song" in 1958. Bennett was unimpressed but released the song anyway. In the first seven weeks, they sold 4.5 million records! For a time, it was the fastest selling record in history. "The Chipmunk Song," perhaps best known to listeners as "Christmas Don't Be Late," featured a selfish Alvin who kept insisting that he wanted a Hula Hoop, a popular toy of the time. David Seville's irritation with Alvin was often expressed by stretching out the sound of Alvin's name. The "Aaalllvvinnn!" gimmick actually came from how Bagdasarian would yell at his son, Adam, when the young boy was making too much noise.

Publicity art from the first season of the ALVIN AND THE CHIPMUNKS Saturday morning series. Note the early design of the Chipettes.

© Ross Bagdasarian

The Chipmunks had another popular hit the next year with "Alvin's Harmonica" in 1959. Once again the stubborn little Chipmunk kept interrupting the song. This time the reason was that he wanted to play his harmonica.

The first Chipmunk long playing album was SING ALONG WITH THE CHIPMUNKS (later reissued as LET'S ALL SING WITH THE CHIPMUNKS). It featured the two previous hits as well as the Chipmunks singing their versions of a number of popular songs. There was the "Old MacDonald Cha Cha Cha" and a rock and roll version of "Whistle While You Work." The album cover showed The Chipmunks drawn to look like actual chipmunks although they wore sport coats. Alvin was already sporting an "A" on his coat.

Chipmunk songs were hugely popular and eventually the Chipmunks released 11 albums and won five Grammy Awards. The Chipmunks racked up several gold and platinum records for high sales. They were so much in demand that Bagdasarian got together with Bob Clampett and created hand puppets of the three characters so that they could perform their musical hits on shows such as THE ED SULLIVAN SHOW. Clampett, a former Warner Brothers director, had achieved success with his own hand puppets of Beany and Cecil.

THE CHIPMUNKS TOON UP!

Bagdasarian knew he could further broaden the Chipmunk success story if could get them into animation. However, he had no desire to start his own studio. He contacted Format Films. Format Films was created in 1959 when Herb Klynn and Jules Engel left UPA taking with them dozens of talented people. So even though they were a new studio, they had experience in TV and limited animation.

Working with the staff, Bagdasarian redesigned the Chipmunks into the appearance that is known today. THE ALVIN SHOW premiered October 4, 1961 in a prime time evening slot on CBS. Each show had four segments. The first was a fairly standard cartoon adventure, usually a domestic situation. Two other segments were built around songs that the Chipmunks sang in sort of an early music video format where a storyline framed the song. The third segment featured an inventor known as Clyde Crashcup who invented things that already existed like the wheel and the bathtub.

THE ALVIN SHOW would be well received by parent watch dog groups today. It was a show that was generally non-violent and often educational. When David Seville and the Chipmunks visited foreign countries, there was always accurate information provided about cultural aspects of the country. Either Seville or Simon was the source for these informational insights.

Many of the regular segments emphasized that these were kids and that troubles and adventures can occur in their own backyard. One time the Chipmunks encounter a friendly eagle who cannot fly. They teach him by strapping cymbals to his wings and telling him to clash them together. Another time, they battle a neighbor's dog who is intent on destroying Dave's garden. A common storyline, used no less than three times, has Alvin planning to leave home.

The Chipmunks were also travelers. Stories found them visiting a number of countries including Italy and Spain. They also went camping, took cruises and visited a haunted house.

The musical segments not only featured songs that Bagdasarian wrote but favorites like "Home on the Range" and "While Strolling Through the Park." Only one season of shows was made and after that first season, the series was moved to Saturday morning where it was continually rerun until 1965. Bagdasarian never considered a Chipmunk feature and this was before the time when animated specials flooded the airwaves.

The last Chipmunk album was released in 1967. Bagdasarian retired and devoted more time to his real estate holdings and his vineyards. The popularity of the Chipmunks continued to decline with no new material being released. Bagdasarian died in 1972 and most people felt that was the end of the Chipmunks.

A NEW GENERATION

In 1977, one of Bagdasarian's sons, Ross Jr., took over the family business and decided to revive the Chipmunks. He began working with Janice Karman, who later became his wife, developing new material for Alvin, Simon and Theodore. He was genuinely surprised to find there wasn't much interest in the Chipmunks. Finally they found a receptive audience in Fred Silverman who agreed to rerun THE ALVIN SHOW for the Fall 1979 season on NBC Saturday morning. The show was well received.

Ironically, considering their musical origins, it was a stunt by a radio disc jockey that revived strong interest in the Chipmunks. The DJ took a new wave record, boosted the speed, and played in on the air as an example of "Chipmunk Punk." The gimmick struck a chord with listeners and radio shows and record shops were flooded with requests for this "new album" which really didn't exist.

A small record distributor contacted Ross Jr and the result was the release in June 1980 of the first new Chipmunk album since 1967, CHIPMUNK PUNK. It was a

"I'm still hounded by fans wherever I go, swamped by the paparazzi, unable to go anywhere without being recognized, I've got no private life."
— Alvin in THE CHIPMUNK ADVENTURE presskit.

"My dad created the characters that captured the fancy of the public. We've tried to continue that theme of fun and love that children and parents seem to respond to."
— Ross Bagdasarian, Jr.

15

collection of top tunes "sung" by the Chipmunks. The new voices were supplied by Ross, Jr. and wife Janice. The album went gold by August 1980. By April 1981 it went platinum. It received the National Association of Recording Merchandisers' award for best selling children's album. RCA signed the Chipmunks to an exclusive recording contract. The next album, URBAN CHIPMUNK, released the Summer of 1981, also went platinum. More albums followed including A CHIPMUNK CHRISTMAS and CHIPMUNK ROCK.

Following the new-found success of the Chipmunks, the Bagdasarians were able to convince NBC to produce a prime time animated special starring the trio. December 14, 1981, saw the return of the Chipmunks to TV in A CHIPMUNK CHRISTMAS. The special was a pleasant Christmas story about Alvin giving his harmonica to a seriously ill child, only to have to replace it in time for a big holiday show.

This special featured a new design for the Chipmunks. Chuck Jones was involved in the early stages of production and helped soften the look of the Chipmunks. Also softened were their personalities. The special was directed by Warner's veteran Phil Monroe. Writers Bagdasarian, Karman, Hal Mason (and Jones), aged the Chipmunks slightly, making them less frantic and childish. Even the music had slightly changed. In the Sixties, the Chipmunks did "hip" rock and roll versions of songs. For the Eighties, the Chipmunks took modern rock songs and made "kiddie" versions of them.

The special was successful and there was discussion about doing an animated special using music from the URBAN CHIPMUNK album to be titled URBAN CHIPMUNK or THE CHIPMUNKS AT OPRYLAND. This special was never made.

"(My dad) liked the sound that he'd come up with in ("The Witch Doctor") and decided to make characters. He didn't know whether to make them into hippos or elephants or beetles or what."

— Ross Bagdasarian, Jr.

L.A. Mayor Tom Bradley officially declared October 25, 1982 as "Chipmunk Day" in honor of Alvin, Simon and Theodore and the release of their new album, CHIPMUNKS GO HOLLYWOOD. There was even a "paw print" in cement ceremony at the parking lot of Tower Records using costumed characters. December 1982 saw the repeat of their Christmas special.

SATURDAY MORNING FEVER

In 1983, the Chipmunks returned to Saturday morning TV in a brand new show for NBC. This time, Ross Jr. contracted with Ruby-Spears to provide the animation. Former Hanna-Barbera writers, Joe Ruby and Ken Spears, who were instrumental in the development of Scooby-Doo, had formed their own studio which was responsible for Saturday morning shows including FANGFACE, DRAGON'S LAIR and SUPERMAN.

The Chipmunks' designs were further softened into rounder, cuter images. The Chipmunks also become more clothes-conscious, wearing a number of costumes. Also, the Chipettes, female mirror images of the Chipmunks, were introduced to add sexual equality to the show. Janice Karman claims she conceived of the females because as a young girl, when she watched the original series, she thought there should have been girl Chipmunks. The Chipettes were christened Brittany, Jeanette and Elenore. The new Chipmunks were, once again, an immediate hit and became one of the top rated series on Saturday morning.

The new series sometimes featured one story during the half hour and sometimes two different stories. There were no separate music videos, as in the first series, but the new Chipmunks used plenty of music. At the drop of a hat the Chipmunks, the Chipettes or all six could break into an abbreviated version of some new or classic rock song. There were Chipmunk versions of such tunes as Chuck Berry's "Surfin' USA," Michael Jackson's "Beat It," and Billy Joel's "Uptown Girl." Bagdasarian and Karman also wrote new songs for the show, including the theme song, "We're the Chipmunks."

1984 saw the release of another Chipmunk album, this time featuring songs sung on the series. These were the complete renditions of the songs, not the abbreviated versions heard on the show. That February also saw the Chipmunks second prime time special, A VALENTINE SPECIAL (first broadcast as I LOVE THE CHIPMUNKS, VALENTINE SPECIAL). The story featured an upcoming dance and the Chipmunks' attempts to get the Chipettes to join them. Naturally, Alvin is the exception and doesn't want to invite anyone. His brothers put a tape recorder under Alvin's pillow and talk up his "Don Juan" personality. This causes Alvin to become a sleep walker who disguises himself as Captain Chipmunk. Alvin develops an identity crisis, but it all works out in the end. Captain Chipmunk later became a recurring character on the Saturday morning show.

Around a year later, in April of 1985, another prime time special debuted, A CHIPMUNK REUNION. This special dealt with where the Chipmunks came from. It was actually a follow-up to one of the Saturday morning episodes ("The Chipmunk Story") that showed how David Seville found the Chipmunks abandoned on his doorstep and adopted them. In the special, the Chipmunks are able to discover their natural mother. However, they return to David, who is the only family they've known. (Though they do say they'll visit their natural mother from time to time.) *Daily Variety* found the special to be a "surprisingly thoughtful and touching half-hour."

The Chipmunks Saturday morning show continued to be one of NBC's strongest shows, always rating in the top ten. In 1987, Alvin was chosen to host the prime time preview of the new Saturday morning series. ALVIN GOES BACK TO SCHOOL (9/12/86) featured a costumed figure of Alvin taking over a school and attempting to "turn every morning into Saturday morning."

THE CHIPMUNKS THEATRICAL ADVENTURE

One of the biggest years for the Chipmunks was 1987 when THE CHIPMUNK ADVENTURE debuted in theaters across the country on May 22nd. THE CHIPMUNK ADVENTURE was written by Janice Karman and Ross Bagdasarian Jr. It was also directed by Karman. The film was backed with a $17 million campaign that included tie-ins with Burger King, K-Mart and General Mills.

ALVIN

"(My dad) came up with the idea of the Chipmunks when he was driving in Yosemite and this chipmunk almost dared him and his huge car to drive past."

— Ross Bagdasarian, Jr.

Promotional art from the Eighties Chipmunks series.

© Ross Bagdasarian

The story was loosely based on Jules Verne's Around the World in 80 days. In it, a couple offer to pay for a race around the world between the Chipmunks and the Chipettes. As proof of their journey, the youngsters are to leave dolls at each stop. What the Chipmunks don't know is that the dolls contain stolen diamonds. From the seas of Bermuda to the snow capped Alps, the travelers face all kinds of perils and ultimately have a showdown with the crooks, the pair who originally backed the race.

Throughout the film, the Chipmunks and Chipettes break into song. The songs were mostly new, but a few old favorites, like Ross Bagdasarian Sr.'s "Come On-a My House," were heard. A soundtrack album was released by Buena Vista (Disney).

In 1988 another change came to the Chipmunks. DIC began supplying the animation for the series. DIC is one of the largest suppliers of TV animation. Their productions include THE REAL GHOSTBUSTERS and INSPECTOR GADGET. Meanwhile, the Ruby Spears shows were put into syndication in 1988 where they proved as popular as ever.

In 1989 the new series began appearing on home video. The Chipmunks were part of the cast of CARTOON ALL STARS TO THE RESCUE (1990), the famous substance abuse cautionary animated special that was simulcast on all three networks on Saturday morning.

NBC planned a prime time live action/animated special "Salute to Five Decades with the Chipmunks" for November 1990 release which would celebrate everyone from Elvis and the Beatles to Michael Jackson. Also a new Chipmunk album, already released in Canada and Australia, will be released in the U.S. Entitled BORN TO ROCK. It features the Chipmunks singing the music of New Kids on the Block, Paula Abdul and Bruce Springsteen.

THE CHIPMUNKS have lasted seven seasons on Saturday morning and have been renewed for an eighth. The eighth season, which begins in the Fall of 1990 will introduce a new format for the show: ALVIN GOES TO THE MOVIES. It will feature parodies of blockbuster films such as BATMAN, BACK TO THE FUTURE and STAR TREK.

"I want to play my harmonica!"
— Alvin

During the approximately 30 years the Chipmunks have been around, they have won five Grammys (out of 15 nominations) and released 11 gold and platinum albums. Their album sales have totaled over $35 million and merchandise sales near the $300 million mark.

SUPPORTING CAST

Not surprisingly, the most frequent recurring characters were female.

In the original series, a frequent visitor was Daisy Belle. Daisy was a blonde, human girl about the same age as the Chipmunks. She was fond of David and the Chipmunks, but had a crush on Alvin. Unfortunately, this was unrequited love because Alvin regarded her as merely a friend. Alvin seemed to be more interested in older women, especially teenage girls. Also, Daisy and Alvin were at an awkward age and found expressing feelings difficult. June Foray provided the voice for Daisy. (June Foray supplied voices for most major animation studios and is perhaps best remembered as the voice of Rocky, the flying squirrel.)

Other regulars in the early series were Sam Valiant, "Private Nose," a detective. Sam not only was hired by Dave on occasion, but the group bumped into him frequently. Mrs. Frumpington was a self claimed cultural leader who thought Rock and Roll should be banned. Stanley the eagle popped up in several episodes.

As noted, in the new series, the Chipmunks are matched with three girls known as the Chipettes. The female chipmunks are the mirror image of the Chipmunks. Brittany is as vain and self-concerned as Alvin. Jeanette also wears glasses like Simon and is the most reserved and studious Chipette. Eleanor is plump and simple minded like Theodore. According to one episode, the Chipettes came from Australia. In Australia, they were the "pets" and friends of a little orphan girl named Olivia. Olivia lived at Miss Grudge's Orphanage and Miss Grudge desperately wanted to have a successful singing group so she kidnapped the Chipettes right before Olivia was adopted. Fortunately, the Chipettes escaped and made their way to the U.S. where after a variety of odd jobs they got to demonstrate their singing prowess. As successful singers, they got to meet the Chipmunks. There is an underlying rivalry between the two groups although more often than not they work together to solve problems.

OTHER MEDIA

Sixties Chipmunk toys ranged from puppets and dolls to bath toys filled with "Soaky" bubble bath. There was a game called "The Big Record." The Barris Company built a custom car called "Alvin's Acorn" which was shaped like an acorn and had a little TV set and stereo.

Dell Publishing released over two dozen issues of an Alvin comic book between 1962 and 1973, with a special ALVIN FOR PRESIDENT issue in 1964.

The Eighties Chipmunks were especially popular on school related items such as lunchboxes, notebooks, calendars, and so on. That area is targeted for further expansion in 1990 when Target Stores, nationwide, plan to showcase over 250 exclusive Chipmunk products. These items range from sportswear and footwear to linens and backpacks. The Chipmunks have also signed a marketing agreement with Del Monte food products. Negotiations are in progress for a Fast Food outlet promotion in 1991.

In any discussion of other media featuring the Chipmunks, it is necessary to mention the almost two dozen albums recorded by the singing group. Those albums include LET'S ALL SING WITH THE CHIPMUNKS, AROUND THE WORLD WITH THE CHIPMUNKS, THE CHIPMUNKS SING WITH CHILDREN, THE CHIPMUNKS SING THE BEATLES, THE CHIPMUNK SONGBOOK, CHIPMUNK PUNK, CHRISTMAS WITH THE CHIPMUNKS and CHIPMUNKS A GO GO.

Chipmunk merchandise.

© Ross Bagdasarian

SUPERSTAR QUALITY

Alvin and his musical menagerie are one of the few animated entries to experience a successful revival after years of non-work. In fact, the Chipmunks have had several careers, as recording stars, prime time animation series stars, TV special stars and Saturday morning stars. There is something intrinsically appealing about this singing family and it seems that Chipmunk music is once again here to stay.

BETTY BOOP

SELECTED SHORT SUBJECTS: Bamboo Isle, Betty Boop's Rise to Fame, Minnie the Moocher, The Old Man of the Mountain, Snow White

Superstar Summary

THE STAR: Betty Boop

YEAR OF DEBUT: 1930 (DIZZY DISHES)

STUDIO OF DEBUT: Fleischer

SIGNATURE: "Boop-boop-a-doop"

KEY CREW BEHIND THE STAR: Dave Fleischer (director), Grim Natwick (animator), Mae Questel (voice)

CAREER HIGH: SNOW WHITE (1933): The best known of the series of cartoons featuring musician Cab Calloway. This short is filled with nightmarish imagery.

Betty Boop is the sole female cartoon superstar. The major factor that seems to have elevated Betty to this status was sex. Almost half a century after her career in theatrical shorts officially ended, she is still a major merchandised character.

While there are other memorable female characters who appeared in the short cartoons, they were usually supporting characters. Their roles were often as wives, girlfriends, princesses, witches or mothers. Even notable exceptions like Little Audrey or She-ra weren't able to match Betty's longevity or high recognition factor.

With revealing outfits, her suggestive movements and her little girlish voice, Betty might be considered a classic tease. Her actions seemed to constantly promise unbelievable joy but in actuality she never delivered on that promise. Perhaps that obliviousness to her own sexiness added to her appeal. In many ways, she was highly moral almost to the point of prudishness. She was genuinely shocked and offended when some lecherous boss wanted to take her "boop-boop-a-doop" away.

Her trademark phrase, "boop-boop-a-doop" seemed to be a synonym for sex. That was certainly the assumption since she was a parody of the wild "flapper" girls of the period. The Flappers of the Twenties were independent young women who were pushing the boundaries of the traditional roles of women especially in the areas of conduct, dress and sexual freedom. Betty may be the last living example of those carefree and careless women.

During a copyright infringement suit in 1934, a judge offered the following description of Betty: "There is the broad baby face, the large round flirting eyes, the low placed pouting mouth, the small nose, the imperceptible chin, and the mature bosom. It was a unique combination of infancy and maturity, innocence and sophistication."

It was that image as a "girl-woman," caught in dark dreamlike adventures, that made Betty's reputation. In later years, public morality transformed her into an almost matronly homebody. This clean image is almost totally forgotten by today's audiences and merchandisers.

In the beginning, Betty was attired in a short and low cut black mini-dress that revealed one gartered leg. Her black hair was a host of spit curls framing a grotesquely butt-shaped face that hid any suggestion of a neck. Her huge round eyes contrasted with her minuscule nose and mouth. Hoop earrings and often hoop bracelets helped complete the picture.

Perhaps one of the reasons she did not survive domestication, like many other characters, was that generally she had no personality. Obviously, she was a good and nice person, always concerned about others. She got scared but loved to sing and dance. However, she only ran the emotional gamut from A to B and even that was often difficult for her. The emotional shadings of other characters, including Fleischer's version of Popeye, seemed unavailable to her because it would detract from the "pretty girl object" image.

There were suggestions in some of the early cartoons that Betty was a Jewish American Princess. This wouldn't be difficult to imagine especially considering some of the people that worked on her cartoons. A studio blurb from the time suggested she was 16 years old, but certainly a very mature 16.

It is the Lolita-like Flapper that is best remembered and loved by audiences. Her later years produced some pleasant but generally unexciting cartoon efforts that perhaps deserve to be forgotten.

THE BIRTH OF BETTY

The Fleischer Studios were a major producer of silent cartoons and even experimented with early sound films. In 1929, they began a new series called "Talkartoons." It was determined that a strong continuing character would help sell this series. They took one of their silent cartoon dog characters and with some redesigning christened the anthropormophic pup "Bimbo." This ill-proportioned, sometimes goofy looking character kept changing appearance and coloring in the early cartoons. He bears a slight resemblance to the official cute Bimbo version familiar to modern audiences.

It was then decided to add a love interest to the series. In the sixth "Talkartoon," DIZZY DISHES (1930), Bimbo is having trouble being a waiter. He is distracted by the restaurant's entertainment provided by a chubby female dog singer. She is unnamed in this cartoon, but there can be little doubt that this character, who was much more girl than dog, was the beginning of Betty. She had the famous spit curls and the short tight black dress that showed the tops of her rolled stockings. However, instead of the famous earrings, she had long floppy ears. Instead of the little upturned nose, she had a black spot to suggest a dog's nose.

Betty was designed by Grim Natwick, a legendary animator who was later responsible for bringing Disney's Snow White princess to life. Natwick had a strong art background. He was noted for his ability to animate a realistic human figure, while others

Early studio art as Betty comes "out of the inkwell." Note panties.

were still concentrating on the rubber hose arms and legs of standard cartoon characters.

In interviews, Natwick has remarked that the original inspiration for Betty Boop was a song sheet he saw of a performer named Helen Kane. Kane had the same spit curls and had added the phrase "boop-boop-a-doop" to the popular song "I Want To Be Loved By You." Later, Kane sued the Fleischer studio claiming that Betty Boop had damaged her singing career. The Fleischers won by proving that Kane had not been the first performer to "boop-boop-a-doop" although she was certainly the most prominent. Despite the court's decision, Betty Boop's debt to Kane is fairly obvious.

The Betty character went through a process of development. In the early cartoons, she was identified as Nancy Lee or Nan McGrew. Whatever she was called, she began being featured more prominently in the "Talkartoons" series and was becoming more humanized. The sexual suggestiveness was clearly established as a natural part of the character and her virtue was soon threatened by lechers.

One of the Fleischer's other cartoon series, "Screen Song Cartoons," encouraged the audience to sing along as a bouncing ball hit illustrated lyrics. One installment, BETTY COED (1931) was the first time the name "Betty" was used in connection with this girl character. However, it would take almost another six months before she became fully humanized in the "Talkartoon" ANY RAGS (1932). Her dog ears finally became earrings. As Betty had become more human, Bimbo had developed into the familiar short, round, black dog who behaved like a human and was generally considered Betty's boyfriend.

Early studio art. Note long earings, formerly dog ears.

© King Features

BETTY-
BOOP

A *Paramount* STAR
CREATED BY
FLEISCHER STUDIOS

Several actresses supplied the voice for the early Betty. In 1931, Max Fleischer hired a teenager who had recently won a Helen Kane look-alike contest to do the voice of Betty. Mae Questel was that lucky teen and she continued doing the voice until the series ended in 1939. She even supplied Betty's voice in a short lived radio series, BETTY BOOP FABLES. Along with Betty, she also supplied the voices for Olive Oyl, Little Audrey and Casper the Friendly Ghost. She was more recently seen as the mother in Woody Allen's segment of the feature film NEW YORK STORIES (1989).

One of the last Betty "Talkartoons" was CRAZY TOWN (1932). In it Betty and Bimbo, sitting on top of a trolley car, journey to Crazy Town. It's a town where fish swim in the air and birds fly underwater. Betty visits a beauty parlor where females can literally get a brand new head to replace their own and one patron wants Betty's head! This film was typical of the dark-toned humor and dreamlike atmosphere of the early Boop cartoons.

BETTY ON HER OWN

Betty Boop got her own series in August 1932 with STOPPING THE SHOW. Betty performs on stage and does impersonations of Fanny Brice (as an Indian princess with a goose headdress), Maurice Chevalier (when Betty changes into a man's suit on stage, it's revealed she wears a bra under her dress) and Jimmy Durante. Her performance is quite literally show stopping.

Also in 1932, Betty did an unforgettable topless hula number in BETTY BOOP'S BAMBOO ISLE. Her charms are barely hidden by a grass skirt and a well placed flowered lei. Most of the early Bettys had some incident of her standing in front of a light. This was so her silhouette could be seen through her now see-through dress. Other shorts offered a flash of underwear or some suggestive wiggle that would have given even Mae West pause.

Most of Betty's cartoons were just a long string of loosely connected gags. When the time limit for the cartoon ran out, the cartoons stopped, leaving many situations unresolved. An example of this pattern is BETTY BOOP'S CRAZY INVENTIONS (1933). Betty, along with Bimbo and Ko-Ko the Clown, host a big invention show. There are marvels including the Spot Remover Machine, which removes a spot from a handkerchief by cutting a hole around the offending stain. A Self-Threader Sewing Machine goes out of control and sews up the tent where the show is being held. It must still be stitching up the countryside since it is never stopped at the end of the cartoon.

Another key element to the Boop cartoons was their music. Unlike the sweeter, orchestral music found in the Disney and Warners cartoons, Fleischer leaned towards a stronger beat. Jazz played a major part in many of Betty's best vehicles. She had such hot acts as Cab Calloway (MINNIE THE MOOCHER, SNOW WHITE and others) and Louis Armstrong (I'LL BE GLAD WHEN YOU'RE DEAD YOU RASCAL YOU).

One of the most popular Betty cartoons was released in 1934. BETTY IN BLUNDERLAND has Betty putting together an "Alice in Wonderland" puzzle. Out of the puzzle pops the White Rabbit, who Betty follows through a mirror into Lewis Carroll's Wonderland. When she is captured by the Jabberwocky, the famous storybook characters try to rescue her and end up falling back into her puzzle. This was one of the last cartoons where Betty would be able to flash her panties at the audience.

In 1934, the Production Code took effect. Concerned citizens were outraged by the low moral behavior and sexual suggestiveness in movies. Even cartoons could not escape their wrath. (Betty's 1934 RED HOT MAMA was rejected by the British Board of Censors and was not allowed to be screened in England.)

"Betty Boop was really unique in that, unlike other cartoon characters, she didn't really change much physically."

— Bernie Wolf,
animator of the orginal Betty Boop
Fleischer shorts.

A NEW BETTY

Betty was transformed. Yards of fabric were added to the top and bottom of her dress. Her wild animal friends disappeared as did the surreal stories. Her innocent sexuality was replaced with an attitude appropriate to a conservative young homemaker, complete with apron. What so many had failed to do previously finally occurred. They took her "boop-boop-a-doop" away. To domesticate her further, they gave her a cute puppy (Pudgy), a human boyfriend, a grandfather and other family members.

"We have nothing else to do so let's go crazy."

— Betty & Bimbo
in CRAZY TOWN (1932)

In STOP THAT NOISE (1935) she flees the city noise outside her apartment window for the supposed quiet of the country. In SWAT THE FLY (1935) Betty is in her kitchen preparing to bake when she and Pudgy must do battle with a bothersome fly. These domestic situation comedy plots could have been handled by any of a number of cartoon characters since they didn't feature the elements that had made Betty unique.

BETTY BOOP AND GRAMPY (1935) introduced Grampy, supposedly Betty's grandfather, who was "so full of pep" that he outdanced his party guests, including Betty. Thanks to his thinking cap, a graduation mortar board with a light bulb on top, he was able to devise a vast array of Rube Goldberg like inventions. He used this ability to help out Betty many times such as cleaning up her house after a party in HOUSE CLEANING BLUES (1937) or giving Irving, the cruel practical joker, a taste of his own medicine in THE IMPRACTICAL JOKER (1937).

An attempt was made to use Betty's cartoons to spin off comic strip characters into animated series. It had proven quite successful with Popeye. He first appeared in animation dancing the hula with Betty in POPEYE THE SAILOR (1933), a Betty Boop cartoon.

Betty was teamed with Carl Anderson's Henry, Jimmy Swinnerton's Little Jimmy and Otto Soglow's The Little King. Neither Henry nor the Little King spoke in their own comic strips which amused audiences with the pantomimed antics. Fleischer saw fit to give these characters inappropriate voices; Henry got an odd mumbling voice while the Little King got stuck with an effeminate whistling lisp.

BETTY BOOP WITH HENRY THE FUNNIEST LIVING AMERICAN (1935) had Henry helping out pet shop owner Betty because he wanted to buy Pudgy, the dog. BETTY BOOP AND LITTLE JIMMY (1936) has Betty trapped in an out-of-control exercise machine and sending Little Jimmy to find an electrician. BETTY BOOP AND THE LITTLE KING (1936) has the Little King sneaking away from a special performance in his honor to go to a vaudeville house to see Betty's horse riding act.

None of these cartoons had that raw energy that propelled Popeye to stardom. Betty suffered through the next few years with a new supporting cast. Freddie, an effeminate but muscular young man, was supposedly her boyfriend and he was cast in the role of lifeguard or soldier. Billy Boop, Betty's kid brother showed up to get into cute scrapes (BABY BE GOOD/1935). Certainly these characters couldn't compete with the earlier oddball supporting cast like the rough and tumble Gus Gorilla.

One of the last Betty cartoons was MUSICAL MOUNTAINEERS (1939) where Betty runs out of gas and a group of grotesque looking hillbillies help her out with some moonshine. Betty's dancing in this cartoon bears absolutely no resemblance to her sensual wiggling in pre-1934 efforts.

The last official Betty Boop cartoon, YIP YIP YIPPY, was released August 1939. Betty doesn't even appear in the story. There were many reasons for Fleischer ending the series. Besides the waning public interest in the new Betty and the difficulty in coming up with interesting stories, the Fleischers moved their studio to Florida and needed all available manpower to concentrate their efforts on their first feature cartoon, GULLIVER'S TRAVELS (1939). Mae Questel's refusal to relocate to Florida also contributed to the decision. Soon afterwards, Paramount took control of the Fleischer studio and saw no reason to revive the character.

> "I actually lived the part of Betty Boop: walked, talked and everything!"
>
> — Mae Questel

BETTY COMES TO TV

When the pre-1948 Paramount cartoons were sold to TV in the late Fifties, the Betty Boop cartoons were syndicated on local stations. These shorts met the fate of most black and white cartoons in the late Sixties and began to disappear from the small screen. However, with almost no notice, Betty was becoming a hot property again.

The late Sixties was a time of dissidence throughout the U.S. Between the "love generation," pot, "hippies" and the Vietnam war, a large anti-establishment mentality pervaded the nation's youth. The new celebrities were classic stars who disrupted society: W.C. Fields, The Marx Brothers and "sexy" Betty Boop. Other attractions were films that were "enhanced" when one was "high:" Disney's FANTASIA, 2001 and, again, "weird" Betty Boop. She was covered in a number of free thinking publications of the time, including *Rolling Stone*.

The increased attention was noticed by National Telefilm Associates (NTA) who had acquired the rights to the cartoons. Sensing a new market, they had the original black and white shorts "colorized" for TV. This primitive process involved shipping the cartoons to Korea where they were traced frame by frame and the tracings hand painted in color.

Noted film critic, Leonard Maltin found the new cartoons questionable. He stated at the time of their release that "Superficially, the color is quite good, with more to offer than many newly made TV cartoons. But somehow, in the process of transference, a certain amount of detail is lost —detail that would go unnoticed by the average TV-viewing youngster, and probably by most viewers, period."

In the Korean process, many drawings were skipped and backgrounds were simplified. The final results bore little relation to the classic Fleischer styling. Even worse was the bizarre selection of colors which resulted in such oddities as a bright purple wolf in DIZZY RED RIDING HOOD (1931).

The shorts were released under the title of THE BETTY BOOP SHOW. Each half hour contained four cartoons. Unfortunately, these color efforts did little if anything to increase Betty's popularity on TV. Cleaned up and in color, she was just another cartoon.

She was still dynamite in her original form. IVY Films put together a feature called THE BETTY BOOP SCANDALS OF 1974. It was merely a grouping of some of her most bizarre and best cartoons such as SNOW WHITE, MINNIE THE MOOCHER and BIMBO'S INITIATION. (Also included were some live action comedy shorts of the same period, and the first chapter of the original BUCK ROGERS serial.) The film proved moderately successful at theatres and very successful on college campuses. A soundtrack album of the film was released, and sold so well a second album of Boop cartoon soundtracks was issued.

Still trying to catch some of the Boop hype, in 1976 NTA approached producer Dan Dalton with the proposal of editing a compilation feature of the colorized shorts to tie-in with the upcoming presidential election. Originally titled BETTY BOOP FOR PRESIDENT, the film took almost four years to complete. When it finally appeared in 1980, it was retitled HURRAY FOR BETTY BOOP.

"She's hard working and fun at the same time — a true metaphor for the career woman of the Eighties."
— King Features press release, 1985

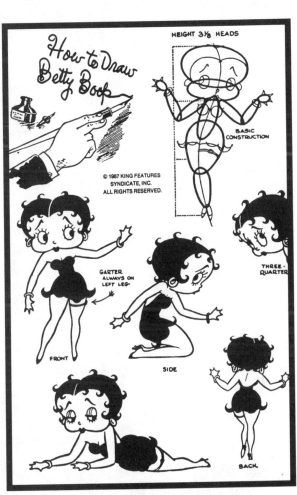

Eighties model sheet.

© King Features

The film features excerpts from 35 different Boop shorts, ending with BETTY BOOP FOR PRESIDENT (1932). Throughout the film, the Devil in a variety of guises tries to prevent Betty from winning the presidential election. Victoria D'Orazi redubbed Betty's voice and Tommy Smothers of the Smothers Brothers narrated the story as Pudgy the Pup. Even though some of the original Cab Calloway songs were kept, there were additional songs by Debby Boone and the Association included in the soft rock soundtrack.

Dalton, along with some other writers, wrote new dialog for the film, making no attempt to match these new words with the previously animated mouth movements. For example, as Betty cleans the kitchen in HOUSE CLEANING BLUES (1937) she asks, "Are your sure Carter started out this way?," a reference to President Jimmy Carter.

New Line Cinema, which distributed the film, spent a minimum of $50,000 on promotion. New York publicist Alan Abel was hired to run a "Betty Boop for President" campaign. This campaign included supporters picketing the Democratic convention in New York. Boop campaign slogans were painted on New York sidewalks and walls. Victoria D'Orazi, the new voice of Betty, toured the country in a Betty Boop costume. This often caused some confusion because of then-current plans to develop a Broadway musical about Betty Boop reportedly starring Bernadette Peters. People were unclear exactly what all this Boop publicity was supposed to be promoting. The film, after a limited series of theatrical bookings, recouped its cost by being sold to cable TV.

BETTY GETS NEWLY ANIMATED

In 1985 Betty starred in a prime time special THE ROMANCE OF BETTY BOOP by Lee Mendelson and Bill Melendez, the team responsible for the Peanuts TV specials. Set in 1939 New York, the story followed Betty's attempt to gain stardom. She deals with millionaires, mobsters and Hollywood. At the end she must decide between being a star and being a wife; no decision is made.

The special has little to reccomend it. Though officially giving "thanks" to Grim Natwick, this new Betty had little of her Boop-boop-a-doop. Mae Questel, upon hearing of the production, offered to do the voice but was refused. The part was played by singer-composer Desiree Goyette, Mendelson's wife.

In 1987, "The Great Betty Boop Talent Search Pageant" was held in connection with a $20 million live action motion picture being produced about the Cartoon Superstar. Edward Lozzi and Associates were involved. However, a year later, the winner complained there was no movie and no contract with the Ron Smith lookalikes that she was promised.

"He likes to boop-boop-a-doop, but I never cared to boop-boop-a-doop..."

— Betty Boop
in STOPPING THE SHOW (1932)

Questel got to "boop-boop-a-doop" again in 1988's WHO FRAMED ROGER RABBIT? Making fun of her plight as a black and white cartoon star, she appears as a waitress in the famous Ink and Paint Club sequence and the final sing-a-long.

As recently as 1990, Betty was being talked about for a new special. King Features, who now owns the character, signed a deal for Big Pictures to produce BETTY BOOP'S HOLLYWOOD MYSTERY. The studio promised the new special would reunite Betty with her original co-stars Bimbo and Koko the Clown. The trio work for Diner Dan and help a detective solve a jewelry heist. Betty's voice was to be provided by Melissa Fahn. Also promised was a return to the "jazz-age surrealism of Max Fleischer's original '30s cartoons."

HER SUPPORTERS

Bimbo was a revised version of the dog character who appeared in the silent cartoon series "Inkwell Imps." Bimbo was assumed to be Betty Boop's boyfriend, despite the fact that he remained a dog while Betty became more human. This mixed love relationship didn't bother early audiences any more than the one between Jessica and Roger Rabbit. Bimbo was a short, black dog who was quite street smart. He wore a longsleeve turtleneck sweater and shoes but no pants.

Ko-Ko the Clown was the famous silent cartoon star of the Fleischers who used to pop out of an inkwell. He was brought out of retirement to become another of Betty's boyfriends and sometime companion to Bimbo. He wore a black clown costume with a black pointed hat. He was a white face clown, the kind most apt to terrify children because they look unreal. Ko-Ko never seemed as sharp as Bimbo.

Grampy was supposedly Betty's grandfather and he frequently upstaged the new Betty. Always full of pep, he was an inventor capable of turning household items into a wild array of useful gadgets.

Pudgy was a small, cute, playful and mischievous white puppy. He really loved his owner, Betty. While he had some degree of understanding, he was obviously just a dog (unlike Bimbo) and never talked.

OTHER MEDIA

Betty was a highly merchandised cartoon star of the Thirties. There were toys, clothing, candy, dolls (including the jointed wooden doll by Cameo), watches, and two Big Little Books (including the unusual MISS GULLIVER'S TRAVELS). In the late Sixties, there was a revival of interest in Betty Boop items which has increased tremendously in the Eighties.

Today, the Betty Boop character is currently licensed for more than 300 products worldwide. There are items geared not only for children (Betty Boop Makeup Kit) but for adults (expensive ceramics, calendars and greeting cards). The line has even been extended to include "Baby Boop." This toddler version is geared for young children and features Baby Boop in strollers, on rocking horses, and the like.

There was a daily newspaper strip in 1934 that lasted a year, and a Sunday version that lasted until 1937 drawn by Bud Counihan. (These strips have been reprinted in recent years by Blackthorne Publishing.) There was one issue of an unauthorized comic book with Betty published in the Seventies. In the Eighties, the Walker Brothers (sons of Mort Walker of Beetle Bailey comic strip fame) tried to revive Betty Boop in an unsuccessful newspaper strip that teamed the classic Betty with Felix the Cat as her pet! In 1990, First Publishing planned to release a graphic novel comic book story entitled BETTY BOOP'S BIG BREAK with new art by Milton Knight.

Betty is also a spokesperson for the Home Shopping Network (a cable network), Hershey's Chocolate and Sumitome 3M video cassettes in Japan. She's also an official NFL cheerleader.

SUPERSTAR QUALITY

Strangely, Betty Boop seems more popular today than at the peak of her theatrical career. Even though Betty's adventures are available on videotape, most fans haven't seen her perform. They are enamored of her classic, sexual, innocent image.

Betty boop-oop-a-doop Boop!

© King Features

BUGS BUNNY

SELECTED SHORT SUBJECTS: *Hare Raising Hare, Rabbit Fire, The Wacky Wabbit, Waikiki Wabbit, What's Up Doc?*

Superstar Summary

THE STAR: Bugs Bunny

YEAR OF DEBUT: 1940 (A WILD HARE)

STUDIO OF DEBUT: Warner Brothers

SIGNATURE: "Eh, What's up, Doc?"

KEY CREW BEHIND THE STAR: Mel Blanc (voice), Tex Avery, Bob Clampett, Chuck Jones, Friz Freleng (directors), Warren Foster, Rich Hogan, Michael Maltese, Tedd Pierce (writers)

CAREER HIGH: THE BUGS BUNNY SHOW (1960) a prime time cartoon show that was entertaining for its combination of classic Warner shorts and new story framing animation.

Bugs Bunny is one of those characters whose great success in so many different forms almost propels him above the rank of cartoon superstardom. Just as Mickey Mouse has come to represent the entire Disney organization, Bugs has achieved a similar recognition as the "top carrot" of Warner Brothers. His value as a character is so high that Warners was able to demand that Bugs get equal screen time with Mickey Mouse in WHO FRAMED ROGER RABBIT? (1988). A national survey in 1989 discovered that Bugs Bunny was the most popular character in the 18 to 49 age group category.

More so than some other characters, there are many different Bugs Bunnys. When people say they love Bugs Bunny, they are not necessarily talking about the same character. There are differences between the more elastic and aggressive rabbit of Bob Clampett and the intellectual counter-revolutionary of Chuck Jones and the more action oriented bunny of Friz Freleng. Other directors including Ben Hardaway, Tex Avery, Frank Tashlin and Bob McKimson also produced significant variations.

Originally, Bugs was a squat, wild, hyperkinetic rabbit not much different from other wacky characters. It was quite reasonable to assume that his natural habitat was an insane asylum. Gradually, the character matured into a taller, more confident gray bunny who was more in control of himself and the situation. In various cartoons, he still might waver between being the aggressor and the victim who retaliates but certain key elements seemed intrinsic to the character.

He was a character who could wield the spoken word with the skill of a surgeon's knife. He could triumph by fast-talking a confused antagonist, substituting a pronoun or assuming an accent. While many other characters depended on pantomime action for their humor, Bugs combined that virtue with a facility for language unmatched by other cartoon personalities.

It was not just his vocabulary and vocal speed that gave him an edge. It was his attitude. His voice suggested the image of a stereotypical, sarcastic New Yorker. It was part argumentative, part disbelieving and part self-assured. This confident, fighting spirit is reflected in two of Bugs' favorite phrases: "What's up, Doc?" and "Of course you know this means war!" (The latter borrowed from Groucho Marx.)

Bugs loved disguising himself as different characters. These impersonations were amazingly effective whether he took on the identity of a policeman or a little old lady. In particular, Bugs loved to cross dress as a woman, a longstanding tradition among many popular live action male comedians. The early cartoons often used gags with Bugs attired in a bra. Later cartoons usually kept him more fully dressed as a woman with elaborate wigs adding to the overall illusion.

Bugs' sexuality has been a subject for some discussion. He seemed to delight in giving his male antagonists long, big, wet kisses directly on the lips. This action might be just another way of Bugs establishing his superiority by violating his foe's private space. He also had a predilection for female disguises and would adopt a female attitude or expression at a drop of the pants. Some state it indicates a possible homosexual preference.

Bugs definitely had a heterosexual side. In HOLD THE LION, PLEASE! (1942) he is married to Mrs. Bugs Bunny (who literally wears the pants in his family). This makes Bugs one of the few cartoon Superstars to actually have a "wife." Other shorts showcase his efforts to get a lady. In HARE SPLITTER (1948) he battles another rabbit to date "Daisy Lou." (Of course before the short is over, Bugs has dressed as "Daisy" to trick his rival.)

That Oscar-winning rabbit!

© Warner Brothers

Sometimes the lady is not what he expected. In THE GREY HOUNDED HARE (1949) the girl turns out to be the mechanical guide for racing dogs, while in HAIR-RAISING HARE (1946) it is a female rabbit robot. (In the latter, upon discovering this fact, Bugs states, "so it's mechanical" and quickly follows after her/it.) There are also several shorts in which Bugs has a number of offspring indicating he could multiply as well as any rabbit. In later years, the comic books introduced a girlfriend for Bugs, Honey Bunny, but she was so unmemorable that even the Warner staff couldn't establish a definite personality for her.

As Bugs evolved, he became smarter and smarter. Rarely did Bugs lose the battle in the final shot although it did happen. Generally, Bugs was able to step aside calmly. He allowed his antagonist's own force and speed to backfire against the enemy. The humor came from what happened to the foolish character who challenged Bugs, not from what happened to Bugs, himself.

THE BIRTH OF THE BUGS

Unlike most other cartoon superstars, the creation of Bugs was not just the vision of one man or even a handful of men. Bugs owes his development as a superstar to more than a dozen talented animators, designers, writers and directors.

The spark behind the Oscar winning rabbit can be traced as far back as the African folk tales which recounted the adventures of a trickster rabbit. The point of these various stories was that a smaller animal through its quickness of mind and body could get the better of larger, more physically powerful and dangerous animals. This trickster rabbit, like Bugs, is a mischief maker with a good sense of humor. Usually, he only caused problems when his well-being was threatened.

It was not surprising that such a character would hold a special appeal for the slaves brought from Africa and placed in a situation where only their swiftness of wit could save them from the cruelties of their new masters. Supposedly, these stories of a trickster rabbit eventually evolved into Uncle Remus' more famous tales of B'rer Rabbit.

In terms of animation, some writers have suggested that the immediate inspiration for Bugs Bunny was Max Hare in the Disney cartoon short THE TORTOISE AND THE HARE (1934). However, that brash, cocky character bears little relation to the smaller, wackier bunny who eventually became Bugs Bunny.

"Now in his 50th year, Bugs (with a Bronx-Brooklyn accent) is probably the cartoon character who works best with dialogue — as seen in the three cartoons in which Bugs, Daffy and Elmer Fudd argue over whether it is rabbit season or duck season."

— Jim Henson, creator of the Muppets

The earliest version of Bugs Bunny appeared in Warners' PORKY'S HARE HUNT (1938) directed by Ben Hardaway and written by Howard Baldwin. Hardaway's nickname was "Bugs" and the model sheet identified the rabbit as "Bug's bunny." Two years later, when it became necessary to name the rabbit, "Bug's bunny" became Bugs Bunny (minus the possessive apostrophe).

Hardaway had a particular inclination for wacky characters, having been involved with the early Daffy Duck and later with the first Woody Woodpecker.

PORKY'S HARE HUNT is similar in spirit to Tex Avery's PORKY'S DUCK HUNT made the previous year which introduced the character of Daffy Duck. This time, instead of a darn fool duck, Porky the hunter is confronted with a pixilated rabbit. The unnamed hare is as physically and vocally insane as the

Seventies licensing art model sheet.

Opposite: Model sheet from CARNIVAL OF THE ANIMALS (1976).

© Warner Brothers

early Daffy Duck. Some of the classic Bugs Bunny character elements appear in this cartoon, including his ability to do magic, to perform histrionic death scenes and the phrase "Of course you know, this means war!"

Other versions of this little white bunny appeared again in 1939. PRESTO CHANGE-O, directed by Chuck Jones and written by Rich Hogan, had him tease a dog using a magician's tricks. HARE-UM SCARE-UM, directed by Hardaway and written by Melvin Millar, found him heckling a hunter who was trying to beat the high cost of meat. However, the character was still too goofy and annoying to be considered a potential star.

It was 1940 that really defined the character and established the basic personality that would launch him to stardom. First, there was ELMER'S CANDID CAMERA, directed by Chuck Jones and written by Rich Hogan. This cartoon established the relationship between Bugs and Elmer Fudd that would provide the springboard for many memorable cartoons.

More important was Bugs' second appearance in 1940. Tex Avery took all the good elements from the previous versions and mixed them with his own unique humor to "create" the character most people would recognize as Bugs Bunny. He, and writer Rich Hogan, made the rabbit smarter and more in-control of himself and the situation in A WILD HARE. One particular item that marks this cartoon as a true beginning of Bugs is the inclusion of the famous line, "What's up, Doc?" It was a phrase that was very popular at the Texas high school Avery had attended.

A WILD HARE, which was nominated for an Academy Award, had Elmer hunting for "wabbits." Unfortunately, the rabbit he finds is Bugs Bunny. Compared with later efforts, Bugs' tormenting of Elmer is mild. It is a Bugs who is now colored in his familiar gray and has been redesigned to look less grotesque, taller and more expressive. This new design was created by Robert Givens.

Also key was Mel Blanc's voice. A mixture of the Bronx and Brooklyn, Mel's original voice work helped to establish the cockiness and brashness of the character. Mel had previously provided goofier voices for the rabbit in some of the earlier shorts. (One of these included the gooney laugh Mel would also use for Woody Woodpecker.)

By 1940, Mel's interpretation was very close to the classic Bugs' voice. Blanc would refine it over the years and be the official voice of Bugs until Mel's death in 1989.

Avery established the basic ground rules for the character and the series. Oddly, he only directed three more Bugs Bunny cartoons before leaving Warners. In those few shorts, he established the foundation of the cool, impudent hero with a jaunty walk and cigar-like carrot for further exploration. Within the next few years, other directors like Chuck Jones, Friz Freleng, Bob Clampett and Frank Tashlin would expand and refine the character. These directors were assisted in this development stage by many key writers at Warners, notably Tedd Pierce, Warren Foster and Michael Maltese.

Bugs Bunny was introduced to the public by name for the first time in the opening titles for ELMER'S PET RABBIT (1941). Elmer makes the mistake of purchasing a supposedly timid rabbit who eventually takes over his house.

"(Bugs is someone who is) minding his own business, and then somebody comes along and tries to disturb him, hurt him, destroy him. When he fights back, he becomes an anarchist, rather like Groucho Marx."

— Chuck Jones, Bugs' director

CARTOON SUPERSTARS

WABBITS! WABBITS! WABBITS!

It was just the beginning of a series of classic cartoons featuring the new star. Each animation unit at Warners was assigned a certain number of Bugs Bunny cartoons to churn out each year in addition to a number of undesignated shorts. As a result, in a year like 1942, there were as many different types of Bugs Bunnys as there were directors who worked with him.

> "In the very first one was 'Eh, what's up, Doc?' and gee, it floored (the audience)! They expected the rabbit to scream, or anything but make a casual remark — here's a guy with a gun in his face!"
>
> — Tex Avery, Bugs' director

THE WABBIT WHO CAME TO SUPPER (1942), directed by Friz Freleng and written by Mike Maltese, had Elmer inheriting $3 million dollars with the restriction that he couldn't hurt animals, especially rabbits. Bugs immediately moves into Elmer's house and makes himself a pest. THE WACKY RABBIT (1942), directed by Bob Clampett and written by Warren Foster, has Elmer prospecting for gold in the desert and discovering that the only gold is in the gold tooth in his mouth. CASE OF THE MISSING HARE (1942), directed by Chuck Jones and written by Tedd Pierce, has Bugs disrupting the magic act of Ala Bama.

While each cartoon featured a recognizable Bugs, each cartoon also had distinctly different styles and points of view. Freleng's cartoon was a series of straight action gags such as Bugs running down stairs to a darkened basement. ("Don't go down there... it's dark!") Clampett's cartoon explored more grotesque territory with Bugs wearing a dried skull to talk to Elmer. Jones' cartoon emphasized that Bugs was only being disruptive because the fat magician had laughingly smashed a blackberry pie in Bugs' face first.

The differences were not consciously noticed by a general audience yet each approach served to develop aspects of Bugs' personality and behavior that blended together to create the familiar image known today. In 1942, Bugs was most frequently seen in a short animated trailer with Porky and Elmer asking the audience in song "Any Bonds Today?" It was a plea to purchase war bonds to help finance the U.S. armed services.

Just as sound had helped make Mickey Mouse a star, World War II catapulted Bugs Bunny into being the new American hero. The Bugs of the Forties captured the energy and flippancy of his time. His wisecracking antics that always defeated the stupid little man with a gun made him a symbol of America's resistance to Hitler and the fascist powers.

> "One of the strengths of Bugs Bunny is that, like all we humans, he has varying 'moods.' At one time he is at peace with the world and slow to react to an invasion of his privacy. At another time, he is in a playful and mischievous mood, full of practical jokes. At other times he is irritable, bugged by the claim that a tortoise can beat a hare."
>
> — Bob Clampett, Bugs' director

Some of Bugs' cartoons directly addressed the situation such as in BUGS BUNNY NIPS THE NIPS (1944) where Bugs very violently defeats an island full of Japanese soldiers. Other cartoons of the same era stuck to more traditional concepts including in THE OLD GREY HARE (1944) which showed an aged Bugs and Elmer of 2000 A.D. reminiscing about their first chase as Baby Elmer and Baby Bugs.

After the war there was no lessening of Bugs popularity. In fact, decades before WHO FRAMED ROGER RABBIT? (1988), Bugs was appearing in films with live action performers. In TWO GUYS FROM TEXAS (1948) he pops out of a rabbit hole to help the hero of the movie, Jack Carson. In MY DREAM IS YOURS (1949), Bugs sings and dances with Jack Carson and Doris Day.

In the mid Fifties, Bugs character finally settled into the familiar mold that most people think of when they think of Bugs Bunny. "He had the intellect of Groucho

32

combined with the zaniness and oddity of Harpo," commented director Chuck Jones comparing Bugs to two of the famous Marx Brothers comedy team. Bugs usually started out in an environment natural for a rabbit. Instead of provoking a fight, he now only fought back if someone was trying to disturb him or hurt him.

The Bugs cartoons of the Fifties produced many memorable gems including the trilogy of cartoons with Daffy Duck based on "Duck Season! Rabbit Season!" Also

Bugs in Warner's special, BUGS VS. DAFFY: BATTLE OF THE MUSIC VIDEO STARS (1988).

© *Warner Brothers*

from the Fifties was Bugs only 3-D cartoon, LUMBER JACK RABBIT (1954), where he wandered into Paul Bunyan territory and discovered giant carrots. WHAT'S OPERA, DOC? (1957) was one of the most elaborately produced cartoons of all time and parodied opera. Bugs also had a significant cameo in DUCK AMUCK (1953) as an animator. Perhaps the crowning achievement for the bunny was winning his one and only Oscar for Friz Freleng's KNIGHTY KNIGHT BUGS (1958), written by Warren Foster, where Bugs outsmarts a dragon and Yosemite Sam.

BUGS BUNNY'S PRIME TIME

Bugs Bunny cartoons started appearing on TV around 1956 thanks to a syndication package acquired from AAP which included 53 cartoons starring Bugs Bunny. Their success was amazing and it prompted ABC to try a prime time series featuring the Oscar winning rabbit. THE BUGS BUNNY SHOW premiered on ABC in October 1960 and ran for two seasons. It was written and produced jointly by

CARTOON SUPERSTARS

Bugs was a frequent cover feature on LOONEY TUNES MERRIE MELODIES COMICS.

© Warner Brothers

Chuck Jones and Friz Freleng, two of the few remaining "original" directors left at Warners. The half hour show included three existing cartoons framed with new animation that tied the three shorts together.

In September 1962, the show moved to Saturday mornings where in various formats (THE BUGS BUNNY/ROAD RUNNER HOUR, THE BUGS AND TWEETY SHOW, etc.) it has remained one of the top rated shows for almost three decades.

The last Warners Bugs cartoon was FALSE HARE (1964) about the Big Bad Wolf wanting Bugs for dinner. Warners officially stopped releasing new cartoons in 1969. Bugs' cartoons in syndication and on Saturday morning were still drawing audiences in the Seventies and it caught the attention of an independent film-maker named Larry Jackson. In 1975, under the banner of Hare Raising Films, Inc., he released a feature entitled BUGS BUNNY SUPERSTAR, featuring several classic Warner cartoons with Bugs, surrounded by documentary footage and new interviews with Freleng, Avery and Clampett. The attention this feature received did not go unnoticed and Warner veteran Chuck Jones was contracted to bring Bugs back to TV in a series of new half hour specials as well as a full length animated film.

For TV, Jones was responsible for all new footage for CARNIVAL OF THE ANIMALS (1976) and A CONNECTICUT RABBIT IN KING ARTHUR'S COURT (1978). His feature film compilation, THE BUGS BUNNY ROAD RUNNER MOVIE (aka THE GREAT CHASE and THE BUGS BUNNY-ROAD RUNNER GREAT CHASE), in development for several years as either a feature or TV special, was released theatrically in 1979. It showcased some new footage of Bugs giving a tour around his mansion and reminiscing about his career, although the majority of the feature was a collection of Jones' Warner cartoons.

Compiling previously shown cartoons with new wraparound, unifying animation was not new for Bugs. Beginning in 1977, several Bugs Bunny half hour specials for TV featured old Warner shorts, often edited to squeeze into a new, forced storyline. BUGS BUNNY'S EASTER SPECIAL and BUGS BUNNY IN SPACE both followed that format and premiered in 1977. Warners produced an additional 15 specials with Bugs ending with BUGS BUNNY'S WILD WORLD OF SPORTS in 1989. During this time, Friz Freleng would direct three more compilation theatrical features, all with old Bugs Bunny cartoons mixed in with flimsy new storylines.

While animation fans complained about the editing of the classic cartoons, these efforts kept Bugs and his buddies highly visible and merchandisable. Adding to that visibility were the many public service spots and commercials with Bugs. (Tex Avery, working at his own commercial animation studio, directed the Kool-Aid spots with Bugs.)

In 1985, Bugs received his own star on the Hollywood Walk of fame. The Fall of that year, he was also featured in much of the art at a special exhibit at New York's Museum of Modern Art. The four month event was in honor of the 50th anniversary of Warner's cartoons (tagged to Porky Pig's debut). A TV special, BUGS BUNNY/ LOONEY TUNES ALL-STAR 50TH ANNIVERSARY, marked the event. TV and movie personalities detailed fictitious accounts of the Toons while creators, such as Friz Freleng and Chuck Jones, added historical insight.

"I'd suspect that Friz's Bugs would be more of a scamp, and Tex Avery's more a controlled lunatic, a brilliant controlled lunatic. Bob Clampett's was a thoroughly amoral lunatic with flashes of greatness."

— Chuck Jones, Bugs' director

34

Bugs Bunny helped present, in animated form, the Academy Award to the Best Animated Short in 1987 and 1990. (The latter featured an entire new animated sequence in which Bugs explains animation.) His appearance in WHO FRAMED

ROGER RABBIT? (1988) stole the scene from Mickey Mouse as they both talked to falling detective Eddie Valiant.

HALF CENTURY HARE

Bugs 50th birthday celebration in 1990 prompted many new projects. 50 YEARS OF BUGS BUNNY IN 3-1/2 MINUTES kicked off the celebration as a short released with NATIONAL LAMPOON'S CHRISTMAS VACATION (1989) in selected theaters. The short was a series of clips compiled from dozens of Bugs' shorts. Warner Brothers prepared a prime time network special featuring a number of live action stars (from Hulk Hogan to Whoopi Goldberg), classic animation and original animation.

> "Bugs is not funny by himself. He really is not funny. ... He's kind of a straight man. But he gets all the credit. He can't even create his own situations. You have to create one for him."
>
> — Fritz Freleng, Bugs' director

Steven Spielberg committed to a new animated project dubbed TINY TOON ADVENTURES which featured the famous Warner characters along with younger versions resembling Bugs and his buddies. In the Fall of 1990, Warner planned to release MERRIE MELODIES STARRING BUGS BUNNY AND FRIENDS, a package of 65 half hour episodes for national syndication featuring classic favorites along with cartoons previously unreleased to syndication.

The year also saw Bugs appear in a special drug prevention cartoon entitled CARTOON ALL STARS TO THE RESCUE, as well as an appearance on THE EARTH DAY SPECIAL (ABC, April 22, 1990). Author Joe Adamson produced a book devoted solely to Bugs' career.

Bugs' crowning achievement in 1990 was his return to the big screen in BOX OFFICE BUNNY, the first new Bugs Bunny theatrical cartoon since 1964. The short found Bugs pursued by Elmer through a multi-theater cineplex built over the rabbit's hole. It was directed by Darrell Van Citters and written by Charles Carney and featured a new voice for Bugs, Jeff Bergman.

BUGS' BUDDIES

Elmer Fudd is a bald, mild mannered, middle aged character with a distinctive speech impediment. Usually, he is cast as a hunter and a natural adversary for Bugs. However, Elmer had no skill at hunting and is genuinely upset when it appears he has actually shot Bugs. Elmer is no challenge for Bugs. There are a handful of cartoons where Elmer is the ultimate victor but they hardly make a dent in the dozens of cartoons where he is a sap. Elmer is a very conservative, gentlemanly person who is totally incapable of preventing Bugs from ruining his secure little lifestyle.

Yosemite Sam is a rip-roaring, pint size Western character with a huge hat and huge red mustache. Unlike Elmer, Sam is extremely aggressive and rough and in theory, he should have no difficulty handling the rabbit. Unfortunately, Sam's quick temper and vanity make him his own worst enemy. With ease, Bugs is able to turn Sam's unthinking violence into a device that trips up the wild character. Although cast in a variety of roles from pirate to Arab chieftain, Sam always retains his Western accent and expressions. He has no patience with animals, from camels to dragons, who never seem to reach his expectations.

Daffy Duck was teamed with Bugs in a number of memorable shorts and the contrast between the characters added to the humor. Daffy is selfish and out of control. Bugs is calm and uses common sense. Despite Daffy's frantic and frequent attempts to be the hero or get the treasure, often at the expense of Bugs, he cannot match Bugs' verbal skill.

Even Bugs couldn't escape being given the obligatory nephew. Clyde first appeared in 1954's YANKEE DOODLE BUGS.

OTHER MEDIA

Like most cartoon superstars, Bugs has appeared in comic books, comic strips, toys, children's vitamins, special video tapes, jewelry, games and assorted merchandise.

Bugs Bunny's first comic book appearance was in 1941, a year after his official birth. He appeared with other Warner stars in the first issue of LOONEY TUNES AND MERRIE MELODIES. Bugs was in every issue until the comic ceased publication in 1962. (It was briefly revived in 1975 with Bugs still the star.)

The BUGS BUNNY comic books started out in 1942 as part of the Dell Four Color series. After 27 different appearances, Bugs was given his own comic series in 1953 beginning with issue #28 and continuing until issue #245 (1983). Besides these issues, Bugs appeared in dozens of specials and giveaways in addition to guest star roles in other Warner Brothers comic book titles including PORKY PIG and YOSEMITE SAM.

The Bugs Bunny newspaper strip first appeared in 1942 as a Sunday page only. In 1948, a daily version of the strip was added. This strip generally featured all of the Warners characters in a situation comedy world. Lately, the strip has been changed to reflect the zany flavor of the original cartoons.

The Six Flags theme parks use the Warner characters as mascots and as expected, Bugs is the main star. Six Flags Magic Mountain, in Southern California, not only has a play area for children themed to Bugs, but the park has been the host to live action stage shows featuring a costumed Bugs with live singers and dancers.

1989 found Bugs cover featured on the debut issue of LOONEY TUNES magazine, for kids. More than 150 different licensees signed up to produce special Bugs Bunny items during Bugs 50th birthday in 1990. DC Comics produced a special three-issue mini-series, while Nintendo released a special videogame.

SUPERSTAR QUALITY

Bugs Bunny is perhaps one of the most influential of all cartoon superstars. Though such stars as Mickey and Felix may have been the source of mimicry within the animation industry, Bugs influence is felt everywhere. Whether it's the person on the street mimicking "What's up, Doc" or a top stand-up comic doing an impersonation, the character of Bugs Bunny is as ingrained upon us as such classic live comics as Groucho Marx, WC Fields and Woody Allen. Bugs Bunny is more than just a studio icon, he represents cartoon characters in general.

The Bugs Bunny comic strip's new look for the Nineties.

© Warner Brothers

Inside the image: © Warner Bros. Inc. 1980

Page from 1980 Warners licensing book. Used to aid merchandisers in drawing character.
© Warner Brothers

SELECTED SHORT SUBJECTS: *Casper Comes to Clown, The Friendly Ghost, Spunky Skunky, There's Good Boos Tonight, True Boo*

Superstar Summary

THE STAR: Casper, the Friendly Ghost

YEAR OF DEBUT: 1945 (THE FRIENDLY GHOST)

STUDIO OF DEBUT: Famous (Paramount)

SIGNATURE: "A g-g-g-ghost!" (How Casper is usually greeted)

KEY CREW BEHIND THE STAR: Joe Oriolo (creator), Irving Sparber, Seymour Kneitel (directors), I Klein, Otto Messmer, Bill Turner (writers)

CAREER HIGH: GHOST OF THE TOWN (1952) - Casper, with his friendly nature, becomes a celebrity, appearing on front pages of newspapers, magazine covers and THE ED SULLIVAN SHOW! Everyone loves Casper in this film.

C asper is one of the must unique of the Cartoon Superstars, if for no other reason, than he is a dead one. Decades before the megahits GHOSTBUSTERS and BEETLEJUICE made the hereafter seem more like Disneyland than a religiously significant location, there was Casper, the friendly ghost. He was also the only major Cartoon Superstar to Debut at the Famous Studio.

Truly a ghost, Casper is generally all white. Over the years, his sheet became form-fitting, outlining his oversized head. In his early shorts, he is somewhat translucent. The later years found him painted solid white. Short, and somewhat chubby, he is portrayed as a young boy.

In 1949, Sam Buchwald, president of Famous Studios, told reporters that Casper was "approximately eight years old... and probably will grow no older." (Unfortunately, the same wasn't true for Alan Shay, then aged 12, who did the character's voice at that time. He inherited the role from the original boy who was forced into early retirement when his voice changed.)

In his early cartoons, the fact that Casper is a ghost is made overly clear. Just as most ghosts, Casper has supernatural powers. He can fly, move through solid objects such as walls and turn invisible. He is found hanging around haunted houses and graveyards. In one short, he's even sitting in front of his own tombstone. These images of death were soon removed, placing Casper in more humorous and "safe" arenas such as a school for ghosts.

He was "the friendly ghost." Casper was easily one of the most kind, sympathetic and forgiving cartoon characters ever created. He pursued friendship with a fervor unequaled in either the human or inhuman world. The ultimate un-bigoted personality, Casper could have out-done Will Rogers who "never met a man" he didn't like. Casper never found anyone he didn't like. He liked everything and everyone, even his fellow ghosts.

This is not to say that Casper was the ultimate "goody two shoes." He had his darker side. This was only raised when he saw his friends in danger. At moments like this, he would become angry and rush to their defense. However, even then about the worst he could do was sternly ask the threat to "leave my friends alone." Such a request would have brought peals of laughter from the average menace, but even a polite ghost seemed to scare the most vicious threat.

In fact, some of the biggest laughs in Casper shorts are from the extreme takes that animals, humans and even inanimate objects do when viewing Casper. In his first short, THE FRIENDLY GHOST (1945), Casper finds a cat and mouse battling. The cat, seeing Casper, throws himself against a wall, mouth wide open. The mouse, seeing Casper, throws himself inside the cat's mouth and closes it! The

mouse then runs into his hole, dragging the cat along. Even more extreme, in PIG-A-BOO (1952) Casper scares a Wolf's skeleton right out of it's body. The Wolf then jumps on the skeleton and rides off!

Critics of this friendly character thought the idea of a cartoon based on a "dead little boy" was in bad taste. The general public, though, found this slightly shapeless, but always hopeful, character to be highly sympathetic. Perhaps they empathized with this gentle soul who only wanted to make friends.

At the end of every short, Casper always succeeded and made a new friend. That was a happy ending every child could appreciate.

THE BIRTH (?) OF A GHOST

Of course there had been ghosts and friendly spirits before Casper, but they had always been secondary players. Felix, Mickey, Porky, and dozens of others have encountered at least one

Artwork from sheet music of Casper's famous theme song.

© Harvey Entertainment

ghost in their many comic adventures. However, Casper was not there to support a star, he was the star.

Casper's origin in the Forties came about when Joe Oriolo, a young animator at the Famous Studio, sold a script to the studio. Famous, which had originally been the Fleischer Studio, had just moved back to New York. (The Fleischers had moved their New York studio to Florida to avoid union problems.) Allegedly Sam Buchwald, President of Famous, was upset that the story department had fallen behind. The studio needed a story for a new short and needed it fast.

Oriolo had been working on a character with a friend (Seymour Reit) that they planned to sell as a comic book or children's book.

Oriolo came up with the concept in the late Thirties as a story he told his children. (It was to help them get over being scared in the dark.) He then enlisted Reit's assistance in putting the book together.

The original design featured Casper wearing a hat and sprouting a bit of a tail. They chose the name "Casper" based on the mild-mannered, unthreatening, Casper Milquetoast character created by cartoonist H.T. Webster. The pair found some interest at publishers, but no final sale materialized.

When he heard the call for scripts, Oriolo and Reit quickly put together a script called "The Friendly Ghost." Famous liked it and the story went into production.

According to Oriolo, he and his friend received a total of $250 for the idea. (The actual amount varied as Oriolo told the story over the years.) According to Oriolo, the sale was for a "one shot" production only. He had thought a cartoon based on the character might increase interest in the book.

Until his death in 1985, Oriolo insisted he had a contract indicating the character was only sold on a "one shot" basis. However, Paramount/Famous had copyrighted the character in the film. Oriolo couldn't find lawyers willing to go up against Paramount. He also always maintained that Buchwald had promised him a contract guaranteeing a percentage of any licensing revenue, but could never get the actual document. Buchwald died in the early Fifties, and by the mid-Fifties, Harvey had purchased the property and films from Famous, making legal action even more confusing.

> **"Anybody else who says they created Casper the Ghost I should hold them for libel for it."**
>
> **— Joe Oriolo, creator**

CASPER'S THEATRICAL DE-BOO

In 1945, THE FRIENDLY GHOST debuted. It was directed by I. Sparber, and written by Bill Turner and Otto Messmer.

Messmer was the creator of Felix the Cat, a character Oriolo would later inherit and develop into a TV superstar.

Casper was re-designed for animation by Famous artist John Walworth. The voice of the famous ghost would be done by various talents including Mae Questel (Olive Oyl, Betty Boop), Norma McMillan, Gwen Davies, Alan Shay and Cecil Roy.

This "Noveltoon" (the series name Famous released all their one shots under) looked like just another one shot cartoon. However, this one shot would be the definitive pattern for all Casper cartoons to come... around 100 of them!

Many books indicate over 200 Casper cartoons, but this figure arises from the syndicated package and includes scores of Famous and Harvey shorts that don't star Casper.

The short begins with a narrator (Frank Gallop) asking if the viewer believes in ghosts as the camera pans an old house. Inside the house is seen Casper, laying on a suit of armor and reading the book "How To Win Friends." The narrator reveals that Casper doesn't like to scare people. The clock strikes twelve, midnight, and all the ghosts go out to do their work. Meanwhile, Casper watches and shakes his head. The narrator states that Casper decided to leave home, "to forget he's a ghost and make friends with the world."

Casper tries to make friends with various animals including a rooster, a mole, a cat and mouse, and a group of hens. All exhibit the extreme takes famous in Casper cartoons. These failures depress Casper greatly. He whines, "I'm just a scary old ghost."

Deciding to end it all (again?) Casper lays down on the railroad tracks in front of a train. However, when the train runs over him, it merely blows him further down the tracks. This final failure is too much for Casper who breaks down and cries.

Suddenly two young children appear, Bonnie and Johnny. They ask if Casper would like to play with them. Casper blushes and happily agrees. After some play time, the children take Casper home. Upon arrival, they introduce the ghost to their mother who does a (more restrained) take and rushes the children under the bed with her. Rejected again, Casper heads towards the door. He repeats his lament of being "only a scary old ghost."

As he reaches the door, it flies open. Standing outside is a mustached, top-hatted villain, one of the type made famous by silent film melodramas. He holds up the mortgage and tells Casper to inform the mother that the mortgage is due.

Before the villain can finish his speech, he realizes he is talking to a ghost. He does a quick take, declares the house is haunted, tears up the mortgage and runs away. Casper resumes leaving out of the door when the mother comes up from behind him. She picks him up and hugs him. The scene dissolves to a new day as the mother is seeing all her children off to school — Bonnie, Johnny and Casper. The friendly ghost is happily dressed in shorts and a hat.

This film features every major element that would be repeated, almost exactly, in practically all future theatrical Casper cartoons. First is the desire to find friends. Next is the sampling of humorous takes as Casper approaches others. Third is the location of an "innocent" (usually a child, or young animal). This character is unprejudiced by the world and thus accepts Casper for "who" he is rather, than "what" he is. Finally, there is the rescue which makes him a welcome commodity by all.

CASPER RISES AGAIN

As stated, the first Casper short was released as a one-shot. However Buchwald thought the ghostly youth was a strong personality. A little over two years after his debut, Casper returned in THERE'S GOOD BOOS TONIGHT (1948).

Once again, Sparber handled direction. The story was credited to Bill Turner and Larry Riley. The short also featured a title card showing Casper sitting by a tree with the wording "Featuring Casper, the Friendly Ghost." Casper's design was slightly altered too, giving him a bit more shape, and larger, more expressive eyes.

In this second outing, Casper joins the animal world. He is first seen sitting at his own grave. As the other ghosts head out to scare people, he is reading "Animal Friends." Once again, in his search for friends, he only manages to scare the various people and animals he meets. Discouraged, he sits down and starts to cry, and begins wishing he were dead!

Suddenly a fox pup comes up to him. Too young to be frightened, the fox and Casper become friends. Casper names his new friend Ferdie Fox and the two play hide and seek, with Casper as "It." Unfortunately for Ferdie, a hunter is also after a fox.

When Casper hears the shooting he races to the aid of his vulpine buddy. Casper flies in front of the hunter and demands he stop shooting at Ferdie, as bullets pass through his ghostly body. The hunter and dog realize that Casper is a ghost, do the appropriate takes and disappear. Casper finds Ferdie but he is too late, Ferdie is dead! Now totally heartbroken, Casper takes the limp body of Ferdie back to the graveyard and buries it next to his own tombstone. Casper sits down and begins to cry again. Suddenly, a ghostly Ferdie springs from the ground and begins to lick Casper. The Friendly Ghost is overjoyed that his friend is back.

At times funny, at times touching, this short is well done and entertaining. It is also somewhat gruesome. In this era when the word "kill" can not even be used in cartoons, to find death as a sort of resolution for friendship is quite eerie.

This short was followed even more rapidly by a third, A HAUNTING WE WILL GO (1949). Directed by famed Disney animator Bill Tytla (FANTASIA's "Night on Bald Mountain" and others), and written by Larry Bourne, this is almost a re-

"I developed the character and gave it to Sam (Buchwald) and he says, 'I'd like to give you a token amount of $175."

— Joe Oriolo, creator

Nineties' promotional art.

© Harvey Entertainment

make of THERE'S GOOD BOOS TO-NIGHT. It opens with Casper attending school in a haunted school house, where the ghosts are singing "A haunting we will go." This scene offers the first sign that ghosts have an organized society of their own.

Casper sits in a corner with a dunce cap on.

After class he attempts to make friends but fails. When he scares a flock of ducks, he sits down dejected and accidentally hatches an egg. The duckling, who Casper names Dudley, is not afraid of the ghost so they become friends. Casper teaches him to swim and fly. Unfortunately, once airborne, he becomes the target of hunters. Casper scares the hunter, though Dudley does get shot. As Casper grieves over his Dudley the other ducks return. They watch in silence as Casper's tears revive the duck. Dudley was only grazed! The short ends with Casper and Dudley happily flying with the flock of ducks.

Now the formula was complete. Casper no longer came from a grave. His friend no longer had to die. But more importantly, his heroic act is witnessed by the masses. Casper was guaranteed to have friends.

THE GHOST WITH THE MOST

Casper was now a full-fledged star, and in 1950 Famous launched the Casper series. It was Famous' first, wholly owned success story. The Casper series of the Fifties reflected newer economies. The artwork was generally less detailed, and Casper was not quite as transparent. Casper also was now being drawn with eyelashes many times, giving him a bit more feminine look.

The storylines were still as strong, and repetitious, as ever. Casper traveled the world always in search of, and finally finding a friend.

"Here was an appealing cartoon with story, animation, speed and charm, with a wee character about which a whole series of cartoons could easily be made."

— Un-named newspaper reviewer commenting on the then newly released CASPER THE FRIENDLY GHOST (1945)

There were some exceptions. GHOST OF THE TOWN (1952) has Casper save a child from a burning building at the beginning of the short. The rest of the film shows how the city honors him from front page headlines to an appearance on THE ED SULLIVAN SHOW! (An animated version of Sullivan appears.) Once on stage, the entire audience, many clad in Casper T-Shirts, sing his theme song.

Another entry from 1952, TRUE-BOO has Casper play Santa Claus for a poor boy on Christmas Eve. When the boy asks for toys, Casper begins making toys out of ordinary objects laying around the house. The mother sees Casper, grabs her son and barricades themselves into the bedroom. However the crying boy makes the mother think twice and she asks Casper to return. All three have a very merry evening... and Casper didn't have to save anyone!

One subtle change occurred when Casper became a series. The ghosts become a bit better organized. In the first three shorts, Casper decides to go out on his own. Most of the Fifties' entries feature a fairly regimented ghost society. The shorts often open with scenes of this society which is usually either military or scholarly. These scenes offer some good humor as the ghosts show that bureaucratic thinking is not always correct. When Casper declares he doesn't want to scare people, he is kicked out (literally in some shorts).

The series debuted with two entries in 1950 that were less strict with the formula, CASPER'S SPREE UNDER THE SEA and ONCE UPON A RHYME. Both were written by I. Klein. UNDER THE SEA was Tytla's final entry. In it, Casper finds that while creatures on land are afraid, the fish in the water are not. (This helps him save his friends from fishermen.)

RHYME was once again in the hands of Sparber. It has Casper enter a book of Mother Goose rhymes. Once there, he scares some, rescues others and generally becomes a hero. The end has Mother Goose write a special rhyme for Casper.

1951 saw the series grow to five shorts. The titles that year were BOO HOO BABY, TO BOO OR NOT TO BOO, BOO SCOUT, CASPER COMES TO CLOWN and CASPER BOW WOW. Several had clever or fun touches.

CLOWN tells the story of Casper and a bear cub he calls Brownie. Casper trains him to be a juggling bear and sings a pleasant song called "Brownie is a juggling bear." Both end up performing a successful circus act.

CASPER BOW WOW starts out with Casper on trial in the "Spookreme Court." The sequence is done all in rhyme and ends with Casper being found "guilty of friendship." He is sentenced to "life with humans!" He promptly goes out and makes friends with a dog. This is a good example of the fun the writers had with ghost society.

> "Sam Buchwald copyrighted the character when the first film was produced, without informing Oriolo of his intentions."
>
> — Shamus Culhane, animator-director at Fleischer/Famous

All were directed by Sparber except BOO HOO BABY which introduced director Seymour Kneitel to the series. Sparber and Kneitel would direct all the theatrical shorts through 1959.

In 1952 the total grew to six shorts. Several featured animal worlds such as PIG-A-BOO, which had Casper rescue the three pigs—Momma, Poppa and Son—from the wolf.

Another one was SPUNKY SKUNKY. A group of animal kids won't let the little skunk play baseball because he "stinks." The skunk, depressed, jumps off a cliff. Before Casper can catch him, the skunk lands in a can of paint. Believing he's a ghost, the skunk merrily plays with Casper. Casper keeps up the pretense by helping the skunk "walk through" things.

When the paint washes off, the skunk realizes he's not dead and runs from Casper. However by now, the Wolf has shown up and is threatening the kids. The skunk tries to save them by spraying the Wolf with a scent in the form of a red cloud. This only makes the Wolf go after the skunk with a gas mask. Casper arrives in time to save the skunk.

The happy ending finds both the skunk and Casper playing baseball with all the animals. The animals do where clothespins on their noses, though.

The Casper series peaked with seven Casper films each year for 1953 and 1954. In 1954 work began on a 3-D Casper short. The film, BOO MOON, was only released in "flat" prints.

From 1955 through 1958, the series usually offered five to six new Caspers a year.

Casper changed graveyards in 1958 when Harvey Publications (who had been publishing Casper comics) bought out the entire film library of Famous. The new company retitled the old Famous shorts to Harveytoons.

The final theatrical year, 1959, offered only four Casper tales, DOING WHAT'S

FRIGHT, DOWN TO MIRTH, NOT GHOULTY and CASPER'S BIRTHDAY PARTY. That same year, Casper came to TV!

TV GHOSTS

In 1959, toy manufacturers and cereal producers were looking to animation to sell their product. Mattel developed a series called MATTY'S FUNDAY FUNNIES. The series featured an animated "Matty" Mattel and his sister "Sue Bell" promoting toys in between Harveytoons that consisted of the Casper theatrical shorts as well as those of Famous' Baby Huey (about a gigantic duckling also looking for friends), Herman and Katnip (an ultra violent battle between mouse and cat) and Little Audrey (about a cute little girl, similar to Little Lulu).

"With the Casper series you never knew what picture you were working on because they were all exactly the same."

— Lee Mishkin, animator at Famous

EYES IN CENTER OF HEAD — FAIRLY LARGE WITH PUPIL TAKING UP ABOUT 2/3 OF EYE

SHOW SLIGHT CHEEK (ONLY ON ONE SIDE AT A TIME)

KEEP NOSE AND MOUTH VERY SMALL

LITTLE CASPER IS SHORT, CHUBBY, SQUAT AND COMPACT

Model sheet from CASPER THE FRIENDLY GHOST, his debut.

Opposite: Early model sheet of Casper.

© Harvey Entertainment

The ABC series debuted in October of 1959 and for the first year ran in the late afternoon on Sundays. In the Fall of 1960 the series shifted over to Friday nights in prime time at 7:30, where it ran for another year. MATTY'S FUNNIES moved to Saturday nights for the Fall of 1961. The Harveytoons only aired on the series for a few months, however, for at the beginning of 1962, Mattel decided to begin airing new, made-for-TV cartoons starring Bob Clampett's BEANY AND CECIL.

The library was re-packaged and debuted back on TV in 1963 as THE NEW CASPER CARTOON SHOW, on Saturday morning.

Another collection of these shorts, called HARVEY CARTOONS, went into syndication.

The Saturday morning series featured new cartoons created by Harvey, with some older Famous theatricals, mostly Modern Madcaps, mixed in. 26 Episodes were produced. The new episodes were directed by Seymour Kneitel and used the talents of many of the original Famous Studios crew.

The new cartoons featured many of the popular Harvey Comic characters such as Wendy, the Good Little Witch, Spooky, the Tuff (sic) Little Ghost, and The Ghostly Trio. Titles included RED ROBBING HOOD, in which Casper helps a young king regain his throne. LITTLE LONESOME GHOSTS found Casper helping a lost ghost find his mother. In PROFESSOR'S PROBLEM, Casper proves there is a "man in the moon" by taking a scientist there!

The series ran on ABC from 1963 through 1969. At that time, these cartoons were mixed into the syndicated package.

A decade later, Casper returned to Saturday mornings in a new series, CASPER AND THE ANGELS. This Hanna-Barbera series brought Casper into the distant future. The premise found Casper in the year 2179A.D.. Here he assisted two futuristic female law officers ("the Angels") in their fight against crime. The Angels are Maxi, an intelligent young Black woman, and Mini, a tall, thin, redheaded, Caucasian woman who was a bit of an airhead. They worked for the Space Police and solved crimes with the assistance of Casper and another ghost, Hairy Scary. Hairy was a large, shaggy ghost with an Ed Wynn inspired voice. He loved to scare people even though he was a bit of a foul-up.

A typical adventure such as "The Cat Burglar" would find Hairy disguising him-self as a bej-eweled woman to lure a thief into the open to be arrested by the Angels. Although Casper was smart in the series, of-ten suggesting a plan, he was passive phys-ically.

It was never explained why the Space Po-lice allowed him and Hairy to team with two of their top patrol women. Casper was voiced by Julie McWhirter in the series.

Hanna-Barbera brought Casper back into prime time TV the same year

in CASPER'S HALLOWEEN (1979) and CASPER'S FIRST CHRISTMAS (1979). These specials featured a number of original songs as well as Hairy Scary from the Saturday morning series, CASPER AND THE ANGELS.

In HALLOWEEN, Casper befriends a group of orphans, helping them have a fun Halloween in spite of Hairy's rowdy ghost gang. In CHRISTMAS, Casper is de-termined to stay awake to see Santa. He's hindered by Hairy Scary, who doesn't believe, and helped by a num-ber of classic Hanna-Barbera characters including Huck-leberry Hound, Yogi Bear, and Snagglepuss. Both spe-cials conclude with Hairy seeing "the light" and assisting in the true spirit of each holiday.

"Harvey's greatest period of success lies just ahead because generations of parents and children alike continue to be drawn to the nonviolent worlds of Casper, Richie Rich and other clas-sic Harvey characters."
— Jeffrey Montgomery, new owner of Casper

Once again, Casper was laid to rest. In 1982, Tom Cart-er Productions, an animation studio located in Southern California (then working on the still unreleased HUCK'S LANDING feature) entered into discussion with Harvey. The youthful, self-made millionaire Carter was set to purchase the rights of the Harvey characters. However, he passed on the deal when it was discovered the film library was still tied up for another 5 to 7 years. This meant the only way

"He always says 'hello' and he's really glad to meet-cha. Wherever he may go, he's kind to ev'ry living creature."
— Casper theme song, lyrics by Mack David

Carter could derive revenue from the Harvey properties would be to go into production on new material.

The Carter studio closed later that year when allegations arose over an investment venture Carter was involved with.

By 1989 most of the film rights were free and a 25-year old Jeffrey Montgomery acquired Harvey Publications. Montgomery set up Harvey Entertainment in Southern California. The new owner immediately set out to step up publication of the successful Harvey characters and begin production on a number of products featuring the characters which included not only Casper, but also Hot Stuff, the Little Devil, Richie Rich, the Richest Kid in the World, Little Dot and Buzzy the Funny Crow. Future plans for the Friendly ghost include a feature film in development at the time of writing, release of his shorts on videotape and in syndication and a possible new TV series.

CASPERS CO-GHOSTS

In the original cartoon series, Casper had no continuing co-stars. However in his popular series of comic books, he appeared with such regulars as Wendy, the Good Little Witch, Spooky, the Tuff (sic) Little Ghost, Nightmare (a ghostly horse), The Ghostly Trio and others. Some of these characters found their way into animation when Harvey produced a new series of shorts for Saturday morning in the early Sixties. In particular, the Ghostly Trio acted like three adult uncles who were disgusted by Casper's lack of interest in scaring people.

"He created Casper the Friendly Ghost in 1944 for my sister, who was afraid of the dark."

— Donald Oriolo, son of Joseph Oriolo

Later, Harvey sued the producers of the GHOSTBUSTERS film claiming Fatso, one of the Ghostly trio, was being used in the famous movie logo. Harvey lost.

OUT OF THE GRAVE

Casper proved one of the most popular merchandised characters to come from Famous. He was found on books, records, and toys of all kinds. Due to his exposure on MATTY'S FUNDAY FUNNIES in the early Sixties, he was used for dozens of Mattel toys, including a talking doll. (You'd pull the string and Casper would say "Booooooo," "Won't you be my friend," and other lines.)

For awhile in the Seventies, Palisades Amusement Park in New Jersey featured "Casper's Ghostland" with Casper, Wendy, Nightmare and the Ghostly Trio. One ride was Wendy's Cups and Saucers.

Casper has been very popular as a mascot for the Cub Scouts and the American Dental Association. Sometimes he combined both roles, such as in the special comic book "The Friendly Cub Scout Casper, His Den and Their Dentist Fight the Tooth Demons" produced in 1974 for the ADA. In it, Casper enters the nightmare of cub scout Charlie to defeat tooth demons with a giant toothbrush, tube of flouride toothpaste and dental floss.

Casper was an honorary astronaut who flew to the moon painted on the outside of Apollo 16. In 1988 Casper rose again via a giant Casper balloon. It debuted in the Pro Football Hall of Fame Festival Grand Parade in Ohio. The 55 foot long balloon was made available for other events.

For Harvey comics, Casper has been a continual superstar. Casper appeared in comics first in 1949 when CASPER THE FRIENDLY GHOST debuted from St. John. By the sixth issue, Harvey had taken over the line and Casper continued to appear not only in this title but in dozens of others including CASPER'S GHOST-LAND, CASPER T.V. SHOW, CASPER AND NIGHTMARE, CASPER AND SPOOKY, CASPER DIGEST and many others. He also guest starred in other Harvey titles. Casper remained in comics as long as Harvey was publishing them through the Eighties. Now he is appearing in a new line via Harvey Entertainment.

SUPERSTAR QUALITY

Casper has lasted almost half a century, and shows no signs of diminishing in popularity. His cartoons are highly repetitious. His personality isn't brash, hyper or sly. Yet in spite of all this, Casper is a well remembered and well loved character. There isn't a ghost of a chance he will ever truly disappear

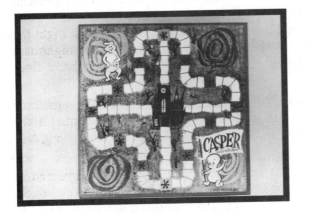

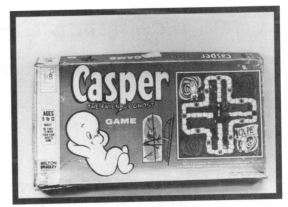

Top left: Sixties lunch box.

Top right: 1959 Casper game.

Bottom left: Game board from 1859 Casper game.

Bottom right: Variety of Casper merchandise

© Harvey Entertainment

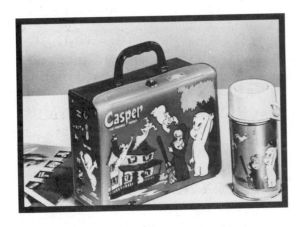

COYOTE
AND THE ROADRUNNER

SELECTED SHORT SUBJECTS: *Beep*

Prepared, Fast and Furry-ous, Lickety

Splat, Operation Rabbit, Sheep Ahoy

Superstar Summary

THE STARS: Wile E. Coyote & Beep Beep, The Road Runner

YEAR OF DEBUT: 1949 (FAST AND FURRY-OUS)

STUDIO OF DEBUT: Warner Brothers

SIGNATURE: "Beep Beep"

KEY CREW BEHIND THE STARS: Chuck Jones (Director); Michael Maltese (Writer); Robert Gribboek, Maurice Noble (Layout artists); Pete Alvarado, Philip DeGuard, Dick Thomas (Background artists).

CAREER HIGH: LICKETY SPLAT (1961) A happy ending for both. The Road Runner gets away, and the Coyote doesn't get blown up.

"B eep-Beep." Zoom! Pure and simple.

These words instantly bring to mind one of the greatest cartoon teams in history, the Coyote and the Road Runner. They are the past masters of the one-joke premise; a simple situation taken to almost infinite proportions.

Wile E. Coyote actually looks almost nothing like an actual coyote. Real coyotes, to a general eye, look very similar to wolves and some dogs. In fact, some Red Wolves are actually coyotes. Wile E. is a bipedal (two legged), two tone, light brown canine. His long legs and arms cause him to resemble a human (or perhaps Bugs Bunny) more than he does his animal counterpart. Coyote ears are triangular and medium size. Wile E.'s ears are rabbit-like, being quite long. A coyote's tail is long and somewhat bushy. Wile E.'s tail began as a short strappling which soon progressed to nothing more than a "fluff" of tail. No wonder he's mixed up... he's built upside down!

In fact, Wile E. seems a much closer cousin to Bugs Bunny than any real canine. He even has Bugs' wide facial cheeks.

The Road Runner is no closer to his real life influence than is the Coyote. The Road Runner seems more closely designed after an Ostrich with long legs, a long neck and a tail that generally sticks straight up. A real road runner does have the long legs, but its neck is no longer than that of an average bird. Also, its tail lays flat allowing it more speed. Real road runners also don't sport a tuff of "feathers" on their head. The Road Runner's body was basically blue, with purple wings and head tuft.

No matter how hard Wile E. Coyote (his full name) tries, he ultimately fails in his quest. Even his silent partner, the powerful, ever complete Acme Company is of no help — except to the Road Runner. The Coyote has all the desire, all the passion, all the determination of the greatest of heroes. All he lacks is success.

Beep Beep, The Road Runner (his full name) enjoys nothing but success. But, just as the Coyote must work hard for his failures, the Road Runner need do nothing to succeed. To the Road Runner, as the song says, "Running down the road's his idea of having fun." All he has to do is run and run and run. It's all fun for the Road Runner. Occasionally he stops, but only to watch the Coyote fail again.

It's no wonder that the team in this wild and wacky series has become one of the most popular in animation. They are the very essence of today's society. Though we may cheer for the Road Runner's continual escape, it is the Coyote that we

most often identify with in the cartoons. No matter how hard we work, no matter how clever our schemes, we invariably seem to get out-run by someone who hardly tries at all.

Actually, like many classic works, the simplicity of this team's setup hides a much larger view. One can easily laugh at the antics of the Coyote's attempts to catch the Road Runner. However, we often find ourselves feeling more for the Coyote. Some may find this rooting for the villain unusual, but these characters and their situations are the kind of stuff psychologists live to study.

Wile E. Coyote is the ultimate obsessive personality. He must get the Road Runner. In the early shorts, they link this need to food. In later cartoons, it is simply a matter of pride and determination. While the coyote could undoubtedly catch almost any other desert creature with his arsenal from Acme, he continues his single minded desire.

WILE E. COYOTE™ (Appetitus Giganticus)   ROAD RUNNER™ (Speedus Demonius)

TM Indicates Trademark of Warner Bros. Inc. ©1980

Page from 1980 Warners licensing book. Used to aid merchandisers in drawing the character.
© Warner Brothers

The Road Runner is merely amused by the Coyote. In only a few instances in their entire career does the bird ever show any actual fear of or concern for his pursuer. Sticking his tongue out and "beeping" is the Road Runner's way of showing up the Coyote's every scheme and desire.

In the long run, this series is about just that: desire. The Coyote wants the Road Runner more than anything else. He will risk life, limb and falling off that ever-present cliff to obtain it. In this era of "just say no," the Coyote will never break his habit. After all, if a room full of monkeys and typewriters could eventually write Shakespeare, then the Coyote could eventually catch the Road Runner. He actually did, but in an unrewarding way in 1980.

a.k.a. THE COYOTE...
Eatibus Anythingus
Famishus Vulgaris
Hard Hedipus Ravenus
Hungrii Flea Bagius
Caninus Nervous Rex

THE CHASE BEGINS

This classic team began when Chuck Jones and writer Michael Maltese were trying to come up with a chase cartoon to end all chase cartoons. They considered various combinations but Jones had been intrigued by coyotes ever since reading Mark Twain's description of them. Jones' crew consisted of a number of top Warners' talents including the previously mentioned Michael Maltese, one of the greatest writers in animation. He also had Robert Gribboek and Maurice Noble (who would become key to many of Jones' later, artier shorts), who did the simple desert layouts, Pete Alvarado, Philip DeGuard and Dick Thomas, who painted the backgrounds and such key animators as Bob Bransford, Ken Harris, Phil Monroe, Tom Ray, Lloyd Vaughn and Ben Washam.

The first film, FAST AND FURRY-OUS (1949), was originally conceived as merely a series of blackouts. However, all the key elements that would continue repeating through the years appear in this first cartoon, from the use of Acme devices to the Coyote using blueprints to plot out his actions.

ROAD RUNNER

The short opens with the Road Runner (Accelerati Incredibulis) running down the road. Up on a cliff, a Coyote (Carnivarious Vulgaris) searches with his binoculars. Upon sighting the bird, he dons a napkin, grabs a knife and fork and makes chase. When it is obvious he can't outrun his prey, he makes other plans. These plans include a rocket, dynamite, an ACME Super Outfit, disguising himself as a schoolgirl and jet-propelled tennis shoes.

It would be another three years before the team would come back for a film. Wile E. would make his next screen appearance trying to capture Bugs Bunny.

1952 saw the release of their second short, BEEP BEEP.

Road Runner model sheet.

Opposite: Coyote model sheet.

© *Warner Brothers*

Once again, the Coyote hungrily tries for the Road Runner using everything from anvils to rockets. This short features the pair running around inside a mine shaft. Later, Jones would restrict the team to more or less staying on top of the desert.

Later that same year GOING! GOING! GOSH! was released. This time the Coyote tries using giant sling shots, quick drying cement, more anvils and dynamite. The pair was definitely now off and running in their own series.

For the next several years, the chase continued with at least one short every year. The "pun"ish titles included ZIPPING ALONG (1953), READY SET ZOOM (1955), ZOOM AND BOARD (1958), HOT ROD AND REEL (1959), and WILD ABOUT HURRY (1960).

As years went by, the team became more and more standardized and so did the cartoons. Running gags (no pun intended) began cropping up. STOP, LOOK AND HASTEN (1954) finds the Coyote installing a steel plate into the road with a special toaster like mechanism that shoots the plate up into oncoming traffic. Of course the device fails when the Road Runner races by, but as the short continues it does come to life. In LICKETY SPLAT (1961) an initial try at using flying dynamite sticks finds various stray sticks popping up throughout the film at the most aggravating moments for the Coyote.

In 1961, the Coyote and Road Runner received their single Oscar nomination for

BEEP PREPARED. This short has the Coyote trying to trip the Road Runner, using a magnet, and wearing the ACME Bat Man suit. At the finale, the Coyote is blasted into space where he "creates" a new star constellation, a Coyote. The short lost out to ERSATZ, the first foreign cartoon to win an Oscar.

1962 found the pair starring in THE ADVENTURES OF THE ROAD RUNNER. This was an unsold TV pilot, and similar to the popular prime time BUGS BUNNY SHOW (1960-62), it featured old and new animation. The 26 minute film received limited theatrical release as a featurette before being cut up into several "new" shorts.

Wile E. appeared in HARE-BREADTH HURRY in 1963. Though this was built like a Coyote-Road Runner short, it actually co-starred Bugs Bunny who was filling in for a slightly injured Road Runner. Wile E. also found work in another "Ralph Wolf" short we will return to later in this chapter.

WAR AND PIECES, released in 1964, was the last new theatrical short made by Jones and crew. This one finds the Coyote using grenades, rope, invisible paint and a rocket car.

The Warners studio shut down their animation unit in 1963. Ex-Warners' director Friz Freleng teamed with David DePatie to form DePatie-Freleng and rented the old Warners' animation facilities to produce economical cartoons, including the Pink Panther series. Warners suddenly found that there was still some profit to be made from creating new cartoons and hired DePatie-Freleng to revive the classic characters from their early retirement.

a.k.a. THE ROAD RUNNER...
Speedibux Rex
Birdibus Zippibus
Super Sonicus
Fastius Tasty-Us
Burn-em Upus Asphaltus

1965 saw the release of the first shorts under the new studio. The first film, THE WILD CHASE (1965) featured a race between the Road Runner and Speedy Gonzales. Interfering with the race were the Coyote (after the Road Runner) and Sylvester (after Speedy).

"My own favorite cartoons are Jones' Road Runners"

— Richard Williams, animation director of WHO FRAMED ROGER RABBIT?

The director on these shorts was usually Rudy Larriva, a former layout artist. Though these shorts often feature some nice poses and expressions, they lack the life of the early adventures.

These later shorts were often based on topics rather than just series of gags. Everything from giant robots (THE TIN COYOTE has Wile E. building a huge mechanical coyote out of junk) to spies (Wile E. finds a spy's attache case in SUGAR AND SPIES) became key themes. These themes were the closest the series ever got to actual "plots." In fact, SUGAR AND SPIES (1966) was the last theatrical Coyote and Road Runner short produced.

CARTOON SUPERSTARS

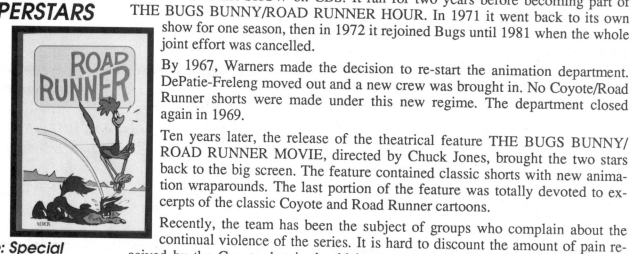

Above: Special school publication featuring original comic strips from the Seventies.

Below: Poster for the 1971 Kite Fun Book.

© Warner Brothers

"The best stuff Chuck ever did was the Road Runners and I think the guy that wrote them, Mike Maltese, should get credit too."

— Harry Love, animation producer/director (Columbia, Hanna-Barbera)

52

That same year saw the team get their own Saturday morning show. Always a staple on the BUGS BUNNY SHOW, in 1966 they received their own half hour THE ROAD RUNNER SHOW on CBS. It ran for two years before becoming part of THE BUGS BUNNY/ROAD RUNNER HOUR. In 1971 it went back to its own show for one season, then in 1972 it rejoined Bugs until 1981 when the whole joint effort was cancelled.

By 1967, Warners made the decision to re-start the animation department. DePatie-Freleng moved out and a new crew was brought in. No Coyote/Road Runner shorts were made under this new regime. The department closed again in 1969.

Ten years later, the release of the theatrical feature THE BUGS BUNNY/ ROAD RUNNER MOVIE, directed by Chuck Jones, brought the two stars back to the big screen. The feature contained classic shorts with new animation wraparounds. The last portion of the feature was totally devoted to excerpts of the classic Coyote and Road Runner cartoons.

Recently, the team has been the subject of groups who complain about the continual violence of the series. It is hard to discount the amount of pain received by the Coyote, but it should be remembered, it is almost totally self inflicted and he returns to the battle relatively unharmed and of his own free will.

The pair continue to work. They have done occasional TV commercials and a cameo in WHO FRAMED ROGER RABBIT? (1988). In the new series TINY TOON ADVENTURES (1990), they have two young counterparts, Calamity Coyote and Little Beeper.

THE RULES OF THE GAME

Jones once stated there were at least nine rules to the series. A look at just three shows how these rules made some order of the Coyote and Road Runner's world.

Rule: *The Road Runner cannot harm the Coyote except by going "Beep-Beep."*

Rule: *No outside force can harm the Coyote — only his ineptitude or the failure of the Acme products.*

Rule: *The Road Runner must stay on the road — otherwise, logically, he would not be called a road runner.*

The creative team thought that the more restrictions they put on the series, the funnier the shorts would become. However almost every cartoon breaks one of the rules. Some of the rules appear broken because Jones and crew kept adding to the list as the series went on. For example the first short has the Road Runner grab a large metal pan so the Coyote will run into it. Other rules were broken when other personnel took over the series.

Finally, even the ultimate rule of the Coyote never catching the Road Runner fell. In SOUP OR SONIC (1980), the Coyote finally catches the Road Runner. (This short was originally part of the TV special BUGS BUNNY'S BUSTING OUT ALL OVER.) After running through a series of ever narrowing pipes the pair emerge from the pipe's tiny end only a few inches high. They run back through the pipes starting at the narrow end heading towards the larger end. At the larger end, the Road Runner comes out full size, but Wile E. comes out still only inches high. He grabs the Road Runner's leg and has a brief moment of joy. Suddenly, he realizes his situation. Looking into the camera with great irritation he holds up two signs: "Okay, wise guys, you always wanted me to catch him — now what do I do?" The cartoon then fades out.

WILE E. COYOTE'S OTHER LIVES

Of the two, Wile E. is the most complex of the characters. So much so, that he actually steps into other roles and interacts with other characters. He is the "Super genius" that tries to capture Bugs Bunny in OPERATION RABBIT (1952). Oddly enough, this cartoon is his second animated appearance. The second Road Runner cartoon didn't

> **"You tend to root for both characters. You want the Road Runner to win because he's an 'innocent' and you want the Coyote to win just because he deserves it after all he's been through."**
>
> **— Jim Henson, creator of the Muppets**

Animation drawings by Chuck Jones.

© Warner Brothers

arrive in theaters until later that same year. He encounters Bugs again in TO HARE IS HUMAN (1956) and the previously mentioned HARE BREADTH HURRY. The Coyote was even less of a match for the quick witted rabbit than he was for the Road Runner.

As "Ralph Wolf," he attempts to steal sheep from Sam, a sheep dog. This series began with DON'T GIVE UP THE SHEEP (1953). This series is similar to his Road Runner series except that at the end of the "work day," both parties quit. He dusts himself off and heads home with his adversary, both planning to "clock in" again the next day for much of the same activity. Other titles in this series include SHEEP AHOY (1954), STEAL WOOL (1957) and READY WOOLEN AND ABLE (1960). It was an amusing concept that the cartoon conceits of the ongoing conflict were merely a 9-to-5 job. It was one of the first indications that toon characters had a much different life outside of the cartoons they appeared in.

Even when he talks, Wile E. has several tongues. His most commonly known is the slightly bland, intellectual tone used in his battles with Bugs Bunny. His Ralph Wolf voice is a bit harsher. This voice is more like a blue collar worker rather than an intellectual "Super Genius". However, he has a number of other "sounds." In several early shorts he has a raspy, creaky laugh.

> **"The Coyote is victimized by his own ineptitude. I never understood how to use tools and that's the Coyote's problem. He's not at war with the gods, but with the minuscule things of everyday life."**
>
> **— Chuck Jones**

More common than his voice are his signs. At any time, as cartoon law provides, the Coyote can pull a sign out from behind his back. These can read anything from "Egad!" to "In heaven's name, what am I doing?"

ON THE ROAD

The Coyote and Road Runner have had additional careers outside of their long running (over 40) short subjects from Warners. In 1958 they debuted in their own comic book entitled BEEP BEEP, THE ROAD RUNNER. It is this comic series that christened the Road Runner with his first name.

The Road Runner spoke in the comic books, but only in rhyme. He also had triplets, three sons, who also spoke in rhyme. Even a Mrs. Road Runner would appear occasionally, all to the distress of the Coyote. The comic book ran 25 years.

> "The Coyote here isn't merely an egotist; he's almost possessed, he's a fanatic."
>
> — Chuck Jones

Both Coyote and Road Runner are also regularly seen in the Bugs Bunny newspaper comic strip.

They are so well known that they have popped up as a gag in other comic strips ranging from the western Rick O'Shay to the surreal Mother Goose and Grimm and even editorial cartoons. In the late 1960's Plymouth used the Road Runner as a design logo for a series of sports cars. For awhile the tireless twosome were popular advertising figures hawking everything from Hershey's chocolate to Donnelly directories to Purolator Courier. The recent appearance of Warners cartoon related merchandise has produced some new Coyote and Road Runner items.

SUPERSTAR QUALITY

Perhaps their crowning achievement was the appearance in the highly successful WHO FRAMED ROGER RABBIT? The film officially takes place in 1947, two years before the team was created. Spielberg and crew agreed that no post 1947 characters would be viewed, explaining the otherwise mysterious absence of TV characters. However director Robert Zemeckis insisted that the Coyote and Road Runner appear. They were his favorite cartoon characters.

> "The Road Runner cartoons began as a parody of chase films which everyone seemed to be doing at the time. I remember Maltese and I thought we were very clever coming up with this biting bit of satire. We figured we'd be considered the Jonathan Swifts of our day. But no one else saw it as that."
>
> — Chuck Jones

To find them, view the end of the film. After Toon Town has been saved and the Toons all come running in to see the dissolved Judge Doom, Wile E. and the Road Runner are seen in the group. They join in and at least dance with the crew through the reprise of "Smile, Darn Ya, Smile."

Of course making audiences smile and laugh is one of the things this team does best. "Beep-Beep." Zoom!

Page from 1980 Warners licensing book.

DAFFY DUCK

Superstar Summary

THE STAR: Daffy Duck

YEAR OF DEBUT: 1937 (PORKY'S DUCK HUNT)

STUDIO OF DEBUT: Warner Brothers

SIGNATURE: "You're dethpicable!"

KEY CREW BEHIND THE STAR: Tex Avery, Bob Clampett, Chuck Jones (directors), Mel Blanc (voice), Warren Foster, Ben Hardaway, Michael Maltese, Dave Monahan (writers)

CAREER HIGH: DUCK AMUCK (1953) — Daffy suffers the ultimate animated nightmare as the animator takes full control changing costumes, scenery, story and more, while stretching Daffy's flexibility to the limit.

SELECTED SHORT SUBJECTS: Ali Baba Bunny, Draftee Daffy, The Great Piggy Bank Robbery, The Scarlet Pumpernickel, Wise Quacking Duck

Daffy Duck is Warners most versatile star. He could be merely zany or certifiably insane, underdog or villain, friendly or selfish. It all depended on the short and director. Daffy went through a short period of development, as do most Cartoon Superstars, but he never seemed to fully "grow up."

Often described, even by himself, as "the little black duck," Daffy was just that, a black duck. His legs and beak were an orange color (sometimes more red or yellow than orange). On his neck there was frequently a band of white. He had no regular attire, but some of his most famous roles were as costumed characters. He spoke in a lisping, spitting form. (In some of his earlier adventures, his spitting gets quite formidable.)

In fact, Daffy is "half" duck. Porky Pig, Mickey Mouse and Huckleberry Hound are basically humans in animal form. Bugs Bunny, Scooby Doo and Yogi Bear are pretty much animals in a human world. Daffy is both. He swims, flies, and dodges hunters as a duck. However, he also holds jobs, wears clothes, and needs money as do humans.

Daffy was either versatile or schizophrenic, suffering multiple personalities. He definitely started out as a "daffy" darnfool duck and even sang about being "looney tune-y" in an early short. However, he soon settled down to being merely wild and crazy. In fact as Bugs, Porky and other characters began to become more settled in their ways, Daffy remained the looniest of the Looney Tune bunch.

When confronted with the spectre of failure or danger, he would merely re-double his speed, volume and efforts. No amount of physical mutilation could prevent his coming back and trying again. Daffy can endure hate but not indifference. Deep down, he has the fear that he is not good enough. By overcompensating, he hastens his own downfall.

As time passed and more directors took their time with him, he began to exhibit different kinds of behavior. Bob Clampett featured a loud, brazen Daffy who could and would do anything for a laugh. Chuck Jones emphasized a Daffy who was a self-centered, greedy and conniving schemer. Friz Freleng had Daffy often become a villainous foil to other characters. Other directors might feature him as anything from a second banana to an everyman.

Unlike other superstars, or cartoon stars in general, Daffy's various styles of behavior were not phases that came and went as he developed. They seemed forever linked with him, reappearing throughout his long career. Only one factor remained constant: Daffy was almost always annoying! Whether wild and zany, greedy and corrupt, a villain or a stooge, Daffy's constant chatter and unconcern for other characters made him an annoying figure. Ironically, he was his own worst enemy and his actions were usually the cause of his setbacks.

Daffy was an intruding character. Whereas most characters lived in their own world and encountered strangers venturing into their territory, Daffy was always the stranger. His cartoons often begin with him arriving somewhere, or trying to get somewhere. Many of his occupations feature this concept such as in THE IMPATIENT PATIENT (1942) where he's a telegram delivery boy or THE UPSTANDING SITTER (1947) where he's a babysitter.

Daffy in BUGS VS. DAFFY: BATTLE OF THE MUSIC VIDEO STARS (1988).

© *Warner Brothers*

He was the most "sexually active" of the Warners crew. (And for that matter of most superstars in general.) Daffy was often married with children. Sadly, it was not always a happy marriage. More than once he was a hen (or duck) pecked husband. He even had a wife who wanted a divorce due to his clowning around that made their egg disappear (THE HEN PECKED DUCK, 1949).

Daffy was also seen as a single duck, frequently on the lookout for women.

Though Daffy was a superstar in his own right, he was also a team player. As often as not, he was one of pair. Throughout his career, Porky was frequently teamed with Daffy. Bugs teamed with Daffy in the Fifties for a series of shorts featuring the two in a battle of wits. The Sixties found him often at odds with the rapid Speedy Gonzales.

It is no doubt that this general versatility of personality is what kept Daffy so busy. Unlike other characters who would become locked into a fairly consistent behavior, the writers and directors could do anything with Daffy... and they did.

THE LITTLE BLACK DUCK BEGINS

Daffy's origins are pretty clean-cut as cartoon superstars go. In the Thirties, the key Warners staff was being assembled. This included such writers as Tedd Pierce, Michael Maltese and Warren Foster. Chuck Jones, Tex Avery, Bob Clampett, Frank Tashlin, Bob McKimson, and Friz Freleng were beginning their work as either animators or directors. (All would eventually become directors.) Also on hand was Carl Stalling, the music master who would create some of the greatest scores in animated history. The Looney Tune factory was getting into full swing.

The studio's main star of this new regime was Porky Pig. He had finally grown up to an adult and was now more human than pig in behavior. 1937 saw the release of just another Porky short entitled PORKY'S DUCK HUNT. However, this film shows much more lunacy than found in other Warners cartoons at the time. Not only is it the debut of Daffy, but some historians consider it the beginning of the "classic" Warners style. Directed by Tex Avery, the main plot was just what the title said.

CARTOON SUPERSTARS

During the Thirties, in the quest for stars, the studios often put the character's name in the title for more recognition. The title also frequently described the short. It wasn't until the late Thirties and Forties that animated shorts began going heavily after titles that were either puns or jokes.

In this debut film, Porky is befuddled by a crazy black duck. The duck bounces and dances around the pond, talks back to Porky and even admits to not following the script. In the end he repeats his dance over the end titles! At the time this was unprecedented. It certainly appears as if the little black duck was being groomed for bigger things.

"Daffy's a little egotistical jerk."

— Mel Blanc

Mel Blanc provided Daffy's lisping voice, a direct copy of producer Leon Schlesinger's. The animators copied it as a gag. They speeded it up slightly. (Sylvester the Cat is an example of how it would sound without being artificially sped up.) It wasn't until the first screening, with Schlesinger, that they had second thoughts. Upon completing the screening, Schlesinger is reported to have said, "Where did you guyth get that crazthy voithe!"

A CONNECTICUT RABBIT IN KING ARTHUR'S COURT
CHUCK JONES ENTERPRISES - 1977
© WARNER BROS.

This character is still pretty much the standard "crazy cartoon character" used in such films. Bugs Bunny's character eventually derived from a similarly silly hare in PORKY'S HARE HUNT (1938). However, this craziness seemed to fit the duck.

Daffy's next appearance was co-starring with another regular Warner's character, Egghead. DAFFY DUCK AND EGGHEAD (1938) was written by Ben ("Bugs") Hardaway and directed by Tex Avery. In it, Daffy is once again the hunted duck. Daffy's back with Porky in PORKY AND DAFFY (1938) as the pair are placed in a boxing ring. This one introduced director Bob Clampett to the little black duck... and Daffy would never be quite the same.

Model sheet for A CONNECTICUT RABBIT IN KING ARTHUR'S COURT aka BUGS BUNNY IN KING ARTHUR'S COURT. Opposite: Model sheet for THE CARNIVAL OF THE ANIMALS drawn by Chuck Jones.

© Warner Brothers

DAFFY GETS A JOB

Clampett gave Daffy his first "job," in the duck's fourth outing, THE DAFFY DOC (1938). Daffy chases Porky through a hospital and accidentally gets caught in an iron lung. This causes Daffy's body parts to begin inflating and deflating as if they were breathing!

The final short of 1938 was DAFFY DUCK IN HOLLYWOOD. Directed by Avery and written by Dave Monahan, the story has Daffy trying to break into pictures. When he's snubbed by a famous director, the Duck sneaks into the editing room and compiles a film of his own.

In 1939, Daffy appears in only two films, DAFFY DUCK AND THE DINOSAUR (directed by Chuck Jones, written by Monahan) and WISE QUACKS (directed by Clampett, written by Warren Foster). While DINOSAUR is a standard duck hunt picture, QUACKS features the first view of Daffy's married life. In fact, Daffy's expecting so Porky comes over to congratulate him.

Daffy's connection to Porky Pig would follow him through most of his career. In YOU OUGHTA BE IN PICTURES (1940), Daffy tries to take over Porky's starring position at Warners. (Something, in reality, he actually did.) PORKY PIG'S FEAT (1943) and DAFFY DUCK SLEPT HERE (1948) have the two share a hotel room with disastrous results. MY LITTLE DUCKAROO (1954) puts the pair in a Western spoof. 1961's DAFFY'S INN TROUBLE finds the two operating competing Inns. The only difference was that by the Fifties, Daffy would be the star, and Porky would play second banana.

Daffy continued growing into the wild and crazy Duck throughout the Forties. THE WISE QUACK-ING DUCK (1943) placed Daffy on the farm with Mr. Meek trying to kill him for a duck dinner. ("Gruesome, isn't it!") In HOLLYWOOD DAFFY (1946) he battled a Hollywood studio guard (patterned after Joe Besser) to try to see movie stars. He fought off a mad scientist (patterned after Peter Lorre) who wanted the wishbone of a duck in THE BIRTH OF A NOTION (1947). Bob Clampett's 1946 THE GREAT PIGGY BANK ROBBERY (written by Warren Foster) had him imagine he was Duck Twacy, the famous "detectative," in a spoof of the popular Dick Tracy comic strip.

This was Daffy's first character satire, something he would come back to in the Fifties.

Clampett is often credited with giving Daffy his craziest lives. It is the Clampett Daffys that feature the incredibly rubbery duck in his most insane adventures. Whether he is trying to hide from "the little man from the Draft board" in DRAFTEE DAF-FY (1945, written by Lou Lilly) or doing a wild scat number in BOOK REVIEW (1946, written by Warren Foster), Clampett's Daffy is totally wacky.

By the late Forties, though, Chuck Jones began to fully develop a new side to Daffy. Jones saw Daffy as a schemer and a coward of gigantic magnitude. Daffy became a close psychological cousin to Wile E. Coyote in that Jones' little black duck was possessed by the idea of winning, at all costs. This character trait was used in two fairly distinct series directed by Jones and written by Michael Maltese.

"THE CARNIVAL OF THE ANIMALS" Chuck Jones Enterprises - 1976

CHUCK'S DUCK

The first was the classic Bugs/Daffy battles in which Daffy continually tried to get the best of Bugs. Sometimes it was convincing Elmer it was Rabbit Season (RABBIT FIRE, 1951; RABBIT SEASONING, 1952; DUCK, RABBIT, DUCK, 1953). Other times it was simply trying to cheat the rabbit (ALI BABA BUNNY, 1957). These verbal battles are considered some of the greatest cartoons ever made. Such lines as "Pronoun trouble," "Shoot me now! Shoot me now!" and the wonderfully subdued comment by Daffy to Bugs, "You're dethpicable," are favorites.

"Daffy, on the other hand, was insane: He never settled down. His personality was very self-serving, as if to say, 'I may be be mean, but at least I'm alive.'"

— Chuck Jones

The other series was a group of satires on popular films and TV shows. Just as Daffy's version of Duck Twacy has remained popular, so have these variations on media... even when the original is long forgotten. The Buck Rogers Comic Strip was lampooned in DUCK DODGERS IN THE 24-1/2 CENTURY (1953). DE-DUCE YOU SAY (1956) had Daffy starring as Dorlock Homes. He was Robin Hood in ROBIN HOOD DAFFY (1958). Even the popular trend of quiz shows got a royal ribbing in THE DUCKSTERS (1950) in which Daffy, the host of "Truth or Aaaagh!," puts contestant Porky through the most horrifying grilling for prizes. Daffy was always cast as the hero but was usually upstaged by his aide-de-camp played by Porky Pig.

Jones and Maltese didn't have a monopoly on the satiric Daffy. Robert McKimson and Warren Foster created several. STUPOR DUCK (1956) has Daffy spoof Superman, while CHINA JONES (1959) made light of the (then) popular CHINA SMITH TV series.

Publicity art for STUPOR DUCK.

© Warner Brothers

During this time, Daffy was still doing his old schtick. RIFF RAFFY DAFFY (1948), directed by Art Davis and written by William (Bill) Scott and Lloyd Turner, found a vagrant Daffy being chased through a department store by policepig Porky. HOLIDAY FOR DRUMSTICKS (1949), directed by Davis and written by Turner, has Daffy getting jealous over the attention a turkey is receiving. DESIGN FOR LEAVING (1954), directed by McKimson and written by Tedd Pierce, features Daffy as another annoying door-to-door salesman. DON'T AXE ME (1957), another McKimson/ Pierce entry, has Daffy and a dog befuddling farmer Elmer.

In the Sixties, Warners would go through a number of changes, but Daffy remained fairly consistent. He battled with Bugs in THE ABOMINABLE SNOW RABBIT (1961), co-directed by Chuck Jones and Maurice Noble and written by Tedd Pierce, and played a stowaway in GOOD NOOSE (1962), directed by McKimson and written by Dave Detiege. In 1963 the studio shut its doors.

David DePatie and former Warners' director Friz Freleng were making cartoons, including the Pink Panther shorts, when Warners asked them to produce additional Warners cartoons. Daffy was part of these new shorts, and was often teamed with Speedy Gonzales. These shorts often centered around Speedy trying to steal something from Daffy, or merely annoying him in a "mouselike" way. Titles included ASSAULT AND PEPPERED (1965), DAFFY RENTS (1966), and SPEEDY GHOST TO TOWN (1967). Warners restarted their own studio in 1967, but it only lasted for two years. Daffy only starred in a few of these, his last being SEE YOU LATER GLADIATOR (1968), also starring Speedy Gonzales. These shorts did not make strong use of Daffy's unique qualities and are not fondly remembered by many fans.

> "As with all characters, the first Daffy didn't look or talk exactly like the later one, but that certain magic was there."
>
> — Bob Clampett

DAFFY TV

With the Warners animated short business seemingly ended, he joined Bugs and the other Warners crew on TV. The shorts sold to TV in the Fifties were still being run successfully in syndication. He'd played a large part on the prime time THE BUGS BUNNY SHOW (1961-63) where he tried continually but unsuccessfully to upstage Bugs. The Bugs Bunny Saturday morning series, which featured numerous Daffy outings, was proving successful. Daffy even got his own series, THE DAFFY DUCK SHOW (1978-81) which primarily featured the Daffy/Speedy shorts that had not previously appeared on TV.

Perhaps of more importance was the string of prime time specials that began in 1976. The continued success of the shorts in syndication and Saturday morning, plus the successful release of the theatrical BUGS BUNNY SUPERSTAR, convinced Warners to go back into the

"Daffy is just like Sylvester, only Daffy is sped up electronically"
— Bob McKimson

animation business. Chuck Jones was brought in and he began work on a number of TV special and feature projects. The first, CARNIVAL OF THE ANIMALS (1976) was all new animation and featured Daffy and Bugs performing the classical music piece on piano. Eventually the specials became a combination of new animation used to bridge old shorts. Daffy was still a frequent player.

When the Warners features began, Daffy cartoons were often included. 1979's BUGS BUNNY/ROAD RUNNER MOVIE featured the classic DUCK DODGERS IN THE 24TH-1/2 CENTURY amongst other Daffys. The other Bugs' features also contained moments from Daffy's career.

In 1980, Daffy again starred in a totally new animated prime time special, DAFFY DUCK'S EASTER SPECIAL. Though it was structured like a normal compilation special, the difference was that all the shorts were new. Daffy starred in THE YOLKS ON YOU, where he and Sylvester fight over a golden egg, and THE CHOCOLATE CHASE, which has him guarding a chocolate factory from Speedy Gonzales.

Daffy was not destined to remain in this world of repeat and new animated compilations. Steven Spielberg had big plans for the little black duck. In the mid-Seventies, Spielberg expressed interest in doing a sequel to the classic DUCK DODGERS. The original plan was to have the short become the start to one of Spielberg's science fantasy features. Sadly, though the short was completed in 1980, it never received the big screen treatment.

Studio art.

© *Warner Brothers*

The short was eventually completed and shown as part of the DAFFY DUCK'S THANKS-FOR-GIVING special in 1981.

The Duck never gave up.

FEATURE FILM FOWL

Daffy received his own feature, DAFFY DUCK'S FANTASTIC ISLAND, in 1983. The feature was based on the popular TV series FANTASY ISLAND. Shipwrecked on a desert island, Daffy and Speedy discover a wishing well that actually grants wishes. The greedy Daffy comes to light and sees a profit from this situation. Soon other Warners characters pay him for wishes, which segues into classic Warner shorts. The plot thickens when Yosemite Sam and the Tasmanian Devil come to the island to recover their treasure, the well.

"DAFFY DUCK"

© WARNER BROS. INC

CARTOON SUPERSTARS

With the release and success of the first GHOSTBUSTERS movie (1985), Warners again considered doing something new with their characters. The first thought was of a new animated feature containing all new animation to be called QUACK-BUSTERS. This expensive plan was moderated to result in yet another mixture of new and classic animation.

"Audiences weren't accustomed to seeing a cartoon character do these things.... People would leave the theaters talking about Daffy Duck."

— Bob Clampett

Then some bright studio person asked, if new animation was to be made to bridge the old animation, and the old animation were shorts, why not make some of the new bridging animation shorts? Work began on both the full length feature QUACKBUSTERS and two new shorts, both starring Daffy. The shorts were titled THE DUXORCIST and THE NIGHT OF THE LIVING DUCK.

The first one, THE DUXORCIST actually received some theatrical release in the Fall of 1987. The short was about Daffy exorcising a demon from a pretty lady duck. It featured the original Carl Stalling music of the Forties and Fifties. Critics were delighted with Warner's return to shorts.

The second short received a festival screening prior to being attached to a feature. THE NIGHT OF THE LIVING DUCK was a musical dream sequence in which Daffy dreams he is entertaining a night club full of monsters. It was debuted at the New York Film Festival on September 23rd, 1988. A few days later, the feature film DAFFY DUCK'S QUACKBUSTERS debuted. NIGHT OF THE LIVING DUCK appeared in front of the feature, almost as a prologue.

DAFFY DUCK'S QUACKBUSTERS begins with Daffy inheriting a great deal of money. However the benefactor keeps coming back from the dead and removing the money, because of Daffy's selfish ways. Daffy decides to come up with a ghost riddance service. He's joined by Bugs and Porky (and his pet Sylvester) who go out on various jobs and encounter psychic phenomena via classic shorts and the two new shorts. In the end, Daffy loses his money and is back on the street hawking his wares.

Publicity still from THE YOKES ON YOU, a 1980 short first seen in DAFFY DUCK'S EASTER SHOW.

OPPOSITE:Forties movie poster advertising Warners' two main stars.

© Warner Brothers

Story and direction on the feature and two new shorts were by Greg Ford and Terry Lennon. They were produced by Steven Greene

When the feature came to home video in 1989, Daffy starred on a commercial at the front of the cassette. He was hawking the Warners catalog of collectible items. Daffy was seen being trailed by numerous fans and finally escaping to the peace and quite of his dressing room... only to find his chair labeled "Donald Duck!"

In 1990, to celebrate the 50th birthday of Bugs Bunny, Warners released another new theatrical short, BOX OFFICE BUNNY. Though it starred Bugs and Elmer, Daffy was included. By this time, Daffy was being voiced by Jeff Bergman. Bergman took on the daunting task after Mel Blanc, Daffy's original beloved voice, died in 1989.

62

This new short was directed by Darrel Van Citters and written by Charles Carney.

Warners is hoping this might lead to a new series of short subjects for theaters. If it does, Daffy will be there.

CO-STARS

Daffy was often teamed with other Warners characters. His most frequent partner was Porky Pig, the generally calm, stuttering "fat boy" (as Daffy would occasionally call him). Another common partner was Bugs Bunny, who was more a rival than partner.

In his later years, his most common partner was Speedy Gonzales. Speedy was "the fastest mouse in all of Mexico." Created by Friz Freleng, this hyper rodent could outrun anything. When working with Daffy, he would frequently be the thorn in Daffy's side.

There were numerous lady ducks who portrayed Mrs. Daffy Duck.

OTHER MEDIA

Daffy was always one of the most popular Warners characters. Toys, books, records, comics, and all the standard forms of merchandising employed the talents of Daffy. He even helped Bugs Bunny sell Tang, the orange flavored breakfast drink.

He first appeared in comic books in Dell's LOONEY TUNES AND MERRIE MELODIES (1941) which lasted over 200 issues. After several one-shot appearances in Dell's Four Color series, Daffy finally got his own comic book in 1956 called DAFFY, which ran for 145 issues. He appeared in other comic book titles that featured Warner's characters and he made frequent appearances in the long running Bugs Bunny comic strip.

Daffy also appeared as part of a group of other Warners characters on merchandise including games, clocks and lunch boxes.

SUPERSTAR QUALITY

Daffy is almost impossible to dislike. Due to his variety of roles and personalities, it seems everyone has at least one Daffy cartoon on their list of favorite shorts. This wildly flexible (in both body and personality), little black duck has made a big impression in the world of animation. He may be "dethpicable," he may be "looney tune-y," he may be "a darn fool duck," but he's a classic Cartoon Superstar.

"The preservation of (Daffy's) dignity depends on the avoidance of humiliation."

— Chuck Jones

DONALD DUCK

SELECTED SHORT SUBJECTS: *Der Fuehrer's Face, Donald's Applecore, Grand Canyonscope, The Three Caballeros (feature), Trick or Treat*

Superstar Summary

THE STAR: Donald Duck

YEAR OF DEBUT: 1934 (THE WISE LITTLE HEN)

STUDIO OF DEBUT: Walt Disney

SIGNATURE: "Wauk!" "Hi ya, toots!"

KEY CREW BEHIND THE STAR: Walt Disney; Clarence Nash (voice); Jack Hannah, Jack King (directors); Carl Barks (storyman, comic book writer/ artist).

CAREER HIGH: THE BAND CONCERT (1935) where he upstaged Mickey Mouse and started on the road to super stardom.

Donald is perhaps the most versatile of all the Disney characters. Throughout his long career, he has been employed in a variety of different jobs from sailor to homeowner. His wide range of emotions has offered animators wonderful possibilities not available for most Disney performers.

Donald is vain, cocky and boastful and always loves to tease other characters. If the tables get turned, he flies into an uncontrollable rage and becomes his own worst enemy. Although he will attempt to use cunning to achieve his goals, these attempts usually backfire with disastrous results.

Despite his fits of unintelligible anger, Donald always remained a sympathetic character. He was an adult who acted like a child. He operated in a world similar to our own. The only noticeable exception being that his world was often populated with animals who behaved like humans. Donald went to work, brought flowers and candy to his girl friend, and mowed his lawn.

While Daffy Duck could appear in a pond and be frightened by the approach of a befuddled hunter, the opening of hunting season filled Donald with excitement because he was not the prey but the hunter. The wonders of animation allowed Donald to contort into physically unusual positions, but he was never taken to the physical extremes of other non-Disney animated animals.

Clarence "Ducky" Nash, the original voice for the quarrelsome Duck, once stated that unlike Mickey Mouse, Donald Duck would not be a good candidate for a fan club. Said Nash, "he's too full of mischief and might not set too good an example for some children."

It is just that mischief that made him loved from the start. In a 1935 article for the *New York Evening Journal*, critic Gilbert Seldes proclaimed that Donald was "a new character who surpasses Mickey Mouse himself." That same year, the *New York Times* devoted a serious editorial to the fact that the irascible Duck might replace Mickey Mouse in the hearts of the world.

That fear was certainly well founded as Mickey Mouse became more and more sanitized when he became a symbol for the Walt Disney Company. Donald Duck was unfettered by such restraints and his frequent bursts of ill temper, violence and selfishness made the world laugh.

DONALD'S ORIGINS

Donald's first screen appearance was in the Silly Symphony THE WISE LITTLE HEN (1934). It was based on a still popular children's fable which recounted the disappointments of a hen seeking assistance to plant her corn. Donald's purpose was to simply be an amusing prop in the story, like his now forgotten companion, Peter Pig.

This Donald would be barely recognizable by today's audiences. The early Donald Duck with his long bill and stick legs was funny but not likable. Gradually over the years, Donald became shorter and rounder on the theory that a chubby figure is cuter and more likable. His eyes became more expressive, his bill shorter and his head larger in order to provide a wider range of subtle expressions. But even in his first

film, he sported the same sailor suit and unforgettable quack that have been his trademark for over half a century.

The unforgettable quack was supplied by Clarence Nash, whose contribution to the Duck's personality was enormous. "I sat in on some of the story meetings and made some suggestions based on all the things I had discovered I could make Donald do," recalled Nash. Originally, Nash had developed a baby billy-goat bleat by age 13 and had used that voice in theatrical presentations. It was that bleat that became the famous Duck voice when Walt Disney heard the sound and thought it perfect for Donald.

Nash also supplied the voice to Herman the Duck on the Burns and Allen radio show of the 1940s. For Disney, he put the left side of his tongue against his upper left molars, formed a pocket high in his left cheek, opened his mouth, and Donald Duck talked.

Donald, long before Roger, in live action via THE THREE CABALLEROS.
© *Walt Disney Productions*

Audience reaction to Donald's first role was so positive that the Duck appeared in a Mickey Mouse short entitled OR-PHAN'S BEN-EFIT (1934). The gag centered on Donald trying to recite the poem "Mary Had a Little Lamb" to a theater full of raucous mouse orphans. Once again, audience reaction confirmed that Disney had a new star.

Donald's next appearance was in the first full color Mickey Mouse cartoon, THE BAND CON-CERT (1935). Donald's playing of "Turkey in the Straw" on a fife disrupts Mickey's attempts to conduct an outdoor concert rendition of the "William Tell Overture." Even the force of a tornado fails to dim Donald's impertinent spirit.

Also released in 1935 was MICKEY'S SERVICE STATION which established the format for the Duck's appearances until he was given his own series. The format was simple but effective: Donald would join Mickey and Goofy on some project such as building a ship, trying to service a car, hunting a moose or cleaning a clock. The story would split into separate sections showcasing the individual misadventures of each character. These situations provided ample opportunity for Donald's ill temper to further aggravate the problem and served as counterpoint to the more subdued frustrations of Mickey and Goofy.

"We began to have an awful hard time finding stories for Mickey," commented Disney director Jack Hannah who was working as a storyman at the time. "The Duck was very versatile to work with — it was easy to find a situation for him. Donald could be anything. He had every emotion a human being had. He could be cute, mischievous, go from warm to cool at any moment. You could half kill him and he'd come right back. He instigated trouble. Not mean, but he always saw a chance to have fun at other people's expense. That was the essence of his personality, that and his temper. He'd start out looking like he just stepped out of Sunday school, and he'd try so hard to be good, but then he'd get tempted."

DONALD STEPS OUT

Noticing the growing popularity of the Duck, Disney decided to turn out short cartoons that would feature Donald. The first solo Donald cartoon was DON DONALD (1937). It also introduced Donald's long time flame, Daisy Duck. (Though in this first appearance she also spoke in "duck speak.") It was directed by Ben Sharpsteen. He had been directing a large number of the Mickey/Donald/Goofy shorts and would continue to direct Duck shorts co-starring a variety of Disney characters such as THE FOX HUNT (co-starring Goofy) and POLAR TRAPPERS (co-starring Pluto).

To help direct the series, Disney hired Jack King from New York. King was a more-than-competent animation director who had previously worked for Warner Brothers and easily adapted to the Disney style. MODERN INVENTIONS (1937) was the first of King's Donald Duck cartoons.

> "We had to pantomime pretty well in the drawing what the Duck was thinking or doing because if you were trying to do a gag or line of dialog, you were in trouble using just that voice."
>
> — Jack Hannah, director

Donald's brashness made him quite popular during World War II when the U.S., itself, was becoming pretty brash. It was the work of Disney director Jack Kinney, best known for his Goofy shorts, that won Donald his only Oscar. DER FUEHRER'S FACE (1942) was a strong propaganda cartoon in which Donald dreamed he was a good hardworking Nazi in Germany. The dream was so frightening that Donald awoke and gratefully kissed a model of the Statue of Liberty.

Donald's wartime popularity was often called into service as a visual aid. In 1940, he had been drafted to promote the Community Chest charities in a three minute short called THE VOLUNTEER WORKER and to help out the Canadian government in 1942 with DONALD'S DECISION. In the U.S., he starred in THE NEW SPIRIT (1942), perhaps one of the most famous of Disney's educational cartoons. It was commissioned by the Treasury Department to inform wartime citizens of the importance of paying their taxes.

A revised version, THE SPIRIT OF '43 was released the following year.

> "I never really got any great salary at Disney, but the greatest payment for me was that this character became known all over the world."
>
> — Clarence Nash, the original voice of Donald Duck

DISNEY'S "DUCK MEN"

The wartime Donald Duck cartoons were largely the result of the story team of Jack Hannah and Carl Barks. Perhaps more than anyone else, these two shaped the image of Donald Duck as he is known to audiences today. They supplied the stories for such cartoons as DONALD GETS DRAFTED (1942), SKY TROOPER (1942), FALL OUT FALL IN (1943), THE OLD ARMY GAME (1943) and COMMANDO DUCK (1944). These cartoons often dealt with Donald as a private who was being harassed by Sergeant Black Pete. The cartoons poked good-natured fun at the military experience and found instant acceptance by audiences familiar with the situations. In FALL OUT FALL IN, poor Donald, after a wearying march, has trouble setting up his tent and after a frustrating battle gets to sleep just in time to "fall in" for another day's march. SKY TROOPER had Donald trying to parachute and ending up with KP duty.

The story team of Hannah and Barks also produced classic Donald stories that were not related to the military experience. THE PLASTICS INVENTOR (1944) had Donald following a radio program's instructions on how to make an airplane out of plastic. Unfortunately, a rain storm melts the plane once it is airborne.

> ### "The bane of my life was getting anybody to understand the Duck."
> ### — Jack Hannah, director

In 1942, he and Hannah had been approached to draw an original Donald Duck comic book story. Western Publishing wanted to stop using reprints of the Donald Duck comic strip and create some original stories. Working evenings and on weekends, the two men produced "Donald Duck Finds Pirate Gold," based on a feature film project that at one time was designed for Mickey Mouse. The comic was a success and the original printing is a much valued collector's item today.

With the shift to war films, Carl Barks reportedly lost interest in his work at the studio. He left with the intention of starting a chicken ranch. When Western Publishing discovered that Barks had left the studio, he was contacted about supplying ten page Donald Duck stories for the comic book, WALT DISNEY'S COMIC AND STORIES. Barks accepted and continued to write and draw Donald Duck stories for a variety of comic books.

During this time, he was responsible for the creation of many key characters in the Donald Duck universe including the villainous Beagle Boys, the super rich Uncle Scrooge and Magica de Spell, the sorceress. In addition, Barks developed the personalities of Huey, Dewey and Louie and created the Junior Woodchucks.

Early Donald from THE ORPHAN'S BENEFIT.

© Walt Disney Productions

Not limited by Clarence Nash's vocalizations, Barks made Donald more articulate and heroic. Barks adventure story concepts were the basis for the now popular DUCK TALES TV series. Barks retired from comic book work in 1966 and his stories have been frequently reprinted. In recent years, he has had a lucrative career doing paintings of the Duck family.

For nearly five years, Jack Hannah and his story partner Carl Barks submitted stories for the Donald Duck series of shorts. When Barks left to pursue a successful career as a writer and artist of Donald Duck comic books stories, Hannah was moved over to directing the Donald Duck cartoons. Hannah's first assignment was DONALD'S DAY OFF (1944). His directorial signature was so strong that within three years, Hannah became the sole Duck director.

HANNAH'S DUCK

The film image of Donald Duck that is most familiar to modern fans is the work of Jack Hannah. Under Hannah's guidance many of Donald's well known supporting cast made their first and most memorable appearances. These characters included Chip 'n' Dale, Humphrey the Bear, Bootle Beetle and Buzz Buzz the Bee. Six of

Hannah's Donald Duck cartoons were nominated for Academy Awards including the memorable TRICK OR TREAT (1952) in which Donald must battle unsuccessfully against his nephews and a real witch over a closet loaded with Halloween goodies.

There were many classic Donald Duck cartoons directed by Jack Hannah. His previous experience as a storyman on the Duck cartoons helped him shape and edit stories before they went to animation resulting in stronger cartoons. Many of the memorable Hannah Donald cartoons featured the Duck interacting with a number of outstanding supporting characters. Oftentimes these co-stars were extremely tiny.

"We did go to smaller characters with the Duck because it would make it funnier when the situation backfired on him," said director Hannah. "Just having Donald and his nephews made it difficult to come up with story ideas after awhile. You couldn't use much dialogue because you wouldn't be able to understand it."

"Donald Duck is a lovable twerp who never could stay out of trouble... and he usually brought it on himself."

— Jack Hannah, director

Donald's tiniest troublemakers were insects! For example, Buzz Buzz the bee was one of Donald's regular frustrations. When Donald irritates him on the beach, Buzz Buzz sends the Duck into shark infested waters in BEE AT THE BEACH (1950). Bootle Beetle, another small insect, was also often in conflict with the Duck. In SEA SALTS (1949) Bootle is shipwrecked with Donald who cheats when he divides the remaining provisions.

Donald's most popular small co-stars were Chip 'n' Dale, the chipmunks. They troubled Donald many times, especially when he played with small objects such as a remote controlled plane (TEST PILOT DONALD, 1951), or a miniature train (OUT OF SCALE, 1951) or a model ship (CHIPS AHOY, 1956). The Chipmunks also appeared in the only 3-D Donald Duck short, WORKING FOR PEANUTS (1953). They steal peanuts from Dolores, the zoo elephant, and then must deal with the wrath of zoo attendant Donald. The short was later re-filmed in regular format after the 3-D craze died.

Donald model sheet from 1938's DONALD'S BETTER SELF.

© Walt Disney Productions

Humphrey the Bear, who lived in Brownstone National Park, was bigger than Donald and barely as intelligent. Whether he was trying to steal Donald's honey (BEEZY BEAR, 1955), or hibernate at Donald's home (BEARLY ASLEEP, 1955) or just hide from hunters (RUGGED BEAR, 1953), he was less a threat than Donald's smaller foils.

DONALD GOES TO TV AND SCHOOL

The last theatrical Donald Duck short that was part of the series was CHIPS AHOY, in 1956, directed by Hannah. The expense of making short cartoons had grown prohibitive in the 1950s and when production ceased on those efforts, Donald Duck moved over to television. He appeared in numerous episodes of Disney's TV series. These were frequently collections of classic Donald cartoons with a bit

Donald in MATHMAGIC LAND.

Opposite: Publicity art for THE FOX HUNT.

© Walt Disney Productions

of new animation (often directed by Hannah) to connect them. Donald was also a regular on THE MICKEY MOUSE CLUB. Not only did he have the key role of hitting the Mickey Mouse gong in the credits, but his shorts would turn up as the Mousekartoon.

Donald was too versatile and valuable a character to leave in the limbo reserved for unused animated characters, or to remain an occasional star of television. Following up on his earlier successes during the War years in training films, Disney had Donald become a star of educational films.

He was redesigned into a slimmer, trimmer Duck echoing the stylization of many popular cartoon stars of the Fifties. Important information was presented to an audience as a reluctant Donald learned along with the audience in such films as HOW TO HAVE AN ACCIDENT AT HOME (1956), DONALD DUCK IN MATHMAGICLAND (1959), HOW TO HAVE AN ACCIDENT AT WORK (1959), DONALD AND THE WHEEL (1961), THE LITTERBUG (1961) and his final film before he "retired," DONALD'S FIRE SURVIVAL PLAN (1966). These films are still used in schools today.

Donald returned to the big screen in 1983. He was called back into service along with many other classic Disney characters for the new featurette entitled MICKEY'S CHRISTMAS CAROL. In this re-telling of the famous Charles Dickens' story, Donald was cast as the nephew of Uncle Scrooge. 1984 saw a year-long celebration of the Duck's 50th birthday. As part of that celebration, Donald put his web prints in cement outside Mann's Chinese Theater during May 1984. Clarence Nash jetted all over the world for special events and tributes. Nash died in 1985, shortly after the celebration ended.

"Who gets stuck with all that bad luck? No one, but Donald Duck."
— Donald Duck theme song, lyrics by Oliver Wallace

Even more recently, Donald has kept busy in featured roles in a number of productions. DUCK TALES (1987) has Donald show up on occasion to talk with his nephews and rich Uncle Scrooge. In the 1988 blockbuster WHO FRAMED ROGER RABBIT?, he teamed with Daffy Duck in a classic piano duel. 1989 found him attending the Oscar telecast with Mickey, Minnie and Daisy.

DONALD'S FEATURES

More than any other Disney character, Donald was also a feature player. The Duck appeared in five Disney animated features (not counting the recent WHO

FRAMED ROGER RABBIT), more than any other Disney Superstar. His first appearance is a short sequence in THE RELUCTANT DRAGON (1941) where he tries to explain animation to Robert Benchley.

Donald became a true feature star via SALUDOS AMIGOS (1943). The feature was a wartime "good neighbor" film encouraged by the U.S. government to increase goodwill between the Americas (North, Central and South). It is merely a series of short subjects tied together with live action footage shot by Disney and his crew. For Donald's sequence, he visits various sites in South America. Donald's problems with a llama at Lake Titicaca, are some of the best remembered moments.

The film proved so overwhelmingly successful that Disney had to rush into pro-

duction a sort of sequel, THE THREE CABALLEROS (1945). Donald returned along with Jose Carioca, a green parrot, and a new character, Panchito, a Mexican rooster. In CABALLEROS, Donald is the central character and "host." This film featured extensive use of animated characters interacting with live actors. In fact one of the advertising banners read "See Donald Make Love to a Real Woman."

Donald's final theatrical role at Disney was with his standard co-stars, Mickey and Goofy. The trio appeared in FUN AND FANCY FREE (1947). Half of the feature starred the team in a slightly hip version of "Jack and the Beanstalk," narrated by Edgar Bergen with interruptions by Charlie McCarthy. The second half of the feature told the tale of BONGO as narrated and sung by Dinah Shore.

His final Disney feature appearance was in MELODY TIME (1948). Similar to his earlier feature ventures, Donald is seen in only a sequence of the film, "Blame It On the Samba." For this bit he is re-united with his friend Jose (Joe) Carioca as they dance to the music of Ethel Smith.

DONALD'S CO-STARS

As mentioned earlier, Donald's career began as a co-star to the Wise Little Hen and he later moved up to sharing the screen with Mickey, Goofy, Pluto and other stars. However the Duck soon was sur-

rounded by his own supporting cast. His first solo film, DON DONALD (1937) had introduced the world to Daisy Duck. In 1938, DONALD'S NEPHEWS introduced Huey, Dewey and Louie to the film world. They actually had already made their first appearance in a 1937 Donald Duck comic strip. Supposedly just sent on a short visit, the nephews quickly became frequent residents not only because they presented more springboards for stories, but because they brought stability to an increasingly domesticated Donald.

"MODERN INVENTIONS— I think that that was the picture where the man in Canada laughed so hard he left his crutches behind him when he left the theater."

— Clarence Nash, original voice of Donald Duck

CHIP 'N' DALE (1947) introduced Donald to two of his best foils. These pesky, lovable, determined, innocent chipmunks eventually developed their own series of shorts. 1947 also saw the debut of Bootle Beetle one of Donald's bothersome bugs. Buzz Buzz the Bee first stung Donald in INFERIOR DECORATOR (1948). Continually confused and frustrated Humphrey the Bear first bumped into Donald in RUGGED BEAR (1953). He also went on to star in his own shorts with the park ranger, J. Audubon Woodlore.

MOONLIGHTING

When it comes to extracurricular activities, few superstars are as active as Donald. His image has been placed on almost every product imaginable. He even sports his own drink, Donald Duck Orange Juice.

At one time there was Donald Duck rice, Donald Duck bread, Donald Duck macaroni and Donald Duck straws! There's even a firm that issues an expensive line of limited edition, fine art lithographs featuring the Duck. Priced at over $600 each, they usually sell out before the printing!

1936 saw Donald debut on the Sunday comics' page. He got a daily strip in 1938. Al Taliaferro supplied the artwork and originated several key characters including Grandma Duck. Those strips appeared in over 200 papers by the early 1960s. The strips were discontinued by the studio in 1989.

Donald's been a standard in comic books since the late '30s. A publisher is currently producing deluxe hardcover collections of classic Duck comic book stories by ex-storyman Carl Barks exclusively for collectors. The new line of Disney comics, for the first time actually published by Disney, features the dynamic Duck in a number of titles.

SUPERSTAR QUALITY

Donald's recognition as a cartoon superstar is secure. He appears on more total feet of film than any other classic Disney character and his comic book career eclipsed Mickey Mouse's many years ago. His animated cartoons still bring joy to his old fans and to new generations who quickly discover why Donald is still the best animal quacker of them all.

Poster to DER FUEHRER'S
FACE.

© Walt Disney Productions

Superstar Summary

THE STAR: Droopy

YEAR OF DEBUT: 1943 (DUMBHOUNDED)

STUDIO OF DEBUT: MGM

SIGNATURE: "You know what? I'm happy."

KEY CREW BEHIND THE STAR: Tex Avery (creator/director), Michael Lah (animator/director), Bill Thompson (voice), Heck Allen and Rich Hogan (writers)

CAREER HIGH: WHO FRAMED ROGER RABBIT? (1988) — Droopy's small cameo as an elevator operator in Toon Town elevates him to superstar status all over again.

SELECTED SHORT SUBJECTS: *Deputy Droopy, Dixieland Droopy, Northwest Hounded, The Shooting of Dan Magoo, Three Little Pups*

Droopy is an unusual Cartoon Superstar. In fact, he is an unusual cartoon character. Most cartoon characters are brash and aggressive. Droopy isn't. Many animated characters are quick talkers; Droopy isn't. A lot of characters are cute and sweet; Droopy isn't. What type of a toon is Droopy? A very funny one.

While Charlie Chaplin supposedly inspired many cartoon characters, Droopy may have been the only character inspired by Buster Keaton. Both Droopy and Keaton maintained a deadpan expression and unique sense of calm despite the frenetic activity surrounding them.

Droopy was a sad faced dog. His pedigree was questionable and he was variously identified as a basset hound, a blood hound and a police dog. Originally, his features were quite detailed so that every line on his face added more weight to his drooping expression. As he evolved, he became shorter and cuter, with merely a suggestion of those previous lines. Still later, when he ventured into Cinemascope, his small round body became more angular and less attractive.

He was a white dog with a small tuft of red hair on top of his head. His eyes were almost always half closed, giving the appearance of sleepiness or unconcern.

His voice was a rather mush-mouthed and nasal whimper. In Droopy's case, appearances were very deceiving. Droopy had the ability to move and think quickly, although this action usually took place off screen. Generally he was unemotional although he was allowed brief moments when he cut loose.

Just as a deep valley makes a mountain seem higher, Droopy's self control made the activity of his co-stars seem all the more desperate and frantic. Much of the humor came from the actions and reactions of his co-stars to Droopy's lack of action and reaction.

Droopy was often incredibly strong. His most amazing ability was being able to get anywhere and everywhere faster and in better shape than anyone else. One cartoon suggested that the reason for his almost magical appearances was because there were hundreds of Droopys. Audiences knew better. There was only one Droopy and he was generally a force for good in the world.

HELLO, FOLKS

The creation of Droopy is credited to Fred "Tex" Avery. In the 1930's, Avery set the style for Warner Brothers cartoons. Avery's style was marked by the fact that the rules of logic, gravity, time and space no longer applied. He felt that the funniest humor resulted from having cartoon characters doing things that could not be duplicated by human actors. It was Avery who first started the use of signs that would pop up with questions like "Exciting, isn't it?" or "Silly, isn't he?"

While at Warners, Avery created the lunatic Daffy Duck. After some false starts by other directors, it was Tex Avery who shaped Bugs Bunny into a superstar. (In the first Droopy cartoon, the Wolf frequently refers to Droopy as "Doc.")

It was while he was at Warners that Avery explored the contrast between a character who was totally in control and a character who was completely out of control. He also experimented with characters having extreme reactions.

For a variety of reasons, Avery left Warners by early 1942 and took a directing position with MGM Studios. At MGM, the kings of the studio were William Hanna and Joe Barbera, whose award winning series of shorts with Tom Cat and Jerry Mouse had brought recognition to themselves and their studio. Avery wanted to follow their example by creating a character that would be acknowledged as his own. At the same time, he wanted to push the limits of cartoon animation.

Droopy as seen in licensing art.

© Loews, Inc.

He was so successful in the latter goal that even Hanna-Barbera's Tom and Jerry series began seeing elements of Averyism.

While at MGM, Avery tried to develop series for several characters including Screwy Squirrel, who starred in five films, and George and Junior, who were teamed for four films. He developed a wide array of one-shot characters who might have spun off into series of their own with little effort.

The most successful and best remembered of Avery's cartoon creations at MGM was Droopy. The stone faced basset hound first appeared in the third cartoon that Avery made for MGM, DUMB HOUNDED (1943).

"I think voices have an awful lot to do with the success of a cartoon character," Avery once stated. The character of Droopy was built on a voice. Avery was amused by a voice he heard on the radio show, FIBBER MCGEE AND MOLLY. Bill Thompson did the voice of Wallace Wimple, a henpecked husband who referred to his wife as "Sweety Face, my big fat wife." What made the character of Wimple amusing was the meekness of his voice. Thompson did several other voices for the radio show and is best remembered by animation fans for supplying the voice of the White Rabbit in Disney's ALICE IN WONDERLAND and the Little Ranger in the Donald Duck cartoons.

"The old radio show had a funny little mush-mouth fellow, so we said, 'hell, let's put a dog to it.' It was the voice! We thought so much of it. It was a steal; there ain't no doubt about it... Bill Thompson, who did the voice... couldn't give us exactly the voice he did for the show, for legal reasons, but he came close," Avery told animation historian Joe Adamson.

Avery, himself, also occasionally provided the voice for Droopy.

DROOPY ON SCREEN

In DUMB HOUNDED, Droopy was still in an early stage of development although most of the key elements of the character were evident. A wolf convict escapes from Swing Swing Prison and the police bloodhounds are sent to track down the crook. The prison gate opens and a loud, frantic mass of dogs pours out. Following this flood is a slow-moving, sad-faced little hound walking on all fours. "Hello, all you happy people. You know what? I'm the hero," comments the dog directly to the audience. There is no doubt that he is a dog. Later, he embarrassingly reappears from behind a fire hydrant and engages in "dog talk" with another dog.

By the middle of the cartoon, Droopy has given up his dog-like habits and walks on his hind legs rather than on all four legs. He even takes a moment out to read a Dick Tracy comic book.

As the Wolf goes to greater and greater extremes to escape from Droopy, he discovers something unusual. No matter how fast he runs, no matter how far he goes, no matter what devices he uses, Droopy always appears at the same spot the Wolf has reached. In fact, while the Wolf is out of breath, Droopy is calm and relaxed as if he had been waiting for the Wolf to finally show up. When questioned about his almost magical appearances, Droopy answers, "Let's not get nosy, bub."

Later, Droopy again addresses the audience directly and states, "I surprise him like this all throughout the picture."

Droopy eventually captures the Wolf by tossing a huge boulder off a high building that smashes the crook flat. When he is given his cash reward, Droopy indulges in an uncharacteristic moment of uninhibited joy and then quickly returns to his natural sad state and tells the audience, "I'm happy."

Unknowingly, Avery developed the character that would be remembered long after many other characters had been forgotten. Droopy is elaborately detailed in this first cartoon. Emphasis is given to making his face look sad with heavy bags under the eyes and drooping jowls. He is an oddly proportioned shape in the beginning of the film but eventually takes on the short build more familiar to cartoon fans.

It wasn't until 1945 that Droopy made his next appearance in THE SHOOTING OF DAN MCGOO. It was a parody of the Robert Service poem. The Wolf tries to steal Droopy's girlfriend, the sexy redheaded human female character who in recent years has been dubbed "Red." While they appeared in several Droopy cartoons, the Wolf and Red also appeared in their own cartoons noted for their sexual suggestiveness.

In the early Droopy cartoons, Droopy was an unlikely aggressor. He usually represented the forces of law and order and needed to bring the Wolf to justice. In NORTHWEST HOUNDED POLICE (1946) Droopy is identified as Sgt. McPoodle of the Mounted Police but he still behaves like Droopy in a revamping of the

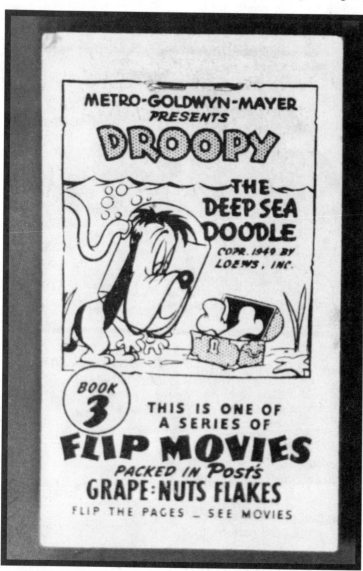

1949 Grape Nuts Flakes give-away flip book.

© Loews, Inc.

earlier DUMB HOUNDED. In SENOR DROOPY (1949) Droopy from Guadalupe battles the Wolf in a bullfighting arena, The Chili Bowl, for the hand of the live action actress, Lina Romay.

SPIKING THE FORMULA

WAGS TO RICHES (1949) changed the Droopy format. A new character, Spike the Bulldog, was introduced. This Spike was quite different from the tough, but good-hearted Spike in the Tom and Jerry cartoons. It was clear that Spike was the aggressor. This change allowed Droopy to be more innocent and even more passive. Basically, similar to Bugs Bunny, Droopy could now sit back and allow his enemy's own actions to defeat him.

When their master dies, Droopy is left the entire estate. However, if Droopy dies, the whole inheritance goes to Spike. Naturally, Spike uses every trick he can think of from filling a room with gas and giving Droopy a cigar to covering Droopy's mouth with cream and trying to get him declared a mad dog.

Interestingly, this cartoon was remade by Hanna and Barbera in 1956 after Avery had left the studio. Hanna and Barbera took animation drawings made for the original and made new cels and backgrounds for them so that the film could be made in Cinemascope. Even though Avery is still credited as director on the remake, the simplified drawing style and subtle changes in composition and pacing make the cartoon much weaker than the original.

"(DIXIELAND DROOPY) was a cutey-cutey. This was almost a (Chuck) Jones."

— Tex Avery

Avery continued to produce Droopy cartoons into the Fifties including DROOPY'S GOOD DEED (1951) where Spike and Droopy compete for the honor of being Best Scout and a chance to meet the President. DROOPY'S DOUBLE TROUBLE (1951) introduced Droopy's look-alike brother, Drippy, who has a powerful punch, as Spike discovered in a series of mistaken identity gags.

Avery not only kept speeding up the pacing of the cartoons, but soon discovered such work often required him to spend all Saturday and Sunday at the studio to get the precision he required. In 1952, due to extreme overwork, Avery had to take a recuperation period of almost a year. During this rest period, ex-Disney director Dick Lundy stepped in to direct one Droopy cartoon, CABALLERO DROOPY (1952) where Droopy and the Wolf battle for the privilege of serenading a pretty girl.

"You'd never see the little fellow get there, but he'd just be there."

— Tex Avery

Avery returned to MGM and directed THREE LITTLE PUPS (1953) which started as a parody of THE THREE LITTLE PIGS. The Three Little Pups were Snoopy, Loopy and Droopy who kept getting interrupted from watching their TV program by a new Wolf character. This Wolf character was a dog catcher in this film and his voice was supplied by Daws Butler. It has been suggested that this slow talking Southern Wolf character was the vocal inspiration for Huckleberry Hound, also voiced by Daws Butler. At one point, Avery considered turning this short into a series, but never did.

"I told (Tex), ...'Let's make some more Droopys.' He couldn't get enthusiastic about them until I laid them out, then he got excited."

— Michael Lah, animator and later director on Droopy

Avery made several more standard Droopy cartoons such as DRAG-A-LONG DROOPY (1954) with Droopy as a sheepherder and HOMESTEADER DROOPY (1954) where his infant son must rescue him from Dishonest Dan the Wolf. These were considered part of the "Western" Droopys that were a homage to Avery's up-

77

bringing in Texas. MGM animation writer Heck Allen, who wrote these two Droopy shorts among others, was also fond of Westerns and became a Western novelist after he left animation.

The last Droopy cartoon fully directed by Avery was DIXIELAND DROOPY (1954). It was the story of John Pettibone (Droopy), an obscure musician whose love of Dixieland music lifted him from the depths of the City Dump to the heights of the Hollywood Bowl. This success was due largely to Pee Wee Runt and his musical fleas who lived on Pettibone.

"(Tex) did Droopy a lot of times.... Occasionally when (voice actor Bill) Thompson wouldn't show up, or we had to have a line or something, Tex'd just go record it. Couldn't tell the difference."

— Heck Allen, storyman on Droopy cartoons

As were many studios producing theatrical cartoon shorts, MGM was in trouble in the mid-Fifties when demand and revenue for the cartoons greatly diminished. In 1955, Fred Quimby retired as producer and Hanna and Barbera were appointed his successor. Avery left MGM and went to Walter Lantz Studios. Before he left, he co-directed one last Droopy cartoon, DEPUTY DROOPY (1955) in which two bank robbers try to rob the town safe without making any noise to wake the sheriff. Avery co-directed his last Droopy with Michael Lah, who had animated many of Avery's Droopy cartoons.

While Avery was at MGM, there were several Droopy cartoon projects that were either abandoned or rejected by management. Some of those lost Droopy cartoons included DROOPY DOG RETURNS, DROOPY'S DOG LICENSE and DROOPY'S SERENADE.

DROOPY WITHOUT TEX

Lah went on to direct six more Droopy cartoons, all in Cinemascope, that were released in 1957 and 1958. One of his cartoons, ONE DROOPY KNIGHT (1957) was nominated for an Academy Award. Droopy is a brave knight who tries to defeat a dragon for the hand of the princess. His competition is a bulldog named Butch. Butch is similar to Spike and appears in four of Lah's cartoons. The last MGM Droopy cartoon was Lah's DROOPY LEPRECHAUN (1958). While vacationing in Ireland, Droopy is mistaken for a leprechaun by Butch, who wants to catch him and make money.

In 1957, MGM decided to close its cartoon studio. The cartoons already in production, including the last three Droopy shorts, were completed and released in 1958. Hanna and Barbera went on to greater fame in television.

"We previewed (THE THREE LITTLE PUPS) and even (producer Fred) Quimby was enthused. He said, 'Yes, sir, them thing are funny. Every time he opens his mouth, he gets a laugh.'"

— Tex Avery

The MGM Droopy cartoons often popped up in Tom and Jerry cartoon packages shown on TV. The Saturday TOM AND JERRY show on CBS in 1965 sometimes plugged a Droopy cartoon in between two Tom and Jerry classics.

Droopy was revived in 1980 for THE TOM AND JERRY COMEDY SHOW. MGM leased some of their characters to Filmation, the studio responsible for THE ARCHIES and FAT ALBERT. Filmation wanted to recapture some of the wild chases and extreme reactions that had made the MGM cartoons classics. Unfortunately, it was a poorly executed attempt lacking in pacing and humor. One segment of the show was devoted to the new adventures of Droopy. Droopy was often in conflict with Slick the Wolf, a pale imitation of Avery's earlier vibrant character. As a segue, Droopy would sometimes recite a poem. Voice artist Frank

Welker performed the voices for Droopy and Slick. The show only lasted one season.

Like many classic cartoon characters, Droopy got another shot in the spotlight with WHO FRAMED ROGER RABBIT? (1988). His small cameo as an unperturbed elevator operator brought laughter from audiences who remembered his earlier adventures. Animator-Director Richard Williams supplied Droopy's voice.

Droopy's success led to cameos in the two Roger Rabbit shorts. In TUMMY TROUBLE (1989), he again reprises his role as an elevator operator but this time at the hospital. In ROLLER COASTER RABBIT (1990), he has a brief moment as a melodramatic villain who has tied Jessica Rabbit to the rollercoaster track.

Recently Droopy appeared in animated form as a singer in a Hawaiian shirt for a promotion by McDonalds where customers could get a little plastic figure of the famous hound.

DROOPY'S PACK

The Wolf was Droopy's first and perhaps best antagonist. He was an unnamed character who had made a previous appearance in Avery's BLITZ WOLF (1942). The Wolf was everything that Droopy was not. He spoke in a deep, rough, forceful voice. He was physically more impressive and seemed more creative. Unfortunately he lacked self control, especially concerning women. Some of the funniest and most memorable animation moments have been the Wolf's reactions to beautiful women. In fact, outside the Droopy cartoons, the character made an impression in a handful of Avery cartoons that dealt quite openly with sexual desire. In these shorts, he was often called "Wolfie."

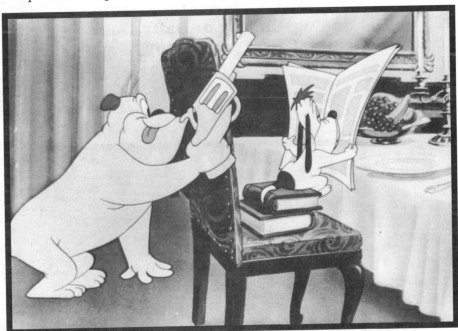

Publicity still from
WAGS TO RICHES.

© Loews, Inc.

He may have inspired two other characters: another unnamed wolf who spoke in a Southern drawl and matched Droopy's pacing for unconcerned behavior and Slick the Wolf, a Filmation character meant to suggest the original Wolf but without class and style.

The Droopy cartoons, especially those with the Wolf, featured an attractive young human woman who in recent years has been christened "Red." She had many names and hair colors over the years but there was no mistaking her smoldering sexuality. She was a talented singer and had no difficulty arousing the Wolf and Droopy. She was also the inspiration for Jessica Rabbit.

Spike, the Bulldog, later became Butch, the Bulldog. This name change may have been to avoid confusion with another MGM Spike (also a Bulldog) appearing in the Tom and Jerry series. Spike was less of a frightening threat to Droopy than the Wolf. Despite his size and guile, it was obvious that Spike was foredoomed to failure since he seemed to lack the intelligence of the Wolf. Spike, though, was a more active threat to Droopy and instigated action.

OTHER MEDIA

Droopy was one of the least merchandised of cartoon superstars. He did appear in OUR GANG and TOM AND JERRY comic books from Dell. Interestingly, sometimes he was labeled "Happy Hound" rather than Droopy. The name was supposed to contrast with his constant expression of sadness.

Like most cartoon superstars, some of his best adventures are now available on videotape.

Because of the revived interest in the character, thanks to WHO FRAMED ROGER RABBIT?, Turner Home Entertainment, who owns the MGM cartoon characters, has begun a new licensing campaign to take advantage of this new-found world-wide fame. They are promoting him in a gaudy Hawaiian outfit as a "party animal." McDonald's released a set of four MGM cartoon plastic figures and Droopy was one of them.

"I hate to say it, but I've never come up with a character as popular as Bugs Bunny or Daffy Duck. The closest I got was Droopy."

— Tex Avery

SUPERSTAR QUALITY

Droopy's unique deadpan makes him one of the most unforgettable cartoon superstars. Proof that less is more, Droopy personifies the old fable that slow and steady can still win the race. As long as the world continues to speed up, Droopy will remain a beacon to audiences who want to watch this amazing hound create his own time. And you know what folks, the audiences are happy.

Left: Publicity still for CABALLERO DROOPY.

Opposite: "Happy Hound" (Droopy) in OUR GANG COMICS. Drawn by famed "Duck Artist" Carl Barks.

© Loews, Inc.

FELIX THE CAT

SELECTED SHORT SUBJECTS: *All Puzzled, Dines and Pines, Flim Flam Films, In Hollywood, Sure Locked Homes (Note: all silent)*

Superstar Summary

THE STAR: Felix the Cat

YEAR OF DEBUT: 1919 (FELINE FOLLIES)

STUDIO OF DEBUT: Pat Sullivan

SIGNATURE: "Right-ee-o!" (and his walk)

KEY CREW BEHIND THE STAR: Otto Messmer (original director, writer, animator), Joe Oriolo (TV producer)

CAREER HIGH: THE FELIX THE CAT TV SHOW (1958) — It introduced his magic bag of tricks and established his image for today's audience, as well as rekindling interest in the classic silent shorts.

F elix the Cat is the original Cartoon Superstar. Created during the age of silent pictures, he is still known around the world today. This black cat with large eyes and a mouthful of sharp teeth certainly proved anything but bad luck.

Like a cat, and many of the other cartoon superstars, Felix had several lives. He was a star of silent theatrical cartoons and early comic strips. There was a brief period of sound cartoons then obscurity. Later TV stardom presented a Felix who was quite different from the famous silent cat. Finally, he starred in a feature which resembled a little of all his lives.

The silent Felix was one of the biggest screen stars during the 1920s. He was as well known and popular as such classic live comics as Chaplin and Keaton. As a silent comedian, Felix seemed to be a bit of both.

Like Chaplin, Felix had a definite personality. This personality was the key to Felix's success. Unlike so many of the other animated characters of the time, Felix was more than just a figure on the screen doing comedy. He would stop and think. He would pace back and forth, hands behind his back, head facing down, in his classic walk. He would look at the audience and wink a large eye. He had desires and morals. He even had a temper. Felix was like a real person and would solve problems with ingenuity and just a touch of mischief.

Unlike Chaplin, Felix wouldn't settle for simple morality tales or camera work. Borrowing a bit from Keaton, Felix played with the aspect of film. The silent Felix cartoons featured wild angles, strange characters and preposterous stories. Only on rare occasion did these strange happenings get explained away as "dreams." Felix's world was definitely surreal, but for Felix it was merely real.

Anything could happen in a silent Felix cartoon. The cat might use his tail as a pencil (OCEANTICS), get mule kicked to Russia (FELIX THE CAT ALL PUZZLED), form his body into a suitcase (FELIX THE CAT GOES WEST), be attacked by eggs (FELIX THE CAT DINES AND PINES) or suddenly wake up in a haunted house (FELIX THE CAT IN SURE-LOCKED HOMES).

The early Felix was a cat most clever. Like T.S. Elliot's Mister Mistoffelees, Felix was a magical cat. He had more control over his body parts than a normal cat. In fact in one cartoon, he is seen waking up and putting on his ears and tail, as if getting dressed.

In particular, his tail was detachable. He was able to use it as a club or a fish hook among other variations. It often emphasized Felix's feelings by becoming an exclamation mark. Felix seemed to be an embodiment of the "cat" spirit. Independent, resourceful, and a little mystical. No matter how surreal his adventures, Felix was always up to the challenge and often just as surreal.

Sometimes down on his luck, sometimes a house pet, and sometimes just a wanderer, the silent Felix was always in charge of his destiny. Like most Cartoon Superstars, Felix seemed largely unflustered by any adversary he might meet. Often, he laughed heartily several times during a cartoon because he enjoyed the oddity of it all.

Felix does differ from many other cartoon characters in his interest and activity in mating. Many a Felix cartoon revolves around him looking for a mate (such as FELIX THE CAT SWITCHES WITCHES) or dealing with his children (as seen in FELIX THE CAT IN FLIM FLAM FILMS). Few other characters had matrimony as regular a theme in their shorts.

When Felix came to TV, he became more Earthbound at least in personality. His design was simplified and made cuter. Though the TV Felix might travel to distant planets and battle such characters as The Master Cylinder, the tube cat was much more domesticated and older. He was now a responsible adult home owner. In TV Land Felix became more of a friend than an adventurer. The only clue to his surreal origins was his famous, magic Bag of Tricks. This along with his familiar cry of "Right-ee-o!" (and equally famous, "It's the profess-or") are what Felix is most known for today.

The bag of tricks was a small yellow carpetbag with a repeating design of small black crosses. It could only be manipulated by Felix. Like Felix's body in the silent cartoons, the bag could transform into a myriad of shapes and functions.

Felix with his creator, Otto Mesmer at a tribute shortly before his death.

THE CREATION OF FELIX

Unlike many Cartoon Superstars, Felix's origin is clearly due to the artistry of one man, Otto Messmer. Messmer was an animator for Australian born Pat Sullivan during the early days of animation. Sullivan had seen Messmer's work when they were both using the Universal camera department for their separate films. Starting around 1915, Messmer worked on a number of shorts with Sullivan, including a series based on the popular live comic, Charlie Chaplin. However, he soon left the Sullivan studio because he was drafted to fight in WWI. Upon his return to civilian life, he came back to the Sullivan studio.

When PARAMOUNT SCREEN MAGAZINE called Sullivan and asked for some help preparing pictures, Sullivan told Messmer that he (Messmer) could submit something. What Messmer came up with was a short cartoon called FELINE FOLLIES (1919). It featured a black cat chasing mice.

This and opposite page: model sheets of the classic Felix.

© Pat Sullivan

Messmer later stated he had used a black cat because, "it saves making a lot of outlines and solid black moves better."

Paramount liked the film and commissioned a second. Messmer went to work and produced MUSICAL MEWS featuring four cats singing on a backyard fence.

The head of Paramount saw something in the black cat character and signed the Sullivan studio to produce a series of shorts in August 1919. Paramount's John King coined the name of Felix basing it on "felicity" (which means good luck) and "feline" (meaning cat). Traditionally, a black cat meant bad luck. By early 1920, the contract was expanded and the press release clearly promoted Pat Sullivan's Felix the cat. This contract called for one short every four weeks.

Sullivan didn't begin copyrighting the films until the mid-twenties, so it is difficult to date many of the early titles.

Initially, Messmer did all the animation himself, though he did have assistants and a cameraman. He thought up the stories, created the animation, and even drew the posters. Messmer also created the Sunday comic pages which ran for years after the film series disappeared.

The shorts proved immediately successful with both audiences and critics. Theaters reported that the films often gave the audiences non-stop laughs. Critics were amused with the astonishing visuals served up by Messmer.

"He (Felix) would go to Arabia, to Mars — not just the barnyard. That's what made him famous."

— Otto Messmer

Messmer discussed how he viewed Felix's role in the shorts. "I had that kind of feeling, like Chaplin, that no matter how big the picture was he [Chaplin] stood out. He attracted attention, the other guys in the stories didn't. So I figured the same way with a cat." Later it was reported that Messmer and Sullivan based Felix on the Rudyard Kipling short story "The Cat that Walked by Himself" (first published in 1902).

In 1922, Sullivan sold the series to Margaret Winkler, a lady who sold films on a state by state basis. This practice generally meant more money for the film maker.

In 1924 production was stepped up to one every two weeks. At this point Messmer began to bring on additional animators. Key to this new group was William Nolan. (Nolan would eventually leave to head up a new series of Krazy Kat cartoons in 1926.)

Messmer's original Felix design was very angular. This rough edged alley cat was quite different (in appearance) than what is generally recognized as Felix. It was Nolan who took these shapes and rounded them out. This made Felix both easier to draw and more visually appealing.

"Being famous is hard work. There's no money in it unless you are deadly serious about it."

— Pat Sullivan

Messmer continued to be the driving force. Whereas Sullivan was busy making deals and selling the property to a large number of licensees, Messmer ran the studio. One employee reported how Messmer thought up each short, giving key drawings to the animators. He would then animate and discuss new ideas out loud. He even went to the bank for payroll.

When the Winkler contract was up, Sullivan went with Educational Pictures in an even more lucrative deal. It has been reported that Messmer was producing the films for around $3,000 each while the Sullivan studio was making over $12,000 on every film.

By 1926, Felix had hit his stride. Educational Pictures was advertising him heavily, merchandise was appearing, even songs were being written about him. Some historians have stated that Felix was the most popular film star next to Chaplin. Like the best of Cartoon Superstars, Felix was loved by all ages.

Messmer later talked about what he thought was the reason for Felix's success. "I used an extreme amount of eye motion, wriggling eyes and turning his whiskers, and this seemed to be what hit the public — expressions!" Messmer also gave Felix a boy-like quality. "I think instead of just having him chase a lot of things around and bumpin' each other, which might be funny, I made him act as a little boy would wonder... how high is that star, how deep is the ocean, what makes the wind blow? I used all those things for a theme," Mesmer explained.

As with many stars of silent films though, Felix was not quite ready for the changes that

would take place with the advent of sound. Though Felix had conquered many a mouse in his films, it was a rival studio's mouse that eventually claimed the first life of this classic character.

In 1928 sound was becoming more and more established. Disney had made a big success with Mickey Mouse. Messmer and Educational talked with Sullivan about going to sound, but Sullivan was unconvinced. When Educational discovered that Sullivan would not produce sound films, they dropped the studio and Felix.

Sullivan, who had reportedly become less and less involved with the business and more involved with his outside activities, suddenly found no studio interest in his star. He began to set the wheels in motion to start a new studio in California which would include sound cartoons when his wife died in a tragic accident in 1932. Less than a year later, Sullivan himself died of pneumonia.

It had allegedly been stated many times during their relationship that Sullivan would leave the studio to Messmer. However, upon the death of Sullivan, it was discovered he had no will. Messmer has said many studios were interested in the Felix property and had hoped to deal with him. Unfortunately, Messmer was merely an employee and had no legal claim to the character. Felix ended up being owned by distant relatives of Sullivan in Australia!

FELIX IN COLOR

The first studio to obtain the rights to Felix for a new series was the Van Bueren studio. This small New York outfit had previously done the (human, not the famous cat and mouse) Tom and Jerry cartoons. By the mid-thirties, they had decided to buy known properties rather than develop their own. Their first two purchases were Toonerville Trolley, a popular comic strip of the period, and Felix the Cat, which was still being run as a comic strip. The silent Felix's were also still being run with newly recorded musical sound tracks in some theaters.

"Otto came up with the ideas, supervised, directed, and every Friday he'd go to the bank and pick up the payroll."

— Al Eugster, animator on the original Felix

Van Bueren's key creative person at the time was Burt Gillett, the director of Disney's THE THREE LITTLE PIGS. He, along with Tom Palmer, oversaw production of the three Van Bueren Felixes: FELIX THE CAT AND THE GOOSE THAT LAID THE GOLDEN EGGS, NEPTUNE'S NONSENSE and BOLD KING COLE. These three 1936 shorts featured only some of Felix's original personality. The street smart character was eliminated. He was now no different than other animated animal characters.

Van Bueren's entries were more story and production driven. Felix, originally a bit of a loner, became lost in the massive production of these color spectacles. In fact he is little more than a secondary character in BOLD KING COLE. Also, Van Bueren substituted standard fairy tale settings for Felix's surreal world.

"Messmer was the father but I am the godfather on it."

— Joe Oriolo

Whereas Messmer's Felix, as did Chaplin, served as the center of his universe, Gillett's Felix was just another character in the crowd. The studio gave Felix a boy-like voice and a helpful, happy nature. Felix still had his walk, and shifted his shape occasionally, but Gillett's Felix was clearly a descendant of the "cute" Mickey Mouse school. This was quite a turn-around since Disney's staff obviously studied the original, personality-driven Felix in developing some of their earlier stars such as Mickey.

Felix's color career was cut short at Van Bueren when RKO, the distributor of the Van Bueren cartoons, signed with the Disney studio in 1936. Not needing two animation studios to distribute, RKO chose not to renew their contract with Van Bueren. Once again, Felix's career was stopped due to studio problems.

MR. FELIX ON TV

Felix was the first star of TV. In 1928, RCA engineers used a paper mache figure of Felix to test a broadcast from New York to Kansas. In July of 1940, a huge figure of Felix was whirled for countless hours atop a phonograph turntable. TV scanners transmitted the image to the few homes with TV sets as a reception test. This event inaugurated the world's first TV station, WZXBS, in New York.

Felix with his magic bag of tricks from the popular TV series.

© Pat Sullivan

His real career in TV began in 1958.

Backtracking to 1953, the silent Felix cartoons, with musical soundtracks, were released to TV. They appeared around the country with many other "forgotten" stars such as the human Tom and Jerry. These shorts quickly went by the wayside as more popular and later cartoons began to enter the TV market.

Felix continued to appear in comics, and was still being done by Messmer. One of Messmer's assistants after WWII was another animator, Joe Oriolo, the man behind Casper the Friendly Ghost. Oriolo took over the comic book chores totally in 1954 when Messmer retired. He soon approached Sullivan's nephew and the two became partners, creating Felix The Cat Productions. Sullivan and Oriolo now co-owned the Felix copyright.

By 1958, Oriolo's Felix the Cat Productions began work on a series of new cartoons for TV. These cartoons were the first TV cartoons produced in New York. It is this Felix most people remember.

Oriolo's series consisted of stories told in cliff-hanger style. Each story took five episodes and could be completed in a half hour show. 260 of these four-minute films were produced between 1958 and 1960. Oriolo used such talented veterans as Jim Tyer (Terrytoons), Steve Muffati (Van Bueren and Famous), Frank Endres (Fleischer and Famous) and Robe Grossman (Fleischer).

The character design was simplified for TV animation. Felix's large head now rested on a slender body.

The voice behind Felix, and all the other characters in this series, was Jack Mercer, also the voice of Popeye. Mercer was asked to read all of his lines slowly to help fill up time in the stories.

Joe Stutz, a writer from Famous, was in charge of the story department, which included such talents as Joe Sabo and Ralph Newman, both from Famous.

Back on the big screen in FELIX THE CAT: THE MOVIE, completed in 1987.

© Felix the Cat Productions

Produced quickly and cheaply, this series took the visual design of Felix but altered his famous personality. Most of his classic elements were replaced with more standard cartoon elements. Felix no longer was really a cat. He now owned a house, had a job, needed money, and so on. Gone were his walk, his thoughtful moments, his boldness and his surreal outlook. These were replaced with satirical (sometimes silly) stories and characters. Felix became less mystical, but gained a "magic" bag of tricks.

Most of these cartoons concern the Professor, his assistant, Rock Bottom, and Poindexter, his nephew. Storylines included such elements as trips to the Moon, gold producing plants and time travel. One set of five stories revolved around Felix and Leprechauns. The writers had written these stories so that they could be edited together into a longer format, possibly a feature although this final editing process was never done.

This series, though somewhat different than the original silent Felixes, did keep Felix in the public's eye.

Oriolo is justified in saying he is somewhat responsible for the revived interest in the silent Felixes. In 1988, it was announced that the silent Felix cartoons were to be colored by computer for re-release to TV stations.

GETTING CREDIT...

In 1967, the Canadian government sponsored a retrospective of the Felix cartoons with Otto Messmer in attendance. This was the beginning of a series of tributes to the man behind the cat. Messmer, himself, was the subject of a retrospective at the Whitney Museum of American Art in 1976. From that point to his death in 1983, Messmer received a great deal of attention.

Since his "re-discovery," Messmer has been hailed as the "inventor" of character animation. Rather than being bitter about his almost 50 years of anonymity he seemed somewhat resolved. When asked if he was bothered by his lack of credit on the films, he stated, "No I really didn't. Because you see Disney... anything anybody did there became 'by Walt Disney.' In those days it seemed to be the thing."

FELIX RETURNS TO THE BIG SCREEN

When the animated feature boom began in the mid-Eighties, Joe Oriolo figured an animated feature starring Felix might be a strong contender. Oriolo began production in 1985 along with his son, Don. Don had already worked with his father on a variety of projects, including the 1958-60 Felix cartoons.

The film was entitled FELIX THE CAT — THE MOVIE.

"I patterned him after Charlie Chaplin. The audience loved him. And so did Chaplin. The cartoon format let Felix do things that Chaplin couldn't do on film...."

— Otto Messmer

In 1986, Joe Oriolo died. Don Oriolo, determined to see the project continue, went to Europe to raise funds and acquire a studio. The film was produced in Hungary under the direction of Tibor Hernadi at a cost of over $9 million. New World purchased the film in May of 1987 and planned a Thanksgiving release in the U.S. that same year. However, the film did not get its announced release.

In early 1988, New World listed it for release in other countries. It finally debuted as the opening event of the 3rd Los Angeles Animation Celebration on January 26th, 1989.

The storyline, written by Don Oriolo, was closely related to the TV cartoon series. Unfortunately, the film told a convoluted tale which was not helped by choppy editing. The film begins with a computer animated talking Felix head created by de Graf/Wahrman, Inc. It was a last minute addition to try and provide story exposition that would help audiences understand the movie.

The device made Felix the first classic Cartoon Superstar animated by computer for a theatrical feature.

The feature had Felix being hijacked to a fantasy kingdom of Oriana, a name was supposedly concocted in tribute to Oriolo. While there, he had to rescue a beautiful human princess enslaved by her evil uncle, the Duke of Zill. Eventually he is joined by the Professor and Poindexter who located the hidden passageway to Oriana so they could steal some gold. The Duke uses machines, called master cylinders, inspired by the original Master Cylinder to keep control of the kingdom.

A series of adventures takes place, including an extended period at the Duke's circus where the princess and Felix perform. Felix, with the help of the Professor and Poindexter, rescues the princess, defeats the Duke and returns safely to his own world.

As the new decade began, there were no plans to release the film either theatrically or on video.

SUPPORTING CAST

The silent Felix had no real supporting characters. As Messmer stated, he felt the films should be totally focused on a single character, similar to the Chaplin comedies. The TV version featured several recurring roles.

Most remembered is The Professor. This short, stout, character with a giant moustache, was often cast as a villain. As his name suggested, he was a self-centered, sometimes evil, scientist. He, along with his large, bulldog sidekick, Rock Bottom (the only other talking animal character), were often plotting some terrible scheme.

The Professor's nephew, Poindexter, was a brainy child with huge, round glasses. His name became a slang term among school children for an overly smart peer.

Another recurring villain was The Master Cylinder, a "cylinder" who, at least in one adventure, said he was a former student of the Professor. After a failed experiment destroyed his body, he had his brain put into the mechanical cylinder.

The Professor, Rock Bottom and Poindexter didn't have very consistent lifestyles. Even though The Professor was often evil, Poindexter would frequently get along with Felix. In fact there were times when The Professor hired Felix to babysit the youngster! In some stories, Rock Bottom was merely Felix's annoying neighbor.

CATTING AROUND

As was previously mentioned, Felix began being licensed in the mid-Twenties. Sullivan sold licenses for Felix to anyone who was interested, from dollmakers and toys to cigar manufacturers. That plus the newspaper comic, done by Messmer, kept the cat in front of the public long after the cartoons had disappeared.

On August 14, 1923, Felix became a newspaper Sunday strip drawn by Messmer. On May 9, 1927, a daily strip started and lasted until 1951. Many early comic books reprinted newspaper strips and Felix's first appearances in comic books were in reprints. Eventually he got his own comic book in the Forties often with stories done by Messmer and later Oriolo. The comic lasted through a variety of publishers including Dell, Toby and Harvey. Issues appeared into the 1960s, including a short-lived comic book featuring Felix's nephews, Inky and Dinky.

Felix merchandise helped his fame grow to world-wide proportions. Early Felix merchandise was produced in a wide variety of materials including tin, celluloid, composition, wood, cast iron, china, plastic, hard rubber and stuffed cloth. During the height of his silent screen popularity, Felix merchandise was even more popular overseas, especially in England where many items were produced.

One merchandising oddity is Felix Chevrolet, a car dealership in Los Angeles established in 1921. The showroom has statues of the "silent" Felix and license plates with his feline face. Huge signs with Felix's image decorate the outside of the buildings.

Since the demise of the TV show, there have been efforts, especially in the late Seventies and early Eighties, to spark new interest in the character by releasing new merchandise ranging from wallets and key chains to the more traditional dolls and banks. Unlike characters such as Mickey Mouse and Betty Boop, whose early design has been the basis of successful merchandising, Felix's new items have been inspired by the TV series. His magic bag of tricks is an important accessory.

His new visibility via TV created a new arena for merchandising which continues to this day earning Felix status as one of longest-running licensed characters.

In the early Eighties there was a syndicated live action show with a Felix costume character as host! So strong was his popularity that he was teamed with Betty Boop in the mid-Eighties for a short lived comic strip in which he was Betty's pet.

"...he could be an alley cat one time, save the day for the losing Yankee Baseball Club the next, and then be the pet of a rich princess."

— Otto Messmer

As we enter the Nineties, there seems no end to the popularity of this feline. Home video has finally taken him to heart with the release of tapes featuring his TV adventures.

SUPERSTAR QUALITY

Unlike many of the stars of the silent cartoon days, Felix has survived and flourished although he followed a rocky path fraught with cancellation. He was king of the silents, but lost prominence with the introduction of sound. He once again regained fame through new adventures on TV. His redesigned TV persona is better known today than was his silent visage when he first appeared.

Felix has had a number of lives, but luckily he is a cat, so he doubtless still has several left. This magical cat has a special place in the Cartoon Superstar universe.

Collection of Felix the Cat merchandise from the Eighties.

© *Felix the Cat Productions*

Felix the button from the late Eighties.

© *Felix the Cat Productions*

Felix bubble gum from Japan.

© *Felix the Cat Productions*

THE FLINT STONES

Superstar Summary

THE STARS: The Flintstones

YEAR OF DEBUT: 1960 (THE FLINTSTONES)

STUDIO OF DEBUT: Hanna-Barbera

SIGNATURE: Yabba-Dabba-Doo!

KEY CREW BEHIND THE STARS: William Hanna and Joseph Barbera (producers/writers/directors), Alan Reed, Mel Blanc, Bea Benadaret, Jean Vander Pyl (voices), Warren Foster (writer)

CAREER HIGH: THE FLINTSTONES (1960-66) — Prime time's longest-running animated series; six seasons. The first animated series to be in the top 20 of Nielsen ratings for a whole year.

Y abba-Dabba-Doo!

Described as a "modern stone-age family," THE FLINTSTONES burst upon TV screens and quickly became part of our culture. In a survey of grade school students during the 1980s, less than 30% could identify a picture of the current President of the United States but over 90% could recognize Fred Flintstone.

The Flintstone family originally consisted of Fred and Wilma, husband and wife. They lived in a modest stone slab home in Bedrock. Their neighbors were the Rubbles, Barney and Betty. They had two pets, Dino and Baby Puss. Into this happy family came Pebbles, a little girl to complete this modern stone-age family.

Fred Flintstone is an overweight, middle-aged married caveman. He wears an orange leopard skin and a tie and has dark hair and a "five o'clock shadow" beard stubble. For many years, he worked as a brontosaurus crane operator at the Rockhead and Quarry Construction Company. A top bowler, he belongs to the Royal Order of Water Buffaloes lodge. Fred often talks before he thinks. When challenged, he often increases his volume rather than considering other possibilities. He frequently tries to better his position in life through get-rich-quick schemes or by pretending to be someone else. His schemes generally backfire, leaving him sadder but not necessarily wiser. Despite his being fat, he moves quickly and has a great deal of energy. Fred is well-liked by others and loves his family. His favorite expression of happiness is "Yabba-Dabba-Doo!"

Wilma is Fred's slender, blond wife. She is more intelligent than Fred and less excitable, but loves her husband no matter how badly he sometimes handles things. Wilma is usually the voice of reason trying to rein in Fred's wild ideas. She is more cultured and better mannered than Fred. Despite her affection for her husband, she can be strong-willed when she believes she's right or truly wants something. She is a fairly typical suburban housewife.

Pebbles is their redheaded daughter. In most episodes she is a cute, inarticulate baby. However, over the years she has appeared in different series as an elementary school student, junior high age and a high school teen. She is as beautiful, intelligent and strong-willed as her mother.

Dino is a Snorkasaurus. The purple dinosaur house pet behaves like a family dog. He is especially fond of Fred and is hyperactive. Despite the fact that he can only communicate by barking, he is amazingly expressive. The Flintstones' other pet, Baby Puss is a saber-tooth tiger. He is mainly seen in the credits and other media, such as books.

THE PREHISTORY OF THE FLINTSTONES

In the late Fifties, with syndicated shows such as HUCKLEBERRY HOUND, YOGI BEAR and QUICK DRAW McGRAW, Hanna and Barbera were receiving critical and financial success. They were approached by John Mitchell, vice-president of Screen Gems, with the idea of developing the first prime time animated series. Mitchell told the team that "they couldn't expect to do animal stories forever. Why not try a cartoon about people?"

Hanna-Barbera decided to base the new series on the same concepts underlying such popular live action situation comedies of the time as I LOVE LUCY and FATHER KNOWS BEST. A middle class family and their day-to-day frustrations and joys would serve as the core of the show. In particular, they shaped the show around Jackie Gleason's THE HONEYMOONERS. Gleason's gruff but hilarious Ralph Kramden was the inspiration for the husband. Other characters from that show similarly inspired the wife and neighbors in the Hanna-Barbera proposal.

The Flintstones, Wilma and Fred and the Rubbles, Barney and Betty.

© Hanna-Barbera

Hanna-Barbera experimented with the idea of making the family Pilgrims, Romans, Cowboys and Eskimos but none of the ideas seemed right. It wasn't until Hanna-Barbera cartoonists Dan Gordon and Ed Benedict began to draw sketches with the family in prehistoric furs and using prehistoric devices that the proper direction was determined. Originally the characters were named the Flagstones. The name was changed to avoid confusion with characters of a similar last name in the popular Hi And Lois comic strip. For a long while, the characters were named the Gladstones. At the last minute, the name was finally altered to the Flintstones.

The gimmick of taking a traditional family sitcom and setting it in the days of the caveman provided ample opportunity for clever sight gags and twists on cliched situations. It took eight long weeks to sell the show. While networks and sponsors liked the show, no one wanted to take the risk of handling this new concept.

"I remember distinctly how Joe Barbera had all the storyboards everywhere and did every voice" stated Stanley Ralph Ross, who worked for Wade Advertising representing One-A-Day vitamins. "I was amazed. I went back to the agency and they asked me what I thought. I said, 'well, I wouldn't watch it, but I think it'll be a hit!'"

Finally, ABC decided to take a chance. The initial sponsors for the program were One-A-Day Vitamins and Winston Cigarettes. In the tradition of live action TV stars, the Flintstones promoted their sponsors' products in commercials during the shows.

"I mean we were the only ones that ever had a baby born in animation. And I gotta tell you, that show was such a hit."

— Joe Barbera

The voices were handled by four veterans from the days of radio. Jean Vander Pyl was the voice of Fred's long suffering wife, Wilma. Bea Benaderet, now remembered for her work in such series as PETTICOAT JUNCTION, was the original voice of Betty. Alan Reed took on the voice of Fred and top voice talent Mel Blanc portrayed Barney. Blanc also did the voice for Dino, Fred's dinosaur housepet. Alan Reed was the one who suggested changing the expression "wahoo" in the script to "Yabba-Dabba-Doo!"

THE FLINTSTONES ROCK TV

The show premiered September 30, 1960. The pilot episode was entitled "The Pool Party." It was a typical situation comedy story.

Fred and Barney build a pool together. Half the pool is in Fred's yard with the other half in Barney's yard. As soon as the pool is built, disagreements arise regarding the use of the pool. Unlike the live action situation comedies, these disagreements show the exaggerated, violent slapstick that can be done so effectively in animation. By the end, they are once again best friends, bosom buddies and life long pals.

An early concept drawing of the Flinstones, showing Fred Jr., their proposed son.

© Hanna-Barbera

The other early episodes also had familiar storylines. The boys try to get out of going to the opera so that they can go bowling. Despite their deceptions and the use of the "Flintstone Flyer," the wives discover the truth.

"Hot Lips Hannigan" has Fred use a magician's cabinet to make the wives disappear. He and Barney decide to take advantage of the situation by going to a night club where Fred becomes a singing star.

In "No Help Wanted," Fred gets Barney a job as a furniture repossessor and he's ordered to repossess Fred's TV set!

These standard stories were enlivened by the use of stone age appliances. Whether it was a mastodon's trunk serving as a vacuum cleaner hose or a variety of birds becoming parts of record players, sirens, or cameras, these inventive twists added to the show's appeal.

Critical reaction was mixed. *The New York Times* stated that "the masculine figures are notably unattractive, coarse, and gruff and the women nondescript." It declared the show an "inked disaster." *Time Magazine*, on the other hand, found the pilot "a little too rocky," but generally liked it stating, "In prime evening time, the half-hour ABC show is aimed at adults, but how can children be asked to sleep while Runtasaurus (a sort of paleolithic Pekingese) is on the screen?"

Audiences agreed more with *Time*'s sentiments. The series appealed to all ages. Despite the roughness of that first season, the show was nominated for an Emmy and won a Golden Globe award among other recognitions. It was rated #18, just behind BONANZA, in the Nielsens for the year. It topped such shows as ALFRED HITCHCOCK PRESENTS, THE MANY LOVES OF DOBIE GILLIS, THE BUGS BUNNY SHOW and WALT DISNEY PRESENTS!

The first episodes were written by Hanna and Barbera. The workload on the ever- increasing number of H-B shows grew larger and larger. Former Warner Brothers' writer Warren Foster was brought in to do scripts. Later writers would include Mike Maltese, R. Allen Saffian, Barry Blitzer, Tony Benedict, Herb Finn, Jack Raymond, Sydney Zelinka, Arthur Phillips and Joanna Lee.

The second season continued the same story focus with episodes including "Fred Flintstone Woos Again" in which Fred took Wilma on a second honeymoon, with the Rubbles. Fred and Barney attended charm school in "Social Climbers." "The House Guest" found the Rubbles moving in with the Flintstones when Barney's house was being repaired. Once again the show was rated in the top 25 for the year.

This season also offered "Alfred Brickrock Presents," the first of many TV series satires. The story told of Fred's attempt to prove a neighbor had murdered his wife. Other series that would get the Flintstones treatment included HAWAIIAN EYE (as Hawaiian Spy in "Hawaiian Escapade"), CANDID CAMERA ("Peek a Boo Camera") and FLIPPER ("Dripper").

In one satire, the original cast appeared! "Samantha" featured not only animated versions of the BEWITCHED cast but the voices of Elizabeth Montgomery and Dick York.

The second season also introduced the famous theme song, "Meet the Flintstones" by Hanna, Barbera and Hoyt Curtin. During the first year, the opening song was an instrumental called "Rise and Shine." "Meet the Flintstones" was so popular the studio went back and changed the opening on the old (first season) shows. "Rise and Shine" can still be heard as background music on the early episodes.

The voices of Betty (Bea Benaderet) and Barney (Mel Blanc).

© Hanna-Barbera

"I find my heart more involved in some of the early stuff. The Flintstones, Yogi and the Jetsons."

— Bill Hanna

A NEW FLINTSTONE

These types of adventures continued into the third season, until "Mother-in-Law's visit." In this episode the nation discovered Wilma was pregnant! It was a "first" in animation that has never been duplicated.

The series biggest change came with the birth of Pebbles Flintstones on February 22, 1963 in "Dress Rehearsal."

At one point, Fred and Wilma were going to have a son, Fred Jr. In fact the son was first planned as part of the original family and appears in some of the early books. At this time, a top team of Screen Gems executives met with Hanna and Barbera for several days to determine the baby's sex. The final decision seems to have been made based on merchandising potential. It was determined that girl dolls sold better. In 1963 when Ideal Toy Company released a Pebbles doll and line of accessories, over $20 million came H-B's way.

The show featuring the birth of Pebbles was one of the highest rated shows ever.

The following (fourth) season, the Rubbles adopted a little boy named Bamm-Bamm who was slightly older than Pebbles. Possessing incredible strength and an intimidating looking club, he became Pebbles' protector and boyfriend.

The show's fourth season dealt with the problems of new parents. "Fred's Monkeyshines" had him putting on the wrong glasses and mistaking a monkey for Pebbles. Fred enters Pebbles in a beauty contest in "Daddy's Little Beauty." "Reel Trouble" had Fred boring everyone with his home movies of Pebbles. Once again, this format appealed to all ages.

Wilma and an example of the humorous transposition of modern devices into a caveman setting.

© Hanna-Barbera

This season also saw the beginning of more fantasy oriented tales. In "Ten Little Flintstones", a flying saucer releases Fred Flintstone robots.

To keep pace with live TV shows such as THE ADDAMS' FAMILY and THE MUNSTERS, a set of weird neighbors was introduced in the fifth season. The Gruesomes were Gobby, Creepella and Weirdly who felt that it was the rest of the neighborhood that was weird. Some feel it was during this season that the Flintstones began to lose their focus and eventually their popularity during prime time. The show featured more fanciful plots including haunted houses and space aliens.

Some of the episodes were fun. For example, "Time Machine" sent the Flintstones and Rubbles to the 1964 New York World's Fair. JW Book, Inc., in arrangement with Western Publishing, even issued a special edition souvenir comic book with the Flintstones visiting the 1964 World's Fair. While there, they met other H-B characters including the Jetsons, Huckleberry Hound, Yogi Bear and many others.

"We pretty much split up the (female) voices, Bea (Benaderet) and I, except when it came to do Pebbles, ... I said, 'I'm Wilma and this is my child. I am doing this voice.'"

— Jean Vander Pyl, voice of Wilma

The sixth season brought The Great Gazoo, a scientist from another planet who used magical powers to help Fred and Barney. However, this help usually resulted in further misadventures. During this season the plots went right through the roof! "Fred Goes Ape" had Fred take the wrong pills and turn into an actual ape! There was also a somewhat prophetic episode called "No Biz Like Show Biz" in which Fred dreams Pebbles and Bamm Bamm grow up to be rock stars. They fulfilled Fred's prophecy over a decade later in a Saturday morning series!

THE SATURDAY MORNING STONE AGE FAMILY

In 1966, the prime time show was canceled. By 1967 episodes began being rerun on Saturday morning, where they remained a mainstay for many years.

CBS noticed the continuing popularity of the modern stone age family. So, in 1971, CBS Saturday morning premiered PEBBLES AND BAMM BAMM. This show dealt with the adventures of the pair as teen-agers at Bedrock High School. Fred and the gang were now supporting characters to the teens. New characters included such friends as Moonrock, Penny, Wiggy and "bad guys" like Fabian and Cindy.

The show became part of THE FLINTSTONES COMEDY HOUR in 1972. Other characters including the bad luck Schleprock and the rowdy Bronto Bunch now became part of Pebbles and Bamm Bamm's adventures. The show only lasted one season. A half hour THE FLINTSTONES SHOW ran for one season the next year on CBS Saturday morning.

> "They were identifiable with every family... They weren't rich, they weren't poor, every mid-life American could understand them."
>
> — Joe Barbera

Meanwhile, the early Flintstone shows were syndicated to local markets beginning in 1972 under the title FRED FLINTSTONES AND FRIENDS.

In 1979, NBC acquired the original show and redubbed 13 of the original episodes with Fred Flintstone's new voice supplied by Henry Corden. Gay Autterson redubbed Betty's voice. The original performers had passed away. THE NEW FRED AND BARNEY SHOW lasted from February to September.

In September FRED AND BARNEY MEET THE THING, an hour long comedy show, took its place. A teenage version of the popular Marvel Comics character, The Thing, appeared in his own stories that bore little relation to the comic book stories that originally featured the character. The next year the show was expanded to 90 minutes and retitled FRED AND BARNEY MEET THE SHMOO. The new 30 minutes segment featured mystery comedies based on THE NEW SHMOO, a show that had premiered the previous year.

The Shmoo was a character from Al Capp's Li'l Abner comic strip whose animated personality was different from the source material. Actually, Fred and Barney only met The Thing and The Shmoo in brief segues between segments.

1980 saw the show revamped yet again and retitled THE FLINTSTONES COMEDY SHOW. The show was divided into six segments. "Dino and the Cave Mouse" was meant to be classic chase cartoons in the spirit of Tom and Jerry. "Bedrock Cops" had Fred and Barney as policemen who teamed with the Shmoo to protect Bedrock. "Pebbles, Dino and Bamm Bamm" solved mysteries in the spirit of SCOOBY-DOO. "Captain Caveman" had Betty and Wilma as reporters for a newspaper who were often saved by a super powered Captain Caveman. "The Frankenstones" were the latest set of monster neighbors who had been introduced in a prime time special. "Flintstone Family Adventure" is self-explanatory.

All of these cartoons were tied together by educational segments, jokes and riddles, exercise and health tips and other similar bits such as a dance-of-the-week. The show was reduced to a half hour in 1981 and renamed THE FLINTSTONE FUNNIES. The Frankenstones still plagued the Flintstones. Strangely, three episodes of THE FLINTSTONE FUNNIES aired in prime time. The series lasted until 1984.

THE FLINTSTONE KIDS debuted in 1986 and ignored all previous continuity. Now the Flintstone characters were elementary school kids and knew each other right from the earliest days. One of their favorite TV shows was "Captain Caveman and Son" which provided another segment to the show. This series ran two seasons.

Also in 1986, The Flintstones were given a 25th anniversary party by Taft Enterprises, the company which owned Hanna-Barbera productions at that time. Held at the La Brea tar pits in Los Angeles, costumed Flintstone characters appeared along with video monitors showing key episodes and sequences.

THE FLINTSTONES MOVIES

Despite the cancellation of the prime time show in 1966, Fred Flintstone got a shot at big screen stardom that same year. THE MAN CALLED FLINTSTONE was meant to parody all the highly successful spy movies and TV series including THE MAN FROM U.N.C.L.E. and OUR MAN FLINT.

International spy, Rock Slag has been injured. Fortunately, he ends up in Bedrock where his chief discovers that Fred Flintstone looks exactly like Slag. Enlisting Fred's help, the Chief sends the Flintstones (and the Rubbles) to France and Italy. Fred's mission is to capture the master spy, the Green Goose and stop him from using his secret weapon to take over the world.

Though the story is a little overwritten, the film is pleasant to watch. It featured better animation than on the TV series thanks to a larger budget. The score, by Doug Goodwin, John McCarthy, and Ted Nichols, featured a number of songs. The title song, by McCarthy, was especially memorable. Long unseen, the feature only became available for viewing again in the late 1980s.

> "Well, at first Hanna-Barbera wanted me to imitate Art Carney, and I said 'No. I don't imitate people. But I can use the same type of inflection and give you a different type of voice for him.'"
>
> — Mel Blanc

It took almost two decades until Fred's next feature film appearance. THE JETSONS MEET THE FLINTSTONES appeared on TV in 1987. Elroy Jetson invents a time machine that inadvertently sends his family back to Bedrock. Once they are there, they meet the Flintstones. The Flintstones eventually get sent to the future for some further misadventures. Finally this mismatching is resolved.

A live action Flintstones film is now in the final planning stages. At one time, Jim Belushi was announced as the choice to play Fred. More recent announcements state that John Goodman will do the part.

THE FLINTSTONE TV SPECIALS

Fred and Barney got a cameo role as the caterpillar in Hanna-Barbera's half hour "hip" version of Alice in Wonderland. Entitled ALICE IN WONDERLAND OR WHAT'S A NICE GIRL LIKE YOU DOING IN A PLACE LIKE THIS?, the show was aired in 1967.

> "(Alan Reed) was Fred Flintstone. He had a warm chuckle... and he was just distinctly styled to fit that role."
>
> — Joe Barbera

A FLINTSTONE CHRISTMAS (1977) had Fred helping out Santa Claus after he sprained his ankle on the Flintstones' roof. THE FLINTSTONES' LITTLE BIG LEAGUE (1978) had Fred coaching Pebbles' baseball team in a game against Bamm-Bamm's team, coached by Barney. Fred and friends first met the Frankenstones in THE FLINTSTONES NEW NEIGHBORS (1980) when the Flintstones and the Rubbles win a trip to Rocksylvania. The following week in another prime time special, THE FLINTSTONES MEET ROCKULA AND FRANKENSTONE. This again featured the monstrous new characters.

In 1981, three episodes of the Saturday morning FLINTSTONE FUNNIES were aired as specials. FRED'S FINAL FLING found Fred thinking he only had 24 hours to live due to an X-ray mix-up. In JOGGING FEVER Fred's boss, Mr. Slate, tells the flabby Flintstone to shape up or ship out. WIND UP WILMA (1981) had Wilma end up pitching for Bedrock's pro baseball team.

THE FLINTSTONES 25TH ANNIVERSARY SPECIAL (1986) offered an hour of clips and new animation. Also on hand were a number of live action hosts including Tim Conway, Harvey Korman and Vanna White.

The Flintstone Kids starred in the first animated special to deal with the problems of drugs. 1988's THE FLINTSTONE KIDS' JUST SAY NO SPECIAL found Wilma falling in with a new gang of kids led by Stoney. (Then) First Lady Nancy Reagan appeared at the end of the special.

That same year, The Flintstone Kids also found themselves in a special public service spot to encourage the proper wearing of seat belts. The spot was produced for the AAA Foundation for Traffic Safety.

SUPPORTING CAST

Barney Rubble is Fred's next door neighbor and best friend. He is a short, blonde caveman. Often he is an unwilling accomplice in many of Fred's schemes. Barney is a likable character who is easily intimidated by Fred. He is also a bowler and belongs to the Royal Order of Water Buffaloes and married to the slender, brunette Betty.

Betty is Wilma's best friend. Like Wilma, she tries to act as the voice of reason when Fred and Barney get carried away. Barney and Betty love each other as much as Fred and Wilma do. Barney and Betty have an adopted son, Bamm Bamm, who is incredibly strong. Bamm Bamm is blond, wears a little hat, and is slightly older than Pebbles.

The prime time special, A FLINTSTONE CHRISTMAS and the cast of THE FLINTSTONE KIDS.

© Hanna-Barbera

Recurring characters included Wilma's mother, Mrs. Slaghoople and Fred's boss, Mr. Slate. Besides Dino, a variety of other animals made frequent appearances as pets including Baby Puss, a saber toothed tiger, and Hoppy, the Hopperoo.

One unique element of the series was the inclusion of guest stars via animation. "The Hit Song Writers" from the first season presented noted tunesmith Hoagy Carmichael in animated form. Other stars who voiced their caricatures through the years include James Darren (as James Darrock, a surfer), Tony Curtis (as Stoney Curtis, movie star) and Ann Margaret (as Ann Margrock, singer).

OTHER MEDIA

The Flintstones immediate TV success made them prime material for merchandise. Through the decades, they've been put on just about every item imaginable.

In 1961 a comic strip began (drawn by Gene Hazelton) that ran for decades. There was also a series of comic books from various publishers.

The Flintstones crew were also seen in a number of promotional comics, including a series in 1988 for Denny's restaurants.

Fred and clan were also popular toy figures. Marx produced an elaborate play set featuring figures, vehicles, houses and a Bedrock plastic mat that served as "ground." Other toys included working models of various vehicles and machinery seen in the show.

As did most H&B characters, the Flintstones appeared on educational material prepared for schools. One such example is THE FLINTSTONES DRIVING GUIDE series which promoted automotive safety. The Flintstones were also involved with the Buckle-Up your seat belt safety program.

For awhile, there was a Bedrock City fun park in Custer, South Dakota. The park was open between Memorial Day and Labor Day each year. It had life-size figures of the characters as well as such items as "stone-scrapers" and Fred's car. The Flintstone costumed characters have also appeared at Marineland in Southern California, ice shows and other presentations. Currently, they are at Universal Studios Florida where, in animated form, they are in a new thrill ride.

Food and Fred always went together, so it was only natural that food makers would come to his door. Flintstone Vitamins were introduced and became the leading children's vitamin. Betty was the only major character who didn't appear as a vitamin. The company felt she would be confused with Wilma, so they substituted Fred's car in her place. Fruity Pebbles Cereal is still one of the top-selling cereals for kids. It

spawned a chocolate version, Coco Pebbles, as well as a series of clever animated commercials and print ads.

Top: *The Flinstones attend the 1964 World's Fair in New York.*

Right: *Early Flintstones merchandise.*

Bottom: *Early Little Golden Book showing Fred Jr. as part of the cast. He was cut prior to commencement of production.*

© Hanna-Barbera

SUPERSTAR QUALITY

Fred and family are one of the longest-running cartoon ensembles in TV animation. Starting out as the most successful animated series in prime time, they moved onto feature films, Saturday morning, and prime time specials. It has been proven that when viewers "...ride with, that family down the street. Through the courtesy of Fred's two feet," they'll "have a gay old time!" Yabba Dabba Doo!

This ad for THE MAN CALLED FLINSTONE is a parody of the ad for the then current James Bond film, THUNDERBALL.

© Hanna-Barbera

HECKLE AND JECKLE

SELECTED SHORT SUBJECTS: *Hair*

Cut-Ups, The Fox Hunt, King Tut's Tomb,

Out Again In Again, Taming the Cat

Superstar Summary

THE STARS: Heckle & Jeckle

YEAR OF DEBUT: 1946 (THE TALKING MAGPIES)

STUDIO OF DEBUT: Paul Terry (Terrytoons)

SIGNATURE: "I say ol' chum!"

KEY CREW BEHIND THE STARS: Paul Terry (producer), Mannie Davis and Connie Rasinski (directors), Tom Morrison (writer)

CAREER HIGH: CAT TROUBLE (1947) — The characters and format are finally established.

They're magpies. They look alike. They act alike. One's British. One's from New York.

Those are the only certain facts about Heckle and Jeckle. It is extraordinary that such little information was all that was needed to propel these birds to stardom.

Heckle and Jeckle were one of the few cartoon teams that were, for the most part, an actual team. Unlike Tom and Jerry, the Coyote and Road Runner, the Ant and the Aardvark, and the like, Heckle and Jeckle were not adversaries. They were buddies. They were also impossible to tell apart.

Even though Heckle and Jeckle have two different accents, it is never quite clear which bird is using which voice. They never seem to call each other by name. However, in watching large numbers of the shorts, one gains the impression that Jeckle is British while Heckle hails from New York.

Yet these two indistinguishable magpies proved extremely popular due to their humor. At their best they could be as fast and furious as any Warners or MGM cartoon. These better efforts contain wild chases and crazy characters. At their worst they feature mindless violence and cruel treatment. They might be considered a sort of animated Three Stooges.

In fact, Heckle and Jeckle may be the most antagonistic, violent characters in the Superstar category. Most of their shorts feature them as the instigators to all that will follow. It is they that break the law, disturb someone or desire fun. Other Superstars might heckle their opponents or seek revenge, but only these magpies go out of their way for a fight.

Another oddity in the Heckle and Jeckle format is that there is never a clear superiority. The magpies always have the winning attitude of being in control, but their chases are continual "back and forth" free-for-alls. One moment they are chasing; the next they are the chased. Though they win many of the battles, they frequently lose the war.

Heckle and Jeckle also tapped into a format not being exploited by other characters. The Heckle and Jeckle cartoons were throwbacks to the very early days of animation when anything could happen. For example, an early, silent, black and white Felix the Cat cartoon entitled FELIX SWITCHES WITCHES had the clever cat divide a horse in half, and attach each half to a different half of a bicycle. Both halves worked.

By the 1940s, such illogic was generally unacceptable in cartoons... except for Heckle and Jeckle. Their contemporaries worried about the "plausible impossible," in which cartoon actions were based on a logical but exaggerated reality. Heckle and Jeckle didn't worry if it made sense. They just had fun.

They also were aware that they were cartoon characters. Unlike some of the other Cartoon Superstars, Heckle and Jeckle knew this was "only a cartoon." This belief was not always shared by other characters in the same cartoon. Hence, Heckle and Jeckle seemed to live a charmed life, surviving the non-stop craziness that was unleashed almost as soon as the opening credits finished.

All they really lacked were individual personalities.

THE BIRTH OF THE BIRDS

The reason for this lack of full development is largely due to Heckle and Jeckle's home base for most of their career. This hyperactive pair came from the famous Terry studio. The studio was founded by animation pioneer Paul Terry.

Terry was proud of that fact that his studio could turn out the least expensive cartoons around. This budget mentality had a definite visual effect on the shorts.

The premise for this team of magpies allegedly came from Terry, himself. He thought it would amusing to have identical twins as the key characters of a series. Since most animated teams worked on the idea of the two characters being quite opposite, this seemed a novel idea. Tom Morrison was instrumental in writing the first short and Mannie Davis directed it.

Heckle and Jeckle officially started their career in THE TALKING MAGPIES (January, 1946). Like many "first" appearances, it has key differences from the current conception of the characters. The biggest difference is that Heckle and Jeckle are husband and wife. The New York character is the husband. He wears a hat and carries a suitcase. The other magpie, called "Maggie" in the short, wears a ladies hat, carries a purse and has large eyelashes.

The short starts out with the married couple looking for a nest. A real estate agent sends them to a nest outside the home of Farmer Alfalfa and his dog, Dimwit. Once in the nest, the two begin arguing. In-

HECKLE AND JECKLE

Heckle and Jeckle at play.

© Viacom

side the house the farmer and Dimwit are trying to sleep. Initial attempts to quiet the birds meet with violent returns. The farmer decides to go down and get his gun.

At this point, the short seems to change direction. The male magpie, sans hat, sneaks into the radio and begins "broadcasting" about the virtues of magpies. At first somewhat taken in by the radio, the farmer becomes outraged when the magpie steps out of the device and says "hello." The farmer grabs his gun and chases the bird outside the house. Both birds re-enter the house and fly Dimwit to the roof where they drop him. By this time, neither magpie is wearing any clothes, and so are totally indistinguishable.

More mayhem ensues as the farmer and Dimwit attempt shooting the pair. As each noisy attempt fails, the magpies, still sans clothes, shout "quiet." Finally the farmer and Dimwit take axes to the tree. This not only makes the two magpies fly around them, but magpies from other nests take up the battle which eventually ends up in the house.

Soon the magpies have flown into the tail pipe of the farmer's car. The farmer and Dimwit get in the back seat and, boards in hand, await the birds' exit.

Instead the birds fly out the radiator and push the car backwards down a hill. As the car madly rolls down the hill, the sound of a drum roll and honking horn are heard. The camera cuts to find the two magpies providing the sound effects. When the car crashes, the farmer and Dimwit are sent flying up into the air. They land in the nest outside their house.

Inside the house, on the bed, lie the two magpies. Once again they are in their husband and wife garb. They comment about the noisy neighbors and start laughing.

Though this short is very different from a typical Heckle and Jeckle cartoon, several themes begin that are repeated in later efforts. First is the idea that they start the problem. The farmer politely asked them to hold down the noise only to receive violence in reply.

Second is the idea that they provide their own music and sound effects. In fact the pair seem to enjoy music to the point of flying and walking in definite rhythm.

The final point is the radio gag. The magpies love to pick up an object and pretend it's a microphone, going into some form of announcement, news broadcast, or sporting event.

The unpublished cover to Spotlight's HECKLE AND JECKLE #1 by Jim Engel.

© Viacom

"One day (Paul Terry) came into our room with a big announcement: 'NO MORE MICE! TO HELL WITH MICE! WE ARE THROUGH USING MICE IN OUR CARTOONS.'"

— I. Klein, storyman/animator at Terrrytoons

THE REAL HECKLE AND JECKLE

It wasn't until the end of the year, November, 1946, that a second talking magpies short appeared, THE UNINVITED PESTS. In this short they are both male, and totally indistinguishable. The New York voice is still there, but there is no British voice yet. This other magpie spent several shorts trying to find an appropriate voice.

Dayton Allen provided the original voices for the magpies. A bit of an impressionist, Allen frequently threw in various voices. Heckle and Jeckle could impersonate the vocal tones of a number of current stars and personalities such as Bogart, Groucho, Jimmy Durante, Hugh Herbert, The Shadow (a radio and pulp magazine hero), and others.

THE UNINVITED PESTS, directed by Connie Rasinski, is truly a standard Heckle and Jeckle short. When Farmer Alfalfa and his dog, Dimwit, try to have a picnic, the two magpies horn in. Violence ensues and the farmer and Dimwit lose in the end.

The next released short, MCDOUGAL'S REST FARM, came out only two months later in January, 1947. This short, as did the first one, features a larger number of magpies. It was also directed by the original director, Mannie Davis. The premise is that Dimwit, now without Farmer Alfalfa, is keeping watch over a rest farm for animals. Magpies arrive to build a new home and begin making all sorts of construction noise. When Dimwit approaches them and tells them he is the watch dog, the New York magpie responds that it is okay, "You can watch."

By the end of the short, the field has narrowed to just two birds. Dimwit corners them with a gun. Unable to shoot them, he proclaims he's probably "just a bird dog!"

The series fourth film, HAPPY GO LUCKY (February, 1947) was again directed by Rasinski. By now the pattern was fully set. In this short the two magpies are trying to steal vegetables from a farm being guarded by Dimwit. After several frantic and violent chases, Dimwit gives up and fills a wheel barrow full of vegetables. The magpies gladly accept and give him a gift in return, a cake. The cake's candle is a piece of dynamite. The magpies then go on their merry way.

In the first instance of "justice," Dimwit states he can't eat the candle and tosses it away. It lands under the wheel barrow and explodes. Heckle and Jeckle are left dazed on a tree branch, wondering what went wrong.

Next up was CAT TROUBLE (April, 1947). This short finally gives the other magpie his British voice. It also gave the two magpies a gray coloring under their wings in several scenes. The story follows the pair's attempts to keep a small bird out of the mouth of a cat.

THE INTRUDERS (May, 1947) introduces the other regular to the series, a bulldog eventually named Clancy. Heckle and Jeckle peddle their wares in a park as custodian Dimwit and security guard Clancy try to stop them.

As one can see, once Terry found a winning combination, he moved with great speed. Heckle and Jeckle were soon appearing in a large variety of adventures.

Other 1947 releases included FISHING BY THE SEA where they attempt to get Dimwit's fish. THE HITCHHIKERS finds them getting a ride with two bank robbers, Clancy and Dimwit. There were a total of eight Heckle and Jeckle films that year.

1948 brought more films. In TAMING THE CAT they hassle a bird-eating cat and sing "Just a couple of songbirds" ala Jimmy Durante. OUT AGAIN, IN AGAIN has them escape jail and create a frantic train chase. Clancy earns their wrath as caddies in GOONEY GOLFERS. Total for 1948: six films.

The series continued full steam until 1955 when Terry sold his studio and library to CBS. Before this occurred, a number of standout shorts were released. These include KING TUT'S TOMB (1950), an atmospheric trip into an Egyptian tomb with Heckle and Jeckle as explorers. While deep in the catacombs they see a num-

HECKLE AND JECKLE

"Tom Morrison (writer of Heckle and Jeckle) had no previous experience at animated cartoon-making before joining the Terrytoons staff. His parents were friends of Paul Terry."

— I. Klein, storyman/animator at Terrytoons

Traditional pose of Heckle and Jeckle.

© Viacom

ber of strange things including some alluring female cat dancers. HAIR CUT-UPS (1952) is a mini musical with the pair as barbers who clip the career of Dangerous Dan. The short features the magpies singing the ballad of Dangerous Dan.

Beginning in 1955, the new owners kept production going, but under new hands new characters were being created. Heckle and Jeckle went to a more relaxed pace of only one or two releases per year.

The last Heckle and Jeckle films were produced in the early Sixties. The artwork on these films was decidedly poorer than that for the classic shorts.

"We cartoon characters can have a wonderful life if we only take advantage of it."

— Heckle (or Jeckle)
in THE POWER OF THOUGHT (1949)

One of these, THOUSAND SMILE CHECK-UP (1960), finds the formula still at work. Heckle and Jeckle have a "last chance" gas station at the desert's edge. When Clancy opens one across the road a battle ensues. The magpies end up exploding Clancy's station with an atomic blast!

Heckle and Jeckle merchandise.

© Viacom

THE TV MAGPIES

When Terry sold his studio and library to CBS in 1955, the talking magpies immediately went on the air. Following the success of MIGHTY MOUSE PLAY-HOUSE in 1955, 1956 saw the debut of THE HECKLE AND JECKLE CARTOON SHOW. With opening credits created from a series of chases and battles, the show became a TV staple and appeared on the network on and off through 1971.

After the birds rested for a number of years, Filmation purchased the rights and created a new Saturday morning series starring the magpies and other Terry characters. THE NEW ADVENTURES OF MIGHTY MOUSE AND HECKLE AND JECKLE debuted in 1979 as an hour show. 1980 saw its second season cut to a half-hour. There was no third season.

Filmation failed to capture the unique charm of Heckle and Jeckle. Admittedly, Filmation was not allowed to use the extreme violence that was an important element in the success of the original Terrytoon series.

WHAT IS A MAGPIE?

Heckle and Jeckle are identified as "magpies." Magpies are part of the Crow and Jay family, the primary difference being that jays are more colorful and crows are completely black and have shorter tails. More specifically, Heckle and Jeckle are what are known as "yellow-billed magpies," a type of bird with black and white coloring and a long tail.

The white coloring on Heckle and Jeckle was on their chest. Sometimes the coloring ranged to shades of blue or grey. There are also times when their bodies are completely black, causing some people to remember them as crows.

According to most bird books, the yellow-billed magpie is restricted to some areas of California! It was an unusual choice of bird for a New York animation studio to decide to use. However, by the 1940s, the term "magpie" had taken on the slang meaning of a person who chatters noisily. Certainly Heckle and Jeckle talk more incessantly than many other Cartoon Superstars and perhaps that contributed to the final choice.

"Terrytoons' work schedule was tight, efficient and fast."

— I. Klein,
storyman/animator at Terrytoons

CO-STARS

A staple of animated cartoons is the dumb dog who is easily outwitted and confused by the main character. In the Heckle and Jeckle series, this canine of unknown pedigree was named Dimwit. The name was most closely associated with the comic book adventures of the mischievous birds.

Dimwit was the ultimate stupid character. Almost his every statement started with a slow, "duhhhhh." The quick chatter from Heckle and Jeckle always prodded him to disaster.

Another regular was Clancy, the bulldog. His name is also appears more frequently in the comics than the shorts.

A tough guy character, he was the powerful canine who would be continually outwitted by the birds. Often, he was the boss or associate of Dimwit but even his additional intelligence failed to save him.

Farmer Alfalfa, one of Terry's stars from silent cartoons, appeared in a few of their earliest adventures. He was usually the owner of Dimwit.

Spotlight comic's
Heckle and Jeckle.

© Viacom

IN OTHER WORLDS

The most prolific Terrytoon's character in terms of merchandise was Mighty Mouse. A distant second place was Heckle and Jeckle. They have the dubious distinction of being more prolific than any of the other Terrytoon characters. They appeared on toys and games and children's books.

Their greatest exposure came in comic books. As early as 1947, less than a year after their official debut, they were appearing in TERRY-TOONS COMICS from Marvel. By the mid-Fifties, they graduated to their own title which, under a variety of publishers, lasted until the late Sixties. In the late Eighties, the short-lived comic company Spotlight planned to revive the madcap magpies in their own comic book. However the first issue never actually came out. A new story with the birds did appear in THE MIGHTY MOUSE AND FRIENDS HOLIDAY SPECIAL.

SUPERSTAR QUALITY

Heckle and Jeckle were Paul Terry's favorite characters created at his studio. Though they never fully developed as personalities, these magpies continue to make audiences laugh through new releases in the home video market. These tapes offer the same variable quality that is behind any Terry product. However, they also offer many laughs. "Good job, chums!"

HUCKLE BERRY HOUND

Superstar Summary

THE STAR: Huckleberry Hound

YEAR OF DEBUT: 1959 (THE HUCKLEBERRY HOUND SHOW)

STUDIO OF DEBUT: Hanna-Barbera

SIGNATURE: "Oh, my darling, Oh my darling, Oh my darling, Clementine" (singing)

KEY CREW BEHIND THE STAR: Bill Hanna, Joe Barbera (directors), Daws Butler (voice), Joe Barbera, Warren Foster (writers)

CAREER HIGH: THE HUCKLEBERRY HOUND SHOW (1958-61) — The first animated series to win an Emmy, and the show that popularized the trend of sophisticated humor in TV animation.

SELECTED SHORT SUBJECTS:
Lion-Hearted Huck, The Purple Pumpernickle, Sherrif Huckleberry, Spud Dud, Tricky Trapper

"Now here's a right big Cartoon Superstar, man," as Huck might say.

Huckleberry Hound is not only one of the biggest Cartoon Superstars to come from TV, he is somewhat responsible for the boom in TV animation. Without Huck, there might not be THE FLINTSTONES or THE SIMPSONS.

Huckleberry, or Huck, is a slow talking, slow moving, blue hound dog who walks on two legs. More a human in dog's clothing than an animal, Huck still works like a dog. His innate kindness, gentleness and honesty made him a lovable character.

Huck comes from the line of characters who never get flustered. No matter what the disaster or danger that presents itself, he merely looks at the audience and calmly announces it in his slightly Southern drawl. For example, when his foe crushes Huck flat with a drawbridge, Huck's only response is, "You know, that's a right heavy drawbridge."

This slow, leisurely pace should not be confused with a dull wit. Huck proved to be one of the fastest-thinking, cleverest, and physically able characters around. He could think himself in and out of trouble remarkably rapidly. Unfortunately, his ideas are more clever than workable.

Hearkening back to a Mickey Mouse style, Huck is really a cartoon actor. He is merely a hound looking for a role. He could be a mailman, a knight in shining armor, a rocket scientist, or the heroic Purple Pumpernickel. More than any other of the Hanna-Barbera creations, he is the consummate toon thespian.

HUCK AND HANNA-BARBERA

In the Fifties, movie studios began closing down their shorts department. The MGM studio was no different. For many of their talented staff, this meant unemployment. However, for Bill Hanna and Joe Barbera, the team behind MGM's Tom and Jerry series, it was a new opportunity.

They opened their own studio and developed a technique to create animation on a severely limited budget. Rather than animate the entire figure, only the parts that moved would be animated. This meant multiple layered drawings and cels. For example, the drawing might have the body and head of the character, but no eyes, mouth, legs or arms. These would be separate drawings that "moved."

The studio was filled with top talent. They boasted not only a number of key animators, including Ken Muse, but also voice and writing talent. Their writing staff included two ex-Warner writers, Michael Maltese and Warren Foster. The pair had written many of the most popular Bugs, Daffy and Porky cartoons. The writing became even more vital in these new cartoons that relied so heavily on clever dialog and characterization instead of movement. Many of the key first episodes were scripted by Joe Barbera, himself.

© Hanna-Barbera

For voices they had Daws Butler, who'd worked in cartoons, radio and with Stan Freberg. Long a cornerstone for Hanna-Barbera voices (Yogi Bear, Snagglepuss, Quick Draw McGraw, Peter Potamus, Mr. Jinks, and dozens of others), Daws Butler was key to many of the characterizations. Also on hand was Don Messick, a former ventriloquist and radio voice. Messick would supply the voice of the announcer in Huckleberry Hound cartoons, as well as Pixie, of Pixie and Dixie, and other characters.

The talent and enthusiasm in the studio kept most spirits high, and all were sure their big break was coming; television as a whole was coming out of its brief dry spell after the earlier "golden age." The studio had already received some minor success via their RUFF AND REDDY animated series of shorts. The final missing ingredient was added in 1957: corn flakes.

Kellogg's Cereals, interested for marketing reasons in sponsoring a children's show, was looking for a suitable animated series. Hanna-Barbera was contacted and a show began to take shape. Instead of simply coming up with some live character to emcee the show in the tradition of Howdy Doody and countless live hosts, Hanna and Barbera envisioned an animated host. They also thought of three separate segments, making it easier to script and leaving some flexibility if either sponsor or audience disliked a particular segment.

"Because of time and budget," explained long time Hanna-Barbera producer Art Scott, "we couldn't use a lot of animation. So we borrowed from radio the concept of using a lot of jokes and satire. The characters created were more like stand-up comics than slapstick clowns."

The lead character filled that description perfectly. He didn't move fast; in fact, he didn't even talk fast.

"I had been doing the slow-talking, laconic voice for some time at MGM," explained Daws Butler in a 1979 interview. "At one time we were going to do a series with a wolf using the voice." The wolf in question appeared in a number of Droopy and other Tex Avery cartoons.

"I even used the voice for the big dog, Ruff, in the series Hanna-Barbera was already doing," he continued.

Along with the voice, a slow moving blue hound dog with a necktie was created. All Hanna-Barbera characters were given something around the neck to better camouflage the segmented artwork. He was christened Huckleberry Hound and made master of ceremonies for the other stars: Yogi Bear, Mr. Jinks, the cat, and the "meeces," Pixie and Dixie. Oddly enough, the only thing Kellogg's didn't like was the character's name. They thought it was too long for children. But it stuck.

In the beginning, Joe Barbera was responsible for writing the Huckleberry Hound sequences. By the second season, Warren Foster had taken over. All the segments were directed by the team of Hanna and Barbera.

INSTANT SUPERSTAR

The show opened in syndication during the Fall of 1958 near prime time (6:30pm in New York). It became a surprise hit. Prior to the recent impact of THE SIMPSONS, it is hard for many to remember when an animated TV series has attracted as much attention and press as Huckleberry Hound did. Articles on Huck and his co-stars appeared in dozens of magazines and newspapers, including in *Time*, *Parents* and *The New York Times*.

> **"Disney's trend was more and more toward beautiful art. Huck and the others have restored cartoons to caricature and fun."**
>
> **— Warren Foster, Huck's writer**

Huckleberry Hound became an instant cult hero of sorts. Clubs formed and merchandise flourished. But the biggest surprise was the discovery that a large percentage of the 16 million viewers were college students and adults. Hanna felt the puns and witty dialog gave Huck a "sophisticated feel." Or, perhaps it was that Huck was something different in a TV season that opened with over 20 Westerns and a dozen detective shows.

More than likely, it was Huck's character that caught audiences by surprise. Used to the brash, fast-paced cartoon characters of the past, Huck debuted as a nice friendly sort who was pleasant to be around and easy to get along with. His even temperament and amiable disposition was obviously due to the kind of superhuman patience that could remain blissfully oblivious to the most alarming injuries and disasters.

THE GOOD, THE BAD AND THE HUCKLEBERRY.

© Hanna-Barbera

HUCKLEBERRY HOUND MEETS WEE WILLIE was the first Huck cartoon produced. It features several key "Huck-isms." First, the story opens with a narrator. Second, Huck is up against a formidable opponent. Third, Huck continually talks to the audience. He not only tells viewers what he plans to do, he also shares his personal insights into any situation.

For this initial venture, Huck does the opening narration. At first referring to himself as a "cop," he catches himself and changes the title to "policeman." Officer Huck, in Car 13, is notified of an escaped gorilla called Wee Willie. His orders are to bring Willie in, but not to hurt the gorilla as it is very valuable. Huck arrives on the scene and discovers mass destruction. He approaches Willie in an attempt of true police procedure. Unfortunately, Willie quickly eats Hucks gun and handcuffs and begins working on Huck's arm. "He's a hungry gorilla," Huck informs the audience, "and that's the worst kind."

As Huck's police radio continually informs the officer not to hurt the gorilla, the simian repeatedly bashes Huck. Finally Huck is able to trap Willie in a giant industrial construction can. He places the can in his patrol car and tells headquarters he is proceeding North with Willie. Suddenly, Willie's head bursts from the top of the can and through the car roof. The gorilla's feet similarly crash through the bottom of the can and car. Facing the opposite direction of Huck, Willie begins walking the car away from headquarters.

Calmly, Huck informs headquarters that Willie is "heading South" with a police car and a policeman, "namely me," as the short fades out.

The second short, LION-HEARTED HUCK, adds two more important Huck elements. First, he is given a talking opponent. Rather than reacting to the monkey sounds of Willie, now there is a second voice that can talk not only with Huck but with the viewer. In this case it's a jokester lion with a crazy laugh. This majestic creature delights in telling the viewer how much fun he is having.

The other major element is the addition of a separate narrator, Don Messick. However, in this short, he has little to say.

LION-HEARTED HUCK also features some great humor. First, there is some visual fun when the narrator shows us how the modern lion battles the modern hunter. The lion is found to have monkeys running radar installations.

Huck admires the lion and his humor almost as much as the lion does! As the lion keeps telling viewers how funny his practical jokes are—"These tacks will slow him down, get the point?"—Huck keeps admitting the same—"You gotta admit, that lion's a load of laughs."

The short ends when the lion pulls his "missing motor bit" by removing the motor from Huck's jeep. The lion sits on the stolen property behind a bush and chuckles as Huck gets in the vehicle and tries to start it. To the lion's surprise, the engine does start, sending him flying through the jungle on top of the runaway engine. As he calls out, "What's with this creepy jeep?" all Huck can say is, "That there lion will do anything for a laugh."

By Huck's third short, TRICKY TRAPPER, the Huck formula and character are 99% set. First, he finally sings "Oh my darling, Clementine" (several times, actually). Second, the narrator maintains an active role in the short, continually attempting to describe in serious tones what is and what will happen. The story follows Mountie Huck as he tracks down Powerful Pierre. Pierre is the first of Huck's formidable human foes with both large bodies and somewhat silly names and fussy demeanor. Huck captures Pierre because a Mountie "always gets his man." Huck repeats the phrase endlessly through the short, having been told "not to forget it" by his commander.

The only missing element finally comes in SIR HUCKLEBERRY HOUND, his fourth short. In this cartoon, Huck attempts to rescue a maiden from Hassle Castle. The narrator not only talks to the audience, but to the cast. As he describes Huck's latest foe as a "cruel, vicious, dastardly, horrible, fat knight," the knight looks to the screen disgusted and announces, "Fat! Cheeesh!"

After several forays, Huck defeats the Knight by dressing as a damsel. However when Huck discovers that the rescued damsel is a matronly, love-sick spinster, he locks himself in the tower and begins calling for help.

That fast (or perhaps slow) paced first season found Huck portraying his usual variety of roles. TWO CORNY CROWS went to work each day to bother farmer Huck. SHERIFF HUCKLEBERRY found him trying to bring in Dinky Dalton, who had now grown to gigantic size. Huck also was a fire man, a knight, a cowboy, a sheepherder, and a homeowner, among others.

In all, there were 22 Huck segments seen in the first season. As final tribute to a great year, THE HUCKLEBERRY HOUND SHOW was awarded an Emmy for Outstanding Achievement in Children's Programming.

"We've never tried to educate to children. We've never tried to preach to them. We've just tried to entertain them."

— Bill Hanna

The second season (1959) found Huck in even wilder situations. Thirteen new episodes were made. JOLLY ROGER AND OUT found him fighting pirates. COP AND SAUCER featured Huck trying to arrest aliens. NOTTINGHAM & YEGGS found him in the days of Robin Hood. He was an early settler in GRIM PILGRIM. These all featured more of the absurd humor and puns seen in the first season.

This was the last season that Yogi Bear appeared on the show. Yogi's popularity had quickly grown and he was given his own show in 1960. To replace the bruin, Hokey Wolf and his son Ding-a-Ling were added to the series.

For his third season (1960), Huck appeared in another thirteen original stories. This season included one of his greatest adventures, SPUD DUD. This sci-fi classic tells the tale of a potato that not only had eyes... but a brain. He uses his brain to grow to gigantic size and terrorize the world. Huck is the scientist who must stop the spectacular spud. After several failed attempts, Huck tricks the potato into a rocket and fires it into space. A reporter asks Huck whatever happened to the rocket. Huck looks upward and says it should be flying overhead any moment. Suddenly an explosion rocks the air. Huck says we may never know what happened to the giant potato, and as white flakes fall from the sky, he adds, "but it is rainin' potato chips."

This same season also offered Huck's classic hero of derring do, the PURPLE PUMPERNICKEL. (Huck tells the viewers, "You can call me 'Purp.'")

After defeating the evil greedy king, the Purple Pumpernickel announces things will be better in the kingdom. Of course to make improvements, he will have to raise the taxes. Soon the crowd is booing him as another costumed hero arrives to vanquish the Purple Pumpernickel. Huck states there'll be no problem, 'cause he knows what to do. He then begins running from the new hero.

Other shorts included LEGION BOUND HOUND, putting Huck in the Foreign Legion, KNIGHT SCHOOL, NUTS OVER MUTTS and CLUCK AND DAGGER, a spy spoof.

Sadly this was the last season for new Huck stories. Hanna-Barbera was now busy with their prime time series including THE FLINTSTONES, THE JETSONS and TOP CAT. Yogi Bear would continue on for another year to keep the legacy alive. Though Huck would return, he would only have one other chance to be "the star."

In 1972, Hanna-Barbera was the king of Saturday morning, producing many of the shows on the air. One such show, ABC'S SATURDAY SUPERSTAR MOVIE, featured a different "movie" each week. One episode brought back the classic Hanna-Barbera characters. YOGI'S ARK LARK featured the popular bruin in an air ship setting sail to help the environment. Huck, once the star, was now just along for the ride with such stars as Snagglepuss, Quick Draw McGraw, Peter Potamus and others. The "movie" proved popular enough to become a series.

1973 saw the debut of YOGI'S ARK, but the series only lasted a year. After this Huck became one of the regular co-stars in a line of series that top-lined Yogi or other new stars. These included SCOOBY'S ALL-STAR LAFF-A-LYMPICS (1977), which was later re-run as SCOOBY'S ALL STARS (1978), and SCOOBY'S LAFF-A-LYMPICS (1980). Huck was part of the Yogi Yahooeys team.

1978 saw the debut of YOGI'S SPACE RACE with Huck teamed with the frantic Quack-Up, a Daffy Duck inspired character. The show also had a segment starring THE GALAXY GOOF-UPS. Huck was part of a team, including Yogi, Scare Bear and Quack-Up as a bumbling squad of space policemen. These were soon split into two separate series.

> "It was the voice that made Huck. Daws had that great voice and it became the character."
>
> —Bernie Wolf, animation producer

YOGI'S FIRST CHRISTMAS (1981) was the first of several made-for-TV features that featured Huck as a co-star. The holidays brought another reunion with the half hour YOGI BEAR'S ALL STAR COMEDY CHRISTMAS CAPER (1982).

1985 found Huck as part of THE FUNTASTIC WORLD OF HANNA-BARBERA, a collection of syndicated series on Sunday mornings. Huck not only was one of the costumed characters working the control board between segments, he also appeared in the animated YOGI'S TREASURE HUNT.

The Fall of 1987 saw the launch of "Hanna-Barbera's Superstars 10." This was a new series of made-for-TV features starring their classic characters. Huck was co-star in several including YOGI'S GREAT ESCAPE (1987) and YOGI AND THE MAGICAL FLIGHT OF THE SPRUCE GOOSE (1987).

Huck did get the title role in THE GOOD, THE BAD AND THE HUCKLE-BERRY (1987). Aided by Yogi Bear, Magilla Gorilla, Quick Draw McGraw and other H-B characters, Huck takes the sheriff's job in the Old West town of Two-Bit. The plot was disjointed as Huck dealt with Indians, outlaws, and townfolk. Though it was nice to be a "star" again, it did not add anything to Huck's prestige.

Huck remained pretty much inactive until 1990 when he was cast in the "Fender Bender 500," part of the daily syn-dicated series WAKE, RATTLE & ROLL. The segment features numerous classic Hanna-Barbera characters in-cluding Yogi Bear, Snagglepuss, Top Cat and Magilla Go-rilla in 4x4 races around the world.

"He is a sort of Tennessee-type guy who never gets mad no matter how much he is outraged. He is the fall guy, and a large part of his humor is the way he shrugs off his misfortunes. To Huck, nobody is really bad."

— Warren Foster, Huck's writer

CO STARS

Huck had no regular co-stars in his short subjects. Though he frequently met with similar characters (mean dogs, tough guys, aliens), they were never really the same character twice. In his many later appearances with Yogi Bear, Huck did little interaction with the bear, generally being one of the crowd.

OTHER MEDIA

Huck was one of Hanna-Barbera's merchandised stars during his first three years. Comics, books, toys, dolls and more could be found for the blue hound. Due to his association with Kellogg's, he was a regular subject for cereal promotions and giveaways.

He joined his other Hanna-Barbera friends as a costume character in a va-riety of locations. In the early Sixties, he and Yogi Bear traveled the country visiting schools and shopping centers. In the Seventies and Eighties, he be-came associated with several amusement parks including the Taft parks Kings Is-land, Kings Dominion and Carowinds. He also appeared at Southern California's Marineland and still appears at Great America in Northern California and Uni-versal Studios Florida.

The United States Coast Guard ice breaker "Glacier" named a tiny island "Huckle-berry Hound" in the Antartic's Bellingshausen Sea.

Rare Dell Comics give-away from the Sixties.

© Hanna-Barbera

SUPERSTAR QUALITY

Huckleberry Hound is the classic showbiz story of a top star who is upstaged by one of his supporting players, and thus becomes a supporting player, himself. However, Huck's place as a Cartoon Superstar is secure due to his many years of hilarious work as the star and host of his own show. Huck gave some of the great-est cartoon characters their first break. His history-making show and the attention it brought make Huck one of the most fondly remembered characters of the Fifties and Sixties.

MR. MAGOO

SELECTED SHORT SUBJECTS: *Dick Tracy and the Mob (from Famous Adventures of Mr. Magoo), Fuddy Duddy Buddy, Magoo's Buggy, Mr. Magoo's Christmas Carol, Ragtime Bear*

Superstar Summary

THE STAR: Quincy Magoo

YEAR OF DEBUT: 1949 (RAGTIME BEAR)

STUDIO OF DEBUT: UPA

SIGNATURE: "Oh, Magoo, you've done it again!"

KEY CREW BEHIND THE STAR: Jim Backus (voice); John Hubley, Pete Burness (directors), Phil Eastman, Millard Kaufman, Dick Kinney, Bill Scott (writers)

CAREER HIGH: MR. MAGOO'S CHRISTMAS CAROL (1962) — A charming, tuneful adaptation of Dicken's classic with Magoo perfectly cast as Scrooge.

M
r. Magoo has been the primary source of unintentional disasters and injuries for over 40 years. Attired originally with a long coat, hat and cane, Magoo is a late middle-aged bachelor who is short and bald. Originally he was conceived as a loud, crotchety, difficult-to-please older man whose quick temper and stubbornness propelled him through life. Later cartoon adventures mellowed his personality, revealing a good-heartedness and sentimentality beneath the disagreeable exterior. He became more of a gentleman who was especially courteous towards women, or inanimate objects such as lampposts, which he perceived as women.

The humor in Mr. Magoo cartoons derives from his physical handicap of not being able to see things clearly and how he triumphs over situations and people despite this obstacle. His nearsightedness often seems to border on blindness as he stumbles through life mistaking animals for old school chums, inanimate objects such as stop lights and coat racks for policemen or sales clerks and misreads signs and store logos.

Such activity would bring instant disaster to any other person. But Magoo's stubborn determination that he is right in his assumptions seems to protect him from all harm while often bringing destruction to anyone and anything else in the immediate vicinity. In a sense, Magoo has found how to survive and flourish in an insane world by living happily in his own personal reality.

Magoo is unique among cartoon characters for many reasons but in particular because he behaves as a real human. Unlike other cartoon stars he does not get smashed, stretched, sliced or blown up. In fact, some early critics compared him to the live action comedian W. C. Fields. Both characters had bulbous noses, fought against mindless authority, and had a blustery behavior when challenged.

Unlike Fields' character, Magoo genuinely loves the world and is a man of principle. Especially in the later cartoons, trouble usually began because Magoo was trying to help someone not because he was trying to take advantage of a situation or a person.

MEET MR. MAGOO

In a way, Mr. Magoo owes his existence to Walt Disney. In the 1940s, some of Disney's key animation personnel were dissatisfied with Walt's method of operation. They eventually formed their own animation company, United Productions of America (UPA), and produced educational films. In 1948 this new studio, now headed up by Stephen Bosustow, obtained a contract with Columbia Pictures to produce animated shorts for theaters. Promising a fresh start for animation, talent began pouring in to the studio.

Rather than relying on the cute funny animals that were the staple of other larger animation studios, including Disney and Warners, UPA decided to create distinctive human characters. They wanted to experiment with animation and personalities. The new studio flourished as critics and the Motion Picture Academy heaped praise and Oscars on them.

The first and perhaps the most successful of these creations was the catastrophically myopic Mr. Quincy Magoo. He made his first appearance in the theatrical short RAGTIME BEAR (1949) in which he mistakes a bear for his raccoon-coated nephew, Waldo. That first short, written by Millard Kaufman, was directed by John Hubley, an innovative animator. Hubley later went on to receive several Oscars for films he did for his own Storyboard Inc. His name will always be one of those closely associated with the beginnings of Magoo.

Magoo and McBarker from DePatie-Freleng'S WHAT'S NEW MISTER MAGOO?

© UPA

Magoo's creation was the result of the contributions of many talented people. Supposedly, Hubley originally based the character on a bullheaded uncle of his named Harry Woodruff who could not be convinced he was wrong once he had made a snap judgment. Jim Backus, who was hired to provide the voice for the character, saw elements of his own father in the character, a man who was personally isolated from the rest of the world. To achieve that effect, Backus utilized the voice of one of his earlier voice creations from a popular radio show. The character was "The Man In The Club Car," a loud-mouthed businessman filled with misinformation. All of these elements helped form Magoo's personality.

"We made up a complete biography for the little jerk," commented Backus. "He graduated from Rutgers in 1901. Magoo studied to be a zeppelin commander, but never made the grade. He's a card-carrying Republican and was on the Committee to Re-elect William McKinley."

Despite Backus' success in other areas including his visibility as the millionaire on GILLIGAN'S ISLAND, he was always haunted by the fame of Magoo. "I'd like to bury the old creep and get some good dramatic roles in movies. He is a pain in the posterior. Every time I start to be a serious actor I lose out because someone — usually a producer — says I'm Magoo." Yet despite those feelings, Backus for many years drove around Hollywood with a license plate bearing the letters "Q MAGOO."

MAGOO BECOMES A STAR

Having enjoyed a success with RAGTIME BEAR, UPA used Magoo on and off. He quickly became the most popular of the UPA creations. Columbia Pictures, who released UPA cartoons in theaters, demanded more. Director Pete Burness, who later worked for the Jay Ward Studios, was made responsible for several Magoo shorts a year, including the two Academy Award winners, WHEN MAGOO FLEW (1954) and MISTER MAGOO'S PUDDLE JUMPER (1956).

"My favorite Magoo is FUDDY DUDDY BUDDY where he is playing tennis with a walrus and we wrote a scene where Magoo realizes he is nearsighted and says, 'Gee, I don't care. I like him.' We never did that again... (Hubley) felt we ruined the character."

— Bill Scott, UPA storyman

In the first cartoon, Magoo thinks he is in a movie theater when he has actually just boarded an airplane and is thrust into a real life adventure with an escaped thief. Needless to add, Magoo enjoys the "movie" although he regrets that the "theater" didn't show a cartoon before the "main feature."

In the other cartoon, Magoo and his nephew Waldo have a harrowing time in a newly purchased electric car. Magoo promptly guides it off the road and under water.

Magoo's success outside the studio was not a source of joy inside UPA. The studio had originally formed to create avant garde and experimental shorts similar to the strongly dramatic TELL TALE HEART, based on the short story by Edgar Allen Poe, and the whimsical UNICORN IN THE GARDEN, based on James Thurber's short story. Now they were forced to "churn out" one Magoo after another for financial survival.

Just as other cartoon characters got rounder and cuter, Magoo also softened. The softening was not just in the design of the character, but in his personality

Cover from UPA model guide.

© UPA

as well. As created by Hubley, the character, even if he had been able to see, would still have been a bullheaded, opinionated old man constantly in some trouble because of his stubbornness.

Veering away from this angry origin, writers and directors concentrated more and more on the nearsightedness and made him more lovable and sentimental. Years later, director Burness wondered in an interview if the character might have been even more successful if Magoo had remained "crotchety, even somewhat nasty."

In the early UPA cartoons, the style is darker and more angular and the pacing slower and more deliberate. TROUBLE INDEMNITY (1950) had Magoo so wrapped up in a crime novel he was reading that he took on the persona of a private detective to save Waldo. Waldo only needed a hundred dollars to repair his father's car but found himself caught up in Magoo's film noire world.

Jim Backus, himself, came up with a storyline for a Magoo cartoon, DESTINA-TION MAGOO (1954). In the story, Magoo mistakenly gets in a rocket built by an old school friend who is now a famous scientist. The rocket lands in the LUNA amusement park and Magoo mistakes his own image in a fun house mirror for an alien and the rest of the park for the moon's surface.

The later Magoo cartoons have a brighter color scheme and lighter story lines. BWANA MAGOO (1959) was one of the last theatrical Magoo cartoons. In the story, Magoo mistakes a lion for Waldo and traps Waldo in the cage.

Magoo was extremely popular, sometimes getting top billing over the main feature. Backus traded a raise in salary for billing on the cartoons and became even more famous. His wife Henny was brought in to provide the voice for Mother Magoo, Magoo's 85 year old mother.

In the late 1950's, when UPA stated to diminish its output and closed its New York Studio, the California branch sustained itself by producing material for tele-vision and commercials. Magoo became a key mar-keting device, shilling light bulbs for General Electric. ("It's easy to see, the best bulbs are G.E.!")

Magoo drawing guide.

© UPA

MAGOO'S FEATURE DEBUT

It was somewhat natural that when UPA decided to produce its first full length feature film, Magoo would be called upon to render ser-vice. Two proposals were developed. One was based on the novel *Don Quixote* and boasted a script by famed author Aldous Hux-ley, who is better known for writing *Brave New World*. Don Quixote was not as well known as the other project, so A THOUSAND AND ONE NIGHTS (1959) became UPA and Magoo's first feature.

Regular Magoo director Pete Burness was set to direct, but left in the middle of pre-producton. Disney animator Jack Kinney stepped in to take control. Abe Le-vitow was head animator.

In the story, Magoo played a bumbling Baghdad lamp dealer named Azziz Magoo. He wants his carefree neph-ew, Aladdin, to get married and settle down. Aladdin falls in love with the beautiful Princess Yasminda who is about to wed the Wicked Wazir. The Wazir craves power and wants a magic lamp that is buried in a treasure cave. Only Aladdin, seventh son of a seventh son, has the power to open the cave. The Genie in the lamp helps Aladdin win Yasminda. Unfortunately, Magoo, who is unaware of the magic of the lamp, turns it over to the Wicked Wazir. However, Magoo constantly upsets the Wazir's schemes and helps to finally defeat him.

"The only thing left to do is an X-rated Magoo!"

— Jim Backus, Magoo's voice

Czenzi Ormonde wrote the screenplay. The film featured an extremely strong voice cast including Kathryn Grant (Princess), Dwayne Hickman (Aladdin), Hans Conried (Wazir), Herschel Bernardi (Genie), Daws Butler and Alan Reed.

This film promoted the largest array of Magoo merchandise ever offered including a hand puppet in gown and fez, a life-size rubber mask of Magoo, a lapel pin, a felt fez with Magoo's name on it and a flying carpet toy powered by a balloon.

Movie poster for Mr. Magoo.

© UPA

At the time, Magoo was still spokesman for General Electric and they announced "one of the most ambitious campaigns ever undertaken by a major manufacturer and a motion picture company." Starting with a full page ad in *Life Magazine*, to publicize the film. GE's 300,000 dealers received window streamers and promotion kits with the Genie of the lamp holding a box of GE's Soft White light bulbs.

To further publicize the film, arrangements were made so that Magoo in his 1001 ARABIAN NIGHTS outfit sponsored U.S. Savings Bonds. 40,000 U.S. Post Office delivery trucks, thousands of banks and countless local businesses had a poster of Magoo stating that Bonds were "Your magic carpet to the future!"

Despite all this effort, the film was not a success. It is little remembered today.

MAGOO ON TV

UPA now devoted more time to television production. Between 1960 and 1962, the studio produced 130 individual sequences of Magoo adventures for television. They also did an equal number of Dick Tracy cartoons at the same time. The cartoons were first released as a half-hour series. Some shorts didn't even star Magoo, focusing instead on various secondary characters. In between the shorts there were small animated lead-ins in which a character would tell an initial gag, then announce a cartoon was coming up. Some of these shorts, especially the ones starring Magoo, are highly entertaining although obviously done with a small budget.

In 1962, during the Christmas season, UPA produced the first animated television Christmas special: MR. MAGOO'S CHRISTMAS CAROL. Directed by Abe Levitow, the story concerned Magoo making his Broadway stage appearance as Ebenezer Scrooge in Charles Dickens' classic Christmas tale.

Certainly a high point in the old geezer's colorful career, the special featured many memorable songs by Jule Styne and Bob Merrill. When the special once again received high ratings the following year, NBC decided it was a good concept for a series.

For the network, UPA developed a prime time program entitled THE FAMOUS ADVENTURES OF MR. MAGOO. Premiering on September 19, 1964, the series ran for 26 episodes and cast Magoo as a key character in stories based on famous novels. Magoo was Captain Ahab, Long John Silver, Dr. Watson and a host of other characters. Obviously Magoo was merely playing a role because none of the characters suffered from nearsightedness nor were confused old men like Magoo himself. Several episodes of this series have been retitled and issued to syndication separately, such as MR. MAGOO'S TREASURE ISLAND.

Strangely, in the middle of its first season, the show was moved to a new time slot opposite GILLIGAN'S ISLAND (also in its first season) where Jim Backus was making cult TV history. Audiences obviously had loved MR. MAGOO'S CHRISTMAS CAROL for other reasons than seeing Magoo play a famous role. The series was canceled after one season, while the original Christmas special continued to run for many years.

Magoo disappeared from new productions until 1970 when he appeared in an hour long TV special entitled UNCLE SAM MAGOO, again directed by Levitow. It offered a series of vignettes detailing the history of America.

DePatie-Freleng obtained the rights to revive the character in 1977 for an all new Saturday morning television show called WHAT'S NEW, MISTER MAGOO? on CBS. Magoo was given a talking white dog named McBarker, also voiced by Backus, and nephew Waldo returned. Magoo was once again up to his old antics, mistaking construction equipment for a used car lot with typical disastrous results or detouring from his class reunion to a zoo and never noticing the difference. The show lasted one season. Each half hour contained two adventures and only 13 half hours were made.

In 1987, Warner Brothers announced a live action feature based on the Magoo character. Some insiders were hoping that Jim Backus would portray the character. However when Jim Backus succumbed to Parkinsons Disease in 1989, that hope also died.

The Magoo library, along with a number of other UPA properties, was acquired by Morrison Entertainment Group in early 1989. Plans began to re-market the shorts and characters. Announced plans included a 40th birthday special for Magoo that never materialized, and a possible Halloween special. The Fall of 1989 did see Magoo return to TV in re-runs on the USA cable network. Talk of the live action feature continued.

MR. MAGOO

"The important thing was Magoo's absolute self confidence, the absolute certainty he feels that he is right at all times."

— Pete Burness, director

Two publicity stills for Magoo. Above scene is from MR. MAGOO MEETS MOTHER MAGOO.

© UPA

MAGOO'S CO-STARS

Over the decades, a host of supporting characters appeared and disappeared. Perhaps the best remembered character was Waldo, Magoo's lanky, goofy nephew who was often an unwitting participant in his uncle's escapades. With his upturned hat and protruding upper lip, he was a parody of the college teen characters of the period. In the Sixties, he was given a girlfriend named Millie and a best friend named Prezley who really resembled a cartoonish W. C. Fields.

Magoo had a variety of pets including Bowser the cat who he believed was a watchdog. Later talking dogs including Caesar and McBarker came on the scene. He also had Hamlet, the Hamster, who battled Caesar in a series of shorts that were part of the 1960's TV group.

Like many superstars, Magoo acquired a never-ending supply of relatives including Tycoon Magoo, an extremely rich and amoral man. He would send his un-

fortunate butler, Worcestershire, to try and prevent Magoo from inadvertently interfering with his projects. Mother Magoo was a very hip woman in her late Eighties. She was involved in such activities as racing cars but had to endure the misguided attentions of her well-meaning son who thought she was a helpless, old-fashioned widow.

Taking care of Magoo's two story house was Charlie, a Chinese servant. His ethnic stereotyping, which included huge, buck teeth, might be unappealing for modern audiences. Similar to the other characters in the series, Charlie often did the physical suffering for "Mr. Magloo's" (sic) self-incurred disasters. The shorts that aired on the USA cable network had Charlie re-dubbed to a standard Anglo voice.

Magoo drove a 1913 Stutz Bearcat automobile which proved as durable and memorable as the character himself. It was the one item which appeared frequently in the many versions of his adventures, except for his more literary episodes.

MAGOO'S OTHER SIGHTINGS

Magoo, unlike other Cartoon Superstars did not have an extensive life outside his animated antics. He appeared in a handful of comics in the early 1950s and then briefly again in the early 1960s. The late 1960s saw a Magoo newspaper comic strip that did not receive wide distribution. Later some paperback books were issued containing collections of this strip. There has been some nominal Magoo merchandising, but nothing compared to his fellow superstars. The exception, as noted, occurred during the promotion of his feature, 1001 ARABIAN NIGHTS in 1959.

Magoo's film life is easily obtainable. A large majority of his theatrical work, including his feature, have been on videotape for some time. Recently Kid Flicks began issuing the TV shorts, including the lead-ins, on video.

SUPERSTAR QUALITY

Magoo's career has spanned over 40 years. When he first began to receive recognition, it was reported that Walt Disney asked rhetorically, "How long can one actually look at Magoo's antics?" Luckily this is one time Disney was wrong.

Perhaps the key attraction of Magoo is that no matter how he stumbles, or blunders, no matter the danger, everything always turns out right for him. An audience envies that.

Even though Magoo is basically a one-joke comic, his determined personality has kept him entertaining audiences for decades. Like his limited eyesight, Magoo hasn't let his somewhat limited cartoon lifestyle get him down.

"The Magoo character epitomized what everybody wanted to do. People would like to accomplish things by luck, by chance, by circumstance, but without working for it."
— Stephen Bosustow, President of UPA

Some of THE FAMOUS ADVENTURES OF MR. MAGOO including Magoo as Long John Silver, Cyrano, Rip Van Winkle (before and after his long sleep) and Uncle Sam.

© UPA

MICKEY MOUSE

SELECTED SHORT SUBJECTS: *The Band Concert, Mickey and the Beanstalk (from Fun and Fancy Free), Mickey's Trailer, Thru the Mirror, Two Gun Mickey*

Superstar Summary

THE STAR: Mickey Mouse

YEAR OF DEBUT: 1928 (STEAMBOAT WILLIE)

STUDIO OF DEBUT: Disney

SIGNATURE: "Ha Ha" (falsetto laugh)

KEY CREW BEHIND THE STAR: Walt Disney (voice/producer), Ub Iwerks (animator/designer), Fred Moore (master animator), Jimmy MacDonald (2nd voice)

CAREER HIGH: THE MICKEY MOUSE CLUB (1955) through which Mickey became permanently ingrained in the psyche of the young and created new generations of Mouseketeers.

Mickey Mouse is more than just a Cartoon Superstar. Mickey Mouse has at various times represented everything that was good and bad in U.S. culture. For a distinctly American character, he became an international favorite generating an affection unmatched by any other.

Originally Mickey Mouse was a mouse-like character that resembled other characters of the time including the mice in Paul Terry's AESOP'S FABLES and Pat Sullivan's Felix the Cat. A direct inspiration was Walt Disney's own Oswald the Lucky Rabbit. One thing that made Mickey's design so much more appealing than these previous efforts was that he was primarily composed of round, soft circles without sharp points. This baby roundness had a subliminal effect that made him appealing. During the first few years, his design varied somewhat before settling into the plump, approximately four foot tall figure known today.

Mickey Mouse was as much a hayseed as his creator Walt Disney and was seen as an animated extension of the artist. When Walt became more sophisticated, so did Mickey. Walt's shyness was reflected in Mickey. Physically, Mickey did not do "mouse"-like things. He never lived in a mouse hole. His tail was never caught in a trap. In many ways, he was a human being who had somehow taken on the appearance of a mouse.

Mickey was a genuinely nice guy. He was cheerful and helpful. His extremes of behavior in his earlier cartoons, such as his treatment of animals, were not done out of malice but rather a playfulness. Eventually, due to public pressure, even that minor characteristic was eliminated so that Mickey was purer than a Boy Scout.

Of all the Disney crew of characters, he was the smartest and was usually placed in the position of the leader. He was not a college-educated character. Mickey's intelligence was a common sense mixed with a genuine respect and concern for others. His success on a variety of jobs and projects was due primarily to his hard work rather than his clever mind.

People remember the early Mickey as being a heroic, adventurous character. This image was sparked more by his comic strip exploits. However, there are a handful of examples from his animated output that placed him into situations where he was able to demonstrate his bravery. He was willing to stand up to seemingly impossible odds to do what he felt was right.

Mickey was the most domestic of the Disney characters. Many of his stories revolved around the setting of his home or some mundane recreational activity such as a picnic or a party. He never took the risks that Goofy, Donald Duck and Pluto seemed to take every moment.

Mickey was unambitious. He loved his girlfriend, his dog and his life. He genuinely liked people and put up with irritations that might try the patience of a saint. He was respectable, gentle and moral.

At one time critics found such blandness offensive and the term "Mickey Mouse" was used as an expression of derision. Lately other critics have seen that this vagueness of character may have contributed to Mickey's success. He represented an optimistic affirmation of the basic goodness of the world. He lacked negative characteristics that would detract from that positive image. Mickey became all things to all people.

This positive spirit captured the affection of people struggling out of the Depression. Mickey seemed to have stepped out of a Horatio Alger novel, the poor but honest boy who made good due to hard work.

THE BIRTH OF MICKEY

Walt Disney, with the assistance of animator Ub Iwerks, had been producing a series of cartoons about a live action girl named Alice and her adventures in a cartoon world. In 1927, as a replacement for the Alice comedies, Disney and Iwerks developed a new series about a little black rabbit named Oswald. The character, who resembled an early Mickey Mouse with rabbit ears, was instantly popular.

Mickey Mouse in the Thirties.

When the series became successful, Disney confronted the distributor in New York to try to get more money to improve the project. The distributor, Charles Mintz, not only owned the character but had secretly signed up Disney's animators, except Iwerks, to exclusive contracts. Disney had to accept a new contract at a lower price or lose the character and his crew. Disney refused to negotiate and, supposedly on the train trip from New York back to Los Angeles, instead created Mickey Mouse.

Over the years, Disney elaborated on this magical creation story. Supposedly back in the days when he was working as an artist in Kansas City, he adopted a family of mice, one of whom he trained. That experience subconsciously helped him to

Mickey is the official host of Disneyland.

© Walt Disney Productions

come up with the idea of a mouse character he was going to call "Mortimer." His wife, Lillian, objected to the name feeling it was too pretentious and Walt settled for the more friendly sounding "Mickey." When he arrived in Los Angeles, he had a new character.

In reality, Mickey was probably designed during a meeting with Ub Iwerks shortly after returning to Los Angeles. Walt was responsible for Mickey's personality and Iwerks handled the physical appearance. As mentioned previously, Mickey looked a great deal like Oswald the rabbit with a few changes such as mouse ears and tail replacing rabbit ears and tail.

In 1927, Charles Lindbergh had become a public hero for his solo plane flight from New York to Paris. Hoping to capitalize on this event, Disney's first Mickey Mouse cartoon was entitled PLANE CRAZY. Iwerks animated this film on his own in less than three weeks. This was a silent black and white cartoon about a barnyard Mickey being inspired by Lindbergh's exploit to build and fly his own plane with Minnie. The reaction to the film at a special preview encouraged Walt to begin work on another Mickey cartoon, GALLOPIN' GAUCHO, parodying Douglas Fairbanks' similar film and having Mickey rescue Minnie from the clutches of Black (Peg-leg) Pete.

Unfortunately, the East Coast distributors were unimpressed with the character and Disney was unable to get his cartoons into theaters. At this point, Mickey Mouse might have been forever lost to the world. However, Warner Brothers released a film called THE JAZZ SINGER, basically a silent film but with a few lines of dialog and some Al Jolson songs using a new sound process. The film made an immediate impact on audiences and Disney was convinced to try one more Mickey Mouse cartoon with sound.

MICKEY SQUEAKS!

There had been a few previous experiments in the use of sound in cartoons. The thing that made Mickey Mouse in STEAMBOAT WILLIE different was that it was the first cartoon with a properly synchronized track so that it really seemed that the actions on the film were causing the sound. STEAMBOAT WILLIE tells the story of Mickey Mouse, a member of Captain Pete's riverboat crew. Mickey entertains the ship's only passenger, Minnie, with a musical version of "Turkey In The Straw" played on animals who are squeezed, hammered and twisted.

Walt believed in the film so strongly that he put every penny he and his company had behind the project. A failure would have completely wiped him out financially. When STEAMBOAT WILLIE premiered at the Colony Theater in New York on November 18, 1928, it was a tremendous hit. The Disney studio immediately produced soundtracks for PLANE CRAZY and GALLOPIN' GAUCHO and a new Mickey Mouse cartoon called THE BARN DANCE. One of the first of the new personnel added for the cartoons was Carl Stalling, a theater organist from Kansas City, who provided effective soundtracks for the films. Stalling would later do similar work for the popular Warner Brothers cartoons. Walt Disney himself supplied the squeaks for Mickey Mouse, with Mickey first speaking words in 1929's THE KARNIVAL KID.

Walt continued to personally voice Mickey until 1946 when, because of his overloaded schedule, sound effects supervisor Jimmy MacDonald took over. MacDonald retired in the early Eighties and was replaced by a number of different voice actors.

The early Mickey Mouse cartoons were not much different from those other studios were producing at the time. They all relied on sight gags with little consistency in characters or stories. For instance, in THE KARNIVAL KID, Mickey removed the top part of his head and ears as he would a hat, a typical gag for characters at this time. What helped Mickey survive during this period was the novelty of sound. It grabbed the audience's attention.

Some writers have argued that what saved Mickey from obscurity was the fact that Iwerks left the studio in 1931 to form his own company. This action forced Walt to devote more attention to the character and resulted in stronger stories. Mickey's personality started to blossom. For the most part, Mickey's expressions at the time were pretty much limited to "happy" and "not happy."

MICKEY BECOMES A STAR

Throughout the Thirties, the Disney studio turned out approximately a dozen new Mickey Mouse cartoons a year. In fact, by the end of 1940 Mickey had appeared in over two-thirds of all the theatrical shorts that would star him.

Mickey became a national phenomenon in the Thirties. He was so popular that his use as a merchandising character is credited with pulling the Lionel Train corporation and the Ingersoll Watch Company out of bankruptcies.

Mickey Mouse even received serious consideration as fine art. MICKEY'S ORPHANS (1931) was nominated for an Academy Award, but lost. Over the years, Mickey was nominated four other times, for BUILDING A BUILDING (1933), THE BRAVE LITTLE TAILOR (1938), THE POINTER (1939), and MICKEY AND THE SEAL (1948). In 1932 Disney was presented with an Oscar for creating Mickey Mouse. The only Oscar-winning short Mickey would appear in was Pluto's 1941 LEND A PAW.

MICKEY'S ORPHANS was a typical demonstration that even in his own cartoons Mickey sometimes seemed merely a supporting player. The cartoon tells the story of a dozen or more homeless kittens invading Mickey and Minnie's house at Christmas and how they destroy the house as the mice share the spirit of Christmas with them.

The early Thirties produced some Mickey cartoons in which he was clearly an adventurous hero. THE MAD DOCTOR (1933) pitted him against an evil scientist who was going to experiment on Pluto. THE MAIL PILOT (1933) found Mickey battling Pete in the sky in a wild aerial duel. TWO GUN MICKEY (1934) portrayed Mickey as a pistol-packing cowboy saving Minnie from Peg-leg Pete. Most of the other Mickey cartoons centered on domestic themes and depended upon Pluto for the humor. MICKEY'S GOOD DEED (1932) has Mickey selling Pluto to buy Christmas presents for a poor family. Often some of Mickey's most amazing adventures turned out to be merely dreams including MICKEY'S GALA PREMIERE (1933) where he met famous film stars.

Mickey and Minnie party in the early Eighties.

© Walt Disney Productions

TECHNICOLOR MICKEY

A turning point in Mickey's career arrived in 1935 with the release of THE BAND CONCERT. It was the first full color Mickey Mouse cartoon and centered on the amusing premise of Mickey trying to conduct his band through a performance of "The William Tell Overture" despite the distractions of Donald Duck and a tornado. Just as the novelty of sound had given Mickey a boost, the introduction of color sparked an even greater interest in his cartoons.

These color Mickeys of the late Thirties are perhaps the best remembered, not only because of their strong stories but thanks to their endless repetition on TV and release on home video. These classics include such gems as THRU THE MIRROR (1936), in which Mickey enters an "Alice in Wonderland" world on the other side of the mirror, and BRAVE LITTLE TAILOR (1938) based on the children's tale of a mild tailor defeating a giant.

Mickey's popularity was becoming so great that restrictions were placed on the mouse. As an idol of children, he was no longer allowed to be involved in the roughhouse gags of his earlier cartoons. "Mickey is limited today because public idealization has turned him into a Boy Scout. Every time we put him into a trick, a temper or a joke, thousands of people would belabor us with nasty letters," recalled a Disney writer in *Collier's Magazine* (April 9, 1949).

Mickey's 7th birthday art.

Opposite: Poster for MICKEY'S BIRTHDAY PARTY

© Walt Disney Productions

In the early cartoons, Pluto often stole most of the laughs. Now, Mickey found himself teamed in a series of cartoons with Donald Duck and Goofy who performed the violent slapstick. Cartoons such as MICKEY'S FIRE BRIGADE (1935), CLOCK CLEANERS (1937), LONESOME GHOSTS (1937) and MICKEY'S TRAILER (1938) teamed the trio up for some project. The cartoon would usually split the trio to showcase the individual frustrations of each character. The three friends would reunite by the end to come up with a resolution to the problem.

By the late Thirties, thanks primarily to the contributions of artist Fred Moore, Mickey got pupils in his eyes and jowls so he could become more expressive. This new look was instrumental in allowing Mickey to perform in one of the high points of his career, "The Sorcerer's Apprentice" segment of FANTASIA (1940). Originally planned as another Mickey Mouse short, Disney decided to expand the concept into an entire feature showcasing interpretations of classical music. Using the sorcerer's magic, Mickey tries to get out of the work of filling a vat with water by conjuring up anthropomorphic brooms to help.

"I love Mickey Mouse more than any woman I've ever known."

— Walt Disney

In the early Forties, there was a short lived attempt at giving Mickey three-dimensional ears and having his tail hidden in his pants. Cartoons such as CANINE CADDY (1941) showcase this unusual look.

In 1942 only two Mickey Mouse cartoons were released. No new Mickeys would be produced until 1947. However, Mickey did not disappear. His image appeared on various products, military insignia and posters. At this time, the character of Donald Duck was more in tune with the brash nature of the country and his popularity temporarily eclipsed Mickey's.

The Disney studio was also putting more emphasis on their war efforts and Mickey no longer fit in with the direction the studio was going. Ironically, "Mickey Mouse" was the secret password for D-Day.

During this period, Disney toyed with making a Mickey feature. A number of stories were developed. One of the most detailed featured Mickey and a Parrot locating a pirate's hidden treasure. This adventure was later adapted into a comic book story for Donald Duck. Another story was a giant, musical version of Jack and the Beanstalk. This got far enough into production to finally reach the screen as the second half of FUN AND FANCY FREE. It was Mickey's return to the big screen.

"Mickey was the beginning. Because of his popularity, we were able to go on and attempt things that were to make animation a real art. He had to be simple. We had to push out 700 feet of film every two weeks, so we couldn't have a character who was tough to draw."

— Walt Disney

Mickey's return in 1947 was another of his career high points. Similar in format to the earlier cartoons he had made teamed with Goofy and Donald, MICKEY AND THE BEANSTALK cast the trio as the diminutive heroes of the Beanstalk legend. With Goofy and Donald playing comedy relief, Mickey got one last chance to be the adventurous hero. In the original feature, the story is being told at a live action birthday party hosted by Edgar Bergen and Charlie McCarthy. Later TV repeats would replace Bergen with Disney or Ludwig Von Drake.

From 1947 through 1953, less than a dozen Mickey cartoons were released. Once again, as in earlier cartoons, he was teamed with Pluto who got all the laughs. In fact, in Mickey's last theatrical short, THE SIMPLE THINGS (1953), when Mickey and Pluto go fishing, Pluto's misadventures with a clam gets most of the footage and steals the show.

By this time, Mickey had become the symbol of the Disney studio. As many theatrical characters did, he found new life on TV. Walt Disney's DISNEYLAND TV show on ABC premiered in 1954 and was an instant hit. In 1955, Walt agreed to create a special afternoon children's show also for ABC. THE MICKEY MOUSE CLUB became the most successful children's program of the late Fifties.

MICKEY'S CLUBS

During the peak of Mickey's popularity in the Thirties, movie theaters had Mickey Mouse Clubs which children could join. The club was originated by Harry Woodlin of the Fox Dome Theatre in Ocean Park, California. In a matter of months, over 400 clubs were established at theaters around the country. For Saturday matinees at which a Mickey Mouse cartoon was shown, members had a special handshake, greeting, a code of behavior, a club song ("Minnie's Yoo-Hoo!") and more. Officers of the club included the "Chief Mickey Mouse" and the "Chief Minnie Mouse." A special booklet was prepared for theaters that showed how to start a club, get local merchant support and purchase special merchandise to sell to club members.

Mickey's most famous and popular club was THE MICKEY MOUSE CLUB TV show of the Fifties. The "Mickey Mouse Club" theme became an anthem for an entire generation. The Mouseketeers were superstars and it seemed everyone wanted to have a pair of Mouse ears.

WHAT! NO MICKEY MOUSE?
What kind of a party is this?

by IRVING CAESAR

sung by PHIL HARRIS

also
"MINNIE'S YOO HOO"

1932 popular song re-recorded in 1970 by Phil Harris.
Below: Mickey's early Seventies disco fever.

© Walt Disney Productions

The Mouseketeers

DISCO MOUSE

Also Walking The Dog

New Mickey Mouse animation introduced each day of the week and Mickey's image and name were everywhere including the clothes and mouse ears the cast wore. The series was seen via repeats in syndication up through 1965. The show was re-syndicated in 1975 to surprising success.

This new popularity for the old series inspired Disney to create THE NEW MICKEY MOUSE CLUB in 1976. Twelve new Mouseketeers were chosen. This new series, which sported the familiar Mouse ears in wild colors lasted only a short time.

Another, more successful attempt to revive the Mickey Mouse club premiered on the Disney Channel in 1989. Abandoning the mouse ears and instead stressing contemporary music and comedy, the show became a popular feature on the network.

MICKEY BECOMES DISNEY

With the official opening of the Disneyland theme park in Anaheim, California in 1955, Mickey became the official host for the Magic Kingdom. The costume character would also represent Disney in numerous parades and special events around the world. The job as host expanded further in 1971 with the opening of Walt Disney World in Orlando, Florida, and later Tokyo Disneyland, EPCOT Center and the Disney-MGM Studios.

Meanwhile, the animated Mickey's theatrical cartoons continued to appear on THE MICKEY MOUSE CLUB and the prime time DISNEYLAND TV program, and its successors including WALT DISNEY'S WONDERFUL WORLD OF COLOR and THE WONDERFUL WORLD OF DISNEY.

The MOUSE CLUB featured primarily the black and white shorts, while only the color Mickey cartoons appeared in prime time. Often the prime time series presented special compilations with new wrap-around animation featuring Mickey.

Mickey fit right into the nostalgia craze of the late Sixties and Seventies and made a TV comeback in THE MOUSE FACTORY (1972). The syndicated series featured live action guest hosts and a wild collage of animated and live action bits from Disney's past films. Produced by Disney veteran Ward Kimball, the show ran two seasons.

In 1974 the Disney Studio picked seven black and white Mickey shorts for theatrical reissue. The titles, which included THE MAIL PILOT (1933) and BUILDING A BUILDING (1933) were advertised to be "in glorious black and white," or "filmed in vivid black and white." 1977 saw the release of the short, DISCO MOUSE. It was a compilation of animated clips and wild graphics edited in time to the song, which originated on the NEW MICKEY MOUSE CLUB.

MICKEY TURNS 50

Mickey's biggest boost came in 1978. For decades, Mickey's birthday had been celebrated whenever the studio felt it was time for a promotion. With the establishment of a Disney Studio archives in 1970 under the direction of Dave Smith, an official birth date for the Mouse was finally approved. It was decided the mouse was born on November 18, 1928, the first public screening of STEAMBOAT WILLIE. The studio worked for almost a year to make Mickey's 50th one of the biggest publicity events in the studio's history. They succeeded beyond their wildest dreams as Mickey Mouse mania raged throughout the country!

Throughout 1978, one could hardly avoid the fact that Mickey was turning 50. Editorial, newspaper and magazine cartoonists had a field day as hundreds of gags appeared showing a "50 year old" Mickey. A simple whistle stop train tour, in which Mickey (the Disneyland costume character) was to visit cities on his way from Los Angeles to New York for the re-premiere of STEAMBOAT WILLIE became a national event. Network TV news covered every stop on the trip. Mayors, where the train stopped, proclaimed the day "Mickey Mouse Day." The train was often delayed, and at one location it arrived over six hours late. Even though it was hours past midnight, and raining, when the train stopped, thousands of people were still on hand cheering and hoping to see the Mouse.

A scene from STEAMBOAT WILLIE, and one from the Fifties MICKEY MOUSE CLUB.

© Walt Disney Productions

The Museum of Modern Art in New York held a special retrospective on the Mouse, as did the Library of Congress. A special Super 8mm film was released and songs were written. NBC ran a special 90 minute "Mickey's 50" program which featured clips of the Mouse's most famous cartoons and comments by such luminaries as Bob Hope, Gene Kelly, Edgar Bergen, sadly, in his last appearance, Dick Clark, Johnny Carson, Eva Gabor, former President Gerald Ford and others. On November 13, 1978, Mickey was the first animated personality to be honored with a star on Hollywood's Walk of Fame.

THE EIGHTIES AND BEYOND

1981 saw the debut of ONCE UPON A MOUSE, a featurette released with the animated feature, THE FOX AND THE HOUND. It celebrated Disney's animated and live action films. With the introduction of the Disney cable channel in 1983, Mickey became the official spokesmouse, dragging his FANTASIA costume out of the closet.

After a 30 year absence from the theatrical screen, Mickey returned in 1983 in a new featurette, MICKEY'S CHRISTMAS CAROL. Despite the title, Mickey merely had a supporting role as Bob Crachit in this animated retelling of the Charles Dickens' tale. Since that appearance, Mickey has been more active, primarily in commercials. Some of the first animated commercials featuring Mickey appeared in the mid-Fifties but their limited animation cannot match the lushness of Mickey's latest efforts.

1987 saw Mickey become the first animated character on a $1 bill when the Disney Parks introduced Disney Dollars. Along with other cartoon stars, Mickey made an appearance in 1988's WHO FRAMED ROGER RABBIT? where he was teamed with Bugs Bunny to give advice to a plummeting Eddie Valiant.

> **"I hope we never lose sight of one fact, that this was all started by a mouse."**
>
> **— Walt Disney**

The celebration of Mickey's 60th anniversary in 1988 was another major event; the studio no longer refers to them as "birthdays." Television specials, theme park parades and celebrations and special contests were all part of it. However, even though there was an avalanche of merchandise available, the birthday seemed to be overshadowed by the success of Disney's newer star, Roger Rabbit.

An animated Mickey appeared at the Academy Awards in 1989 with actor Tom Selleck to help present the Oscar for Best Animated Short. Also in 1989, the opening of the Disney-MGM Studio in Florida gave Mickey a new persona: Hollywood Mickey.

Mickey was also the star, albeit in silhouette, of THE MARATHON, a Russian animated film. The short is an amazing tribute to the longevity of Mickey from a country that, up to that time, had never officially seen a Disney film. Of course, some had been smuggled in.

In 1990, a new featurette was made starring Mickey. THE PRINCE AND THE PAUPER once again tapped into familiar territory of a classic story redesigned to showcase Mickey.

> **"Like most superstars, with age he has come a new image — from a scrawny, mischievous rodent to today's human-looking innocent."**
>
> **— US Magazine, September 19, 1978**

SUPPORTING CHARACTERS

One of the most important of Mickey's supporting cast is Minnie Mouse. She was created at the same time as Mickey and shared in his early adventures. She is a good match for Mickey and shares his love of home and family. She also shares Mickey's spunk.

Pete, also known as Peg-leg Pete and Black Pete, is a cat. A big, black villain of a cat, Pete's roots can be traced all the way back to the early Alice comedies. In the first Mickey cartoons, and especially in the comic strip, Pete was the main villain.

Pluto is Mickey's dog, although he also seems to spend time on his own and at Minnie's house and with Donald. A playful pup, he has a wider range of emotions than Mickey. He also had his own series of shorts without Mickey.

Actually being Disney's first star, Mickey appeared with just about every Disney character, including Clara Cluck, Donald Duck, Chip 'n' Dale, Goofy and many more.

OTHER MEDIA

Mickey Mouse established the standards of character merchandising. By 1930, Mickey was already appearing on a variety of items. Today, the number of licensed Mickey Mouse products is almost uncountable. Mickey has appeared on practically every item imaginable from clothes and foods to the more standard toys and games. It has been estimated that in one average day, over five million items with Mickey Mouse on them are sold. Mickey even appears on Postage stamps in foreign countries, an honor not granted to many other characters.

Mickey Mouse had one of the longest-running comic book series of any animated character. Besides that comic book, and guest appearances in other Disney comic books, Mickey appeared in every format of book imaginable. These books ranged from Big Little Books to Waddle Books to coloring books to oversized art collectors' books and more.

In 1937 he starred in a short lived radio show on NBC. THE MICKEY MOUSE THEATRE OF THE AIR featured Mickey and other Disney cartoon stars in songs and skits with live action guests.

Of particular interest to Mickey Mouse fans was the syndicated comic strip which began January 13, 1930. The first episodes were written by Walt Disney and drawn by Ub Iwerks. Later the strip was taken over by artist Floyd Gottfredson who produced many exciting Mickey Mouse adventures with Mickey matching wits with the Bat Bandit, the mad scientists of Blaggard Castle and Black Pete. Gottfredson left the strip in the Eighties. The strip, which had changed from an adventure strip to a daily gag strip, ceased publication at the end of 1989. It re-started in early 1990 as a continuing comedy-adventure strip.

SUPERSTAR QUALITY

Mickey is one of the ultimate Cartoon Superstars. His popularity and influence transfer well to all media, and to all cultures. There are few other figures, real or imaginary, that have created as much good will, inspiration and even investigation. In the animated rat race, Mickey is the top mouse.

Above: Ad promoting Nabisco and Mickey Mouse Cookies.

Below: Disney Studio publication honoring Mickey's 50th.

© Walt Disney Productions

MIGHTY MOUSE

SELECTED SHORT SUBJECTS: *A Fight to the Finish, Don't Touch That Dial, Mighty Mouse and the Pirates, Mighty Mouse in Krakatoa, Mighty's Benefit Plan*

Superstar Summary

THE STAR: Mighty Mouse

YEAR OF DEBUT: 1942 (THE MOUSE OF TOMORROW)

STUDIO OF DEBUT: Terrytoons (Paul Terry)

SIGNATURE: "Here I come to save the day!"

KEY CREW BEHIND THE STAR: Tom Morrison (voice and storyman), Connie Rasinski (director), Jim Tyer (animator), Paul Terry (producer).

CAREER HIGH: MIGHTY MOUSE PLAYHOUSE (1955) — One of the longest-running Saturday morning series.

*ere I come to save the day!"*

Mighty Mouse has thrilled new generations of fans for decades. His popularity saved Terrytoons from obscurity and debt. Without question, he is the best known and most beloved character from Paul Terry's cartoon factory.

His costume was suggestive of Superman in particular and all superheroes in general. He wore a gold leotard with a red cape, boots and pants. Unlike most superheroes, he didn't have an insignia or logo on his chest or cape. Originally a parody of Superman, Mighty Mouse quickly took on a distinctive personality of his own.

While Superman became more complicated, Mighty Mouse became more simplified. He was an ordinary mouse with extraordinary powers. These powers normally seemed limited to flying, super strength and speed with just a degree of invulnerability. On at least one occasion, he also exhibited mystical powers that allowed him to "mentally" command water.

He was equally as effective battling huge sinister cats as handling natural disasters such as floods and exploding volcanoes. He was so powerful that in his early cartoons he often appeared only in the final moments to save the day. He resembled a comet streaking through the sky as he rushed to aid the helpless.

Mighty Mouse's base of operations changed over the years. His home at various times had been a supermarket, a plush skyscraper office and even the Moon. At other times, he was a disguised "mysterious stranger" wandering around the country helping those in distress.

Despite his great powers, Mighty Mouse's personality was much like that of a humble country boy. Even though he was obviously an adult mouse, this modest young boy attitude helped make such a powerful character appealing to children of all ages. It was not unusual that a kiss from a rescued maiden would bring a deep red blush to his entire face. This bashfulness made him tremendously appealing to a variety of Terrytoons' women.

In the early cartoons Mighty Mouse was the object of affection of many female mice including such hot numbers as the Gypsy Princess, Sweet Susette and Krakatoa Katy. ("She ain't no lady when she starts to shake her sarong!")

Mighty Mouse eventually concentrated his affections on Pearl Pureheart.

He was a mouse of few words who took himself and his responsibility as a crusader against evil very seriously. In the heat of battle, he offered no clever quips. Even if his foes resorted to trickery, Mighty Mouse still fought fairly.

While Mighty Mouse may be best remembered for his countless battles against mice-hungry felines, he also battled a large assortment of other recurring bullies including a nameless wolf and Oil Can Harry.

Mighty Mouse had normal intelligence. He solved problems with his strength and common sense, not through analytical planning or new inventions. It is surprising that villains never really took greater advantage of his natural good nature and gullibility.

When the series evolved into a melodramatic format, Mighty Mouse truly became the embodiment of all that was good locked in an endless battle against evil. While he might smile, it was clear he was accomplishing fantastic feats because it was his duty not for personal pleasure. Even in a more recent revival, Mighty Mouse retained the Boy Scout personality that has served him well for almost half a century.

Publicity art.

© Terrytoons

BUILDING A BETTER MOUSE

In the Forties, the popularity of Superman was enormous. At Terrytoons, animator I. Klein came up with the idea for a cartoon to spoof the whole concept of a super-powered savior. Klein conceived the idea of a superpowered housefly. The smallest creature he could imagine would imitate the fabled Man of Steel.

Paul Terry was interested in the idea but, according to some sources, felt that a fly would be too small to animate well or be clearly visible matched against a larger menace. A short while later, Terry himself suggested developing the story using a mouse instead of a fly.

Late in 1942, Terrytoons released the classic THE MOUSE OF TOMORROW. Cruel cats were subjugating innocent mice. One of these poor little mice, chased by a hungry cat, dashed into a supermarket. The mouse bathed in Super Soap, munched Super Celery, swallowed Super Soup and plunged headfirst into Super Cheese. When the mouse reappeared, he was now a Super Mouse! Attired in blue tights and red shorts and red cape, this mouse of tomorrow was able to beat up all the cats and send them to the Moon.

As clever as this origin story is, Terry's storymen had trouble sticking to it. In 1943, the cartoon PANDORA'S BOX revealed that this super mouse became super by swallowing vitamins A through Z. In 1946, the cartoon THE JOHNSTOWN FLOOD suggested that a little mouse ranger had to drink from a jug labeled "Atomic Energy" to be transformed into the amazing mouse. Still later in 1951, the story was again revised in THE CAT'S TALE so that a mouse couple raises an orphan baby mouse left on their doorstep. Soon, they discover that he has powers and ability far beyond mortal mice. This version closely mimicked Superman's origin

"The old cartoons had lots of scenes of Mighty Mouse punching somebody out, but we couldn't do that even if we wanted to."

— Mike Kazaleh, animator on Bakshi version

Late Fifties Mighty Mouse comic book.

© Terrytoons

and was similar to the version of Mighty Mouse's origin officially given in his comic book adventures.

The concept of Super Mouse was instantly popular and another half dozen cartoons were made. One of the most interesting was FRANKENSTEIN'S CAT (1942) in which Super Mouse is contacted in his supermarket headquarters to rescue a bird captured by a monstrous cat living in Frankenstein's castle.

By the beginning of 1944, Super Mouse was rechristened Mighty Mouse. For years, there was speculation concerning the name change. It was suggested that the publishers of Superman threatened a lawsuit for infringement of copyright.

Within recent years, a Terrytoons staffer, Bill Weiss, has claimed that the real reason was the existence of another Super Mouse. While the first animated cartoon was in preparation, a Terrytoons employee left the studio and sold the idea to a comic book publisher. Nedor Publications released *Coo Coo Comics* #1 the very same month THE MOUSE OF TOMORROW appeared. In that first issue was the adventures of Supermouse (one word) who gained his powers by eating supercheese.

The comic book company had been able to copyright the name before Terry could and Terry was placed in the difficult position of producing cartoons that gave free publicity to the comic book character. The name of Terry's creation was officially changed in 1944 with the release of THE WRECK OF THE HESPERUS on February 11. The cartoon is a fairly straight adaptation of the classic poem with Mighty Mouse arriving in the last few minutes to save people from a shipwreck.

When the earlier Super Mouse cartoons were released to TV, they were redubbed and retitled to eliminate references to the original name. Mighty Mouse was now costumed in his familiar red and gold outfit and had started to gain some weight and muscle.

Many of the early Mighty Mouse cartoons followed a format where the champion of justice appeared only within the final moments to save the day. Terry explained that it was a "pattern-made thing" based on the assumption that throughout history people without hope yearn for a magical solution to an insurmountable problem.

AT THE CIRCUS (1944) has escaped lions terrorizing the population and Mighty Mouse showing up at the last minute to recapture the felines. RAIDING THE RAIDERS (1945) begins as a typical Thirties Terrytoon with cute bunnies but when a baby bunny is stolen by vultures, Mighty Mouse turns up at the end to rescue the rabbit.

This concept became limiting to the storymen and animators who began to experiment with different approaches. One approach was having Mighty Mouse disguised as a "mysterious stranger" in a trenchcoat and slouch hat who is in the entire cartoon but at the last minute rips off his disguise. Another approach was a mini-operetta perhaps inspired by the public domain works of composers such as Gilbert and Sullivan, where the characters sang their dialog.

Another difficulty was developing a continuing villain who would pose a real threat to the Mouse of Steel. Several recurring villains were tried including a nameless wolf, an Edward G. Robinson-like cat gang leader, and a Wild West bandit, Bad Bill Bunion. For various reasons, the chemistry just didn't work.

A SQUEAKY MOUSE GETS THE OIL

Finally in the late Forties, a more successful approach was developed for the series. Mighty Mouse director Connie Rasinski had directed one of the eight cartoon series produced by Terry in the mid-Thirties. The series had a black mustached fiend known as Oil Can Harry who chased a helpless heroine named Fannie Zilch. Fannie was rescued in true melodrama fashion by a clean cut hero named Strongheart.

The series, a parody of turn-of-the-century melodramas and silent movie serials, had been fairly popular. The Terry staff re-adapted the concept, substituting Mighty Mouse for Strongheart. Oil Can Harry was transformed into a cat and the object of his misguided affection became the bland, blonde mouse called Pearl Pureheart.

While other story formats continued to be used, it is these melodrama operettas that stand out in the memories of Mighty Mouse fans. One of the reasons for that distinction was the concept allowed Mighty Mouse to appear in all seven minutes of the cartoon, not just the last moments.

The first in the series was directed by Rasinski in 1947 and was entitled A FIGHT TO THE FINISH. A classic example of this series was STOP LOOK AND LISTEN where Mighty Mouse and Pearl are tied to a rampaging bull by Oil Can Harry while Pearl's father desperately drills for oil in his basement to raise money to pay the ransom. Another example was a A SWISS MISS (1950) in which an unconscious Mighty Mouse is about to be shot by the gun that makes holes in Swiss Cheese while Oil Can Harry chases Pearl in the Swiss Alps.

For many cartoon fans, the last official Mighty Mouse cartoon was THE RE-FORMED WOLF (1954). The cartoon is told in flashback as a wolf explains how he became a vegetarian after trying to steal some sheep when Mighty Mouse was around.

MOUSE IN THE BOX

It was considered the last official cartoon because in early 1955, Terry sold his studio and properties to CBS for $3.5 million. The studio stopped production on the "old" characters including Mighty Mouse and Heckle and Jeckle. They developed new characters such as the janitor Clint Clobber, artist Gaston Le Crayon and the lisping elephant, Silly Sidney.

The "old" characters came to Saturday morning TV in a series showcasing their classic adventures entitled MIGHTY MOUSE PLAYHOUSE. This show's success is generally credited with beginning the Saturday morning cartoon ghetto. It was also this show that first presented the famous theme song that became so popular. It premiered December 10, 1955 with some new wraparound animation.

"Here he comes, that Mighty Mouse,
Coming to vanquish the foe
With a mighty blow!
Don't be afraid any more
'Cause things won't be like they've been before"
— Theme song,
MIGHTY MOUSE:
THE NEW ADVENTURES

"Mr. Trouble never hangs around,
When he hears this mighty sound:
'Here I come to save the day!'
That means that Mighty Mouse
Is on the way!"
— Might Mouse theme

"I've always liked the character and I thought it would be a fun thing to do."
— Ralph Bakshi

When the new Terrytoons' characters failed to capture the public's fancy, the studio tried to revive the classic characters. From 1959 until '61, Mighty Mouse appeared in three new cartoons, OUTER SPACE VISITOR, THE MYSTERIOUS PACKAGE and CAT ALARM. These films were created in a simpler animation style and were generally uninspired adventures with some science fiction elements.

In the Sixties, Viacom inherited all of CBS Films' properties and Terrytoons as a cartoon producing plant disappeared although the licensing of characters such as Mighty Mouse continued. MIGHTY MOUSE PLAYHOUSE continued until 1966 when tougher competition finally ended its successful run.

Beginning September 8, 1979, CBS revived the character of Mighty Mouse in a new series of Saturday morning cartoons produced by Filmation. The hour long show was entitled THE NEW ADVENTURES OF MIGHTY MOUSE AND HECKLE AND JECKLE. The settings for the Mighty Mouse stories spanned time and space. Primarily, the storylines still concerned Mighty Mouse saving Pearl Pureheart from Oil Can Harry who was now assisted by a bumbling helper, Swifty the cat.

During the hour, Mighty Mouse appeared in two separate adventures and an episode of a sixteen chapter serial, "The Great Space Race." The serial was later edited into a feature and released on home video.

Most of the Saturday morning cartoons of this period contained educational elements. Mighty Mouse proved no exception with his "Mighty Mouse Environmental Bulletins" concerning such things as littering.

One typical story from the series was GYPSY MOUSE where, by the light of the full Moon, Oil Can Harry was transformed into a werecat who kidnaps the gypsy dancer, Pearl Pureheart. Naturally it takes Mighty Mouse to save the day.

Filmation seemed unable to duplicate the simple charm of the original Terrytoons. Though there was an attempt to inject clever verbal humor, the pacing was slower than that of the classic episodes. The series disappeared after only 16 installments.

In 1983, at the American Film Market, Sandy Cobe of Intercontinental Releasing Corp. promoted an animated Mighty Mouse movie. His promotion included all the merchandising tie-ins from a health food candy bar to kites. Also in the early Eighties, Kaufman's Bobka Company purchased from Viacom the rights to "Mighty Mouse" as a live action film project.

THE NEW ADVENTURES

On September 19, 1987, almost a decade after Filmation's attempt, Mighty Mouse once again returned to CBS's Saturday morning schedule in a new series. MIGHTY MOUSE: THE NEW ADVENTURES was produced by Ralph Bakshi, well known for his animated features. Bakshi had worked as a beginning animator at Terrytoons in the Sixties and had received screen credit for animating one of the last Mighty Mouse cartoons, THE MYSTERIOUS PACKAGE (1961).

"The Bakshi version of Mighty Mouse will help clear the air of the smog of spoiled sugar and superslop."

— Chuck Jones

Bakshi's team for THE NEW ADVENTURES included such new talent as John Kricfalusi, Bob Jacques, Kent Butterworth and Mike Kazaleh, as well as veteran John Sparey, who began his career animating Crusader Rabbit. This group took a highly irreverent approach to the series and tried to recreate the wild spirit of the Warner Brothers cartoons rather than the classic Terrytoons.

While Mighty Mouse still remained the clean cut hero who protected Mouseville, there were significant changes. Mighty Mouse was given a secret identity as Mike Mouse, assembly line worker for Pearl Pureheart's factory. He was also given a mouse kid side-kick named Scrappy, who was constantly getting into trouble.

Former villain Oil Can Harry made one appearance in the second season, but the series relied on new antagonists including The Cow, big Murray and Petey Pate. One of the popular new characters was Bat-Bat, a parody of Batman who drove a Man-mobile along with his youthful companion, Tick, the Bug Wonder.

Many of the cartoons satirized other cartoons. Alvin and the Chipmunks became Elwy and the Tree Weasels in MIGHTY'S BENEFIT PLAN. Saturday morning cartoons in general were satirized in DON'T TOUCH THAT DIAL. In order to meet the demands of Saturday morning's tight scheduling, several of the Bakshi cartoons featured excerpts from the earlier Terrytoons framed with new animation.

"It was the reviews that kept us alive."
— Ralph Bakshi

Bakshi's MOUSE FROM ANOTHER HOUSE gave Mighty Mouse yet another origin. Born in a tough neighborhood that is being demolished, his parents send the baby mouse in a rocket ship to a nicer neighborhood. Adopted by a farm couple, Ma and Pa Squirrel, the baby is raised to become a champion of mice, Mighty Mouse. This version is yet another homage to Superman's origin story.

The one stain on Mighty Mouse's spotless reputation occurred during this series. Reverend Wildmon, head of a self claimed media watch group American Family Association, stated that one cartoon, THE LITTLE TRAMP, showed Mighty Mouse sniffing cocaine. In actuality, it was clear that the Mouse of Tomorrow was simply smelling a crushed flower but the damage had been done. Three and one-half seconds of offending footage were finally removed.

Various Mighty Mouse merchandise including the Mighty Mouse Trace Master, a cereal and a game.

© Terrytoons

The series was a favorite for many fans and critics. It received an award from Action For Children's Television (ACT), only the third animated series ever to receive an award from the parent watchdog group in its 20 year history. However, the ratings were not strong enough to warrant its continuance after a second season (1988-89).

SUPPORTING CAST

Perhaps the most long-lived of Mighty Mouse's supporting cast have been Oil Can Harry and Pearl Pureheart. While other recurring characters appeared, none seem to have made the lasting impression of these two characters.

Conceived as a melodrama villain, Harry was a cat usually attired in a long black coat, often a black hat and a mustache of varying sizes over the years. In the original series, although he was a comic villain, there was never any doubt that he was a bad guy capable of nasty deeds. His obsession with Pearl Pureheart seemed to be his major motivation. Over the years, he softened considerably becoming almost as much a buffoon as his dumb assistant, Swifty, introduced in the Filmation series.

137

Pearl Pureheart is unofficially Mighty Mouse's best girlfriend. She never really seems to be a good match for the mouse. Certainly she lacks the spunk and sexiness of earlier heroines in the series. Over the years, she developed a harder-edged personality, a fact very evident in the Bakshi version. In the original series, this blonde, bland mouse had a father, Colonel Pureheart, which emphasized her image as a helpless Southern belle. In some cartoons she was actually called "Little Nell."

Scrappy, created for the Bakshi series, is an orphan mouse who views Mighty Mouse as a surrogate father. An irritating character with few redeeming qualities, Scrappy is supposedly either a savage parody of Fievel Mouse (AN AMERICAN TAIL) or Jerry (from Tom & Jerry). Few viewers get the joke. However his frequent appearances in the Bakshi version guarantee him a perverse immortality.

OTHER MEDIA

Without a question, Mighty Mouse is the most successful and most visible of any Terrytoons character. He appeared on countless toys, games, books, records and promoted Colgate toothpaste and his own health food cereal and vitamins.

In the late Eighties, he was the mascot for New England Playworld, a short-lived amusement park in Hudson, New Hampshire that featured Terrytoons characters. The park even had a gigantic statue of Mighty Mouse, arms upraised and a big smile on his face.

Mighty Mouse first appeared in comic books in 1945 in TERRYTOONS published by Timely (now known as Marvel comics). After four issues, the character shifted to a variety of different publishers including St. John and Pines, both of which published not only a MIGHTY MOUSE comic book but an ADVENTURES OF MIGHTY MOUSE comic book as well. There were also several special large comic book collections, Later, Dell/Gold Key continued both of those titles with each book coincidentally ending with issue #172.

"This is a great example of how a cartoon character can be reborn. The innovative TV show featured satire on cartoons and guest appearances by other 'retired' characters."

— Jim Henson, creator of the Muppets, commenting on MIGHTY MOUSE: THE NEW ADVENTURES

Some of the comic book adventures are of special interest to collectors because they were done by such moonlighting Terrytoons staffers as Connie Rasinski, Jim Tyer, Carlo Vinci, Art Bartsch and Tom Morrison. Of particular interest was the publication in 1953 of MIGHTY MOUSE 3-D which was the first three dimensional comic book. It helped spur a short-lived but popular fad in the Fifties.

In the late Eighties, a new series of comics was published by the short-lived Spotlight Comics. Just prior to the company folding, Spotlight attempted to put out a special issue using talents from Bakshi's NEW ADVENTURES' crew. Marvel Comics revived the character in his own comic book in 1990.

SUPERSTAR QUALITY

Mighty Mouse is such a strong character that he survived weak stories and animation to capture the hearts of decades of fans. He was a mouse whose actions spoke louder than the few words he was given in his many cartoon appearances. He outlasted every other animal superhero parody, proving that he is the mightiest mouse of all.

Forties movie poster featuring Mighty Mouse and Gandy Goose. This short title is NOT a Mighty Mouse entry.

© Terrytoons

PINK PANTHER

SELECTED SHORT SUBJECTS: *Come on in the Water's Pink, The Pink Phink, Psychadelic Pink, The Return of the Pink Panther (feature title), Super Pink*

Superstar Summary

THE STAR: The Pink Panther

YEAR OF DEBUT: 1964 (THE PINK PANTHER)

STUDIO OF DEBUT: United Artists

SIGNATURE: Da-dum, da-dum, da-dum-da-dum-da-dum (theme music)

KEY CREW BEHIND THE STAR: David DePatie and Friz Freleng (producers), Hawley Pratt (designer and key director), John Dunn, Jim Ryan (main writers), Henry Mancini (theme)

CAREER HIGH: THE PINK PHINK (1964) — Less than a year after his debut as a movie title, the Panther stars in his own short and wins an Oscar!

Pink Panther is a most unique character. Born from a movie title sequence, and featuring no voice, he is perhaps the only cartoon character based on elegance and "style." Like Roger Rabbit, he is one of the few theatrical Cartoon Superstars to be created since the end of the Fifties. His popularity continues on much to the surprise of those who created him over 25 years ago.

As his indicates, this adult panther is pink. His eyes are often large and yellow so they can be more expressive although most people remember them as always being white. He is tall and lean and has a long, snake-like tail. In his early outings, he has a cigarette holder to reinforce the sophisticated image. He also generally walks in time to his music.

The music, "The Pink Panther Theme," by Henry Mancini is one of the most famous cartoon compositions. Not since Laurel & Hardy's "March of the Cuckoos" has a theme brought such instant recognition of a character. Its deceptively simple rhthym and beat are an audio recreation of the Panther's grace, style and wit. Mancini actually appeared with the Panther in PINK, PLUNK, PLINK (1966) when a live action Mancini applauds the Panther's performance at the Hollywood Bowl.

The Pink Panther officially never speaks, however in two shorts a voice was tested. In SINK PINK (1965), while working on an "Ark," he talks briefly in a Rex Harrison-type voice. PINK ICE (1965), in which he handles diamonds, also has him speaking in the same manner. Reportedly impressionist Rich Little supplied the voice. These experiments were unsuccessful with audiences so the Panther remained silent the rest of his screen career.

Actually, though he never speaks, he does make sounds. For example, THE HAND IS PINKER THAN THE EYE (1967) has him scream in pain. In SUPER PINK (1966) he makes "judo" sounds as he approaches some villains.

Not since the early Felix the Cat has a character been so concerned with pantomime. His jaunty, bouncing walk also harkens back to the famous black cat who paced his way to fame. However, he is more elegant and less cat-like than Felix.

He lives in all worlds. As a movie title, he is able to change his shape and costume at a moment's notice. He is given a magical ability to appear and disappear as needed. In these adventures, he is often found waging a battle of wits with an animated inspector who is trying to track him down.

As a full-fledged cartoon character, he also has a great deal of freedom. He is almost always himself, silent, dignified and attempting to remain cool. A bit of a vagabond, his early adventures seem to be about him trying to experience life among the human species. No humans ever seem perplexed at this Panther who is the only intelligent anthropomorphic animal in his cartoon universe. Other animals, including dogs, behave as dogs.

He wanders the world joining in whatever activity fits him. In one adventure he joins the Army (G.I. PINK, 1968). He flies and becomes a kite in SKY BLUE PINK (1967). PREFABRICATED PINK (1967) has him try his hand as a construction worker. In these shorts, not only does he accomplish his work, sometimes at the expense of others, but he shows quite a bit of cleverness and resolve. It's only in his later years that he begins to lose this cleverness.

He can appear at any time. EXTINCT PINK (1969) shows him in prehistoric times as he battles dinosaurs and cavemen over a bone. Medieval times are his home in THE PINK PIPER (1975). However, he seems most at home in the present.

LOVE AT FIRST PINK

© Mirisch-Geoffrey-Depatie/Freleng

The Panther also has the distinction of being one of the few cartoon characters to be multiple-owned. Those who have a piece of the Panther include DePatie-Freleng, the studio that first animated him, Blake Edwards producer of the first feature, Mirisch Productions, the production company of the first feature, and MGM, since they acquired United Artists, who first distributed the picture. Any of these parties can do something with the Panther as long as all the other parties agree. Because of this arrangement, DePatie and Freleng continue to earn money on the character.

The Pink Panther is one of the few key cartoon characters created since the end of the "golden days" of animation in the late Fifties. The fact that he has been able to hold his own shows that this silent cat has more than nine lives.

THE PANTHER SPRINGS TO LIFE

In 1964, two forces were moving towards each other. The first was the studio of DePatie-Freleng. Both men had been at Warner Brothers when the shorts department closed down. They were now in the business of doing commercials. Meanwhile Blake Edwards, a TV and Feature producer was completing his comic farce, THE PINK PANTHER.

The film's story was about a smooth thief, known as the Phantom (ably played by David Niven) attempting to steal the most valuable jewel in the world, "The Pink Panther." The jewel has been so named because of a flaw in it that looks "like a tiny pink panther." The famous, bumbling Inspector Clouseau (Peter Sellers) makes life difficult for the thief by remaining hot on his heels. Unbeknownst to the

Sixties model sheet of the Pink Panther.

Opposite: Two Eighties model sheets of the Pink Panther drawn by Richard Williams.

© United Artists

Inspector, his wife is a lover of the thief. It was a delightful "caper" film with strong elements of farce and slapstick.

DePatie, who was an associate of Edwards, received a call one day from the producer-director. He said his latest film, THE PINK PANTHER was "screaming" for an animated title sequence. Freleng had his crew draw up 80 different designs for a "pink panther." They showed them to Edwards who immediately pointed to one and claimed that "was it." The design chosen was one from the group by Hawley Pratt.

Pratt had been one of the key layout artists in the classic days of Warners. In fact, in the early Sixties Freleng and Chuck Jones had begun giving Pratt co-directing credit on many shorts. Pratt was considered one of the better draftsmen at Warners and even did a large number of childrens and Little Golden Books throughout the Fifties and Sixties.

The studio went to work and created the opening titles. In them, the animated Panther appears out of the flaw in the gem. He is sitting on his haunches (some scenes in the first title make him much more panther-like than human), holding a cigarette in a holder. The panther turns to the audience and smiles, scampering through the credits in an unprecedented manner. At the film's end, he reappears to hold up a "the end" sign.

The title sequence garnered almost as much praise and applause as the film. Supposedly some audiences remained in the theater after the film just to see the opening credits again. At that time, it was unusual for a live action film to have an animated title sequence, although a handful of earlier films had featured animated title sequences, including 1948's ABBOTT AND COSTELLO MEET FRANKENSTEIN.

The publicity impressed United Artists and they decided to take a chance and ordered DePatie-Freleng to make a couple of theatrical shorts based on the character.

The studio went to work on THE PINK PHINK (1964). This short established all the key elements for the series. First, the Panther remained silent. This also meant that no one else could talk in the short. The producers felt that if any of the characters talked, it would appear as if the Panther were mute. Second, the character is very image conscious. In the short he continually tries to paint a house pink, while the owner, a short squat man, attempts to paint it blue. Finally, the Panther demonstrates some magical ability, especially the ability to appear from almost anyplace. This magical ability comes and goes as dictated by the stories.

THE PINK PHINK debuted on December 18th to reasonable success. Most of the critics found it an amusing entry and commented on its origin as a film title. More impressed was the Academy of Motion Pictures Arts and Sciences who awarded the film the Oscar for Best Animated Short. The Panther and DePatie-Freleng were on their way.

They began producing shorts in quick succession, around eight to twelve per year. The peak year came in 1968 with 17 released that year alone!

"We tried several voices with him, but nothing ever worked. Actually, since he was originally created for a main title and didn't speak, there wasn't any reason for him to ever speak."

— Friz Freleng

The first several years of shorts showed a great deal of imagination and styling. This can be credited to a number of key personnel. Hawley Pratt, who had designed the Panther, was the director of the shorts for the first few years. He maintained a crisp tempo. It wasn't the fluid speed of Warners, or the static look of TV. The original Panther shorts projected a fresh look. They were reminiscent of the groundbreaking UPA cartoons, yet distinctly individual. Pratt's world included a society of short, large-nosed humans and squat, stubby dogs. It's a look that is still attractive. Starting with the shorts in 1967, several new directors were added including Gerry Chiniquy, Art Davis and even Freleng, himself.

Also of key importance was the main writer, John W. Dunn. A former Disney storyman, Dunn joined Warners in the early Sixties. He essentially replaced Warners top storymen Warren Foster and Michael Maltese who had gone over to Hanna-Barbera. Dunn scripted some of the best late entry Warners shorts for such directors as Freleng and Jones. In fact, of the six Warners shorts nominated for Oscars in the Sixties, he wrote three of them.

Dunn's Panther was almost always an innocent character who was trying to help. This made him almost Chaplinesque. In SUPER PINK (1966) the Panther is inspired by Super Guy Comics to become a costumed hero. However, with no real powers, he causes a little old lady to be run over by a car, hit by a falling piano as he holds an umbrella over her for protection and crushed by a rock. Finally, after accidentally pushing her car into the path of a train, she goes into a phone booth and comes out in a superhero costume and begins chasing the Panther!

Another Dunn classic is SLINK PINK (1969). Directed by Freleng, it features the recurring idea that the Panther is a homeless character. Here the Panther is seen sleeping on a park bench in the snow. When

"The problem with him is to keep him slim and loose and not let him get dumpy — to keep him so that he's a catlike character."
— Art Leonardi, Panther shorts animator

KEEP HIS PROPS TO THE MINIMUM

he walks and finds a warm house, he sneaks in and manages to avoid the master. However, he's continually seen by the dog. No matter how the dog tries to prove there is a Panther in the house, it always backfires with the dog getting punished.

The series other regular writer, Jim Ryan, found the bizarre side of the Panther. PSYCHEDELIC PINK (1967) has the Panther discover the Bizarre Book Shop where he meets a strange fellow, falls through holes that aren't there and accidentally changes perspective. The Panther has a strange day at the beach in COME ON IN THE WATER'S PINK (1968). He has a beach bag with a never-ending supply of inflatable toys and attractions that makes him the hit of the beach, much to the irritation of a muscle-bound bully. After the bully tries several schemes to get rid of the popular Panther, the muscular man gets pricked and deflates. The Panther picks up the deflated figure, puts it in his beach bag and leaves!

One of the key artists behind the Panther was Art Leonardi. During productions of the shorts, he was considered the top Panther artist. He even contributed scripts to the series. His PINK OUTS (1966) is a string of clever, surreal and sometimes hilarious

CARTOON SUPERSTARS

"Very sophisticated — very cool; he's always on top of things. He's been very sophisticated from the very beginning but, as with all characters, his personality has changed some as we've progressed."

— Art Leonardi, Panther shorts animator

PINK PANTHER AND SONS.

blackouts. Leonardi was often brought back in later years to work on the titles and specials.

After the market for theatrical shorts finally ceased, the next step was TV. In 1969 NBC debuted THE PINK PANTHER SHOW. The show consisted of two shorts starring the Panther and one starring The Inspector. This was another theatrical series done by DePatie-Freleng. It was based on the Inspector Clouseau character created by Peter Sellers. A live action host, assisted by puppets, appeared on the series during its first two seasons.

1971 premiered THE NEW PINK PANTHER SHOW. This half hour series ran through 1976 and again featured theatrical Panther cartoons along with The Inspector and newcomer, The Ant And The Aardvark. This DePatie-Freleng series was similar to the Coyote-Road Runner series only it featured a purple aardvark (drawn more like an anteater) continually trying to catch an ant.

In a special promotional move, General Foods, a heavy sponsor of the show, compiled a group of the cartoons and released them theatrically in 1972. The PINK PANTHER CARTOON FESTIVAL played at theaters around the country.

THE RETURN OF THE PINK PANTHER (1975) brought the Panther back to his theatrical title roots. The film's titles were once again a highlight. They were more elaborate and the Panther was more involved. The Panther did impressions of a number of key stars ranging from Fred Astaire to Boris Karloff to Groucho Marx as he evaded the Inspector. This title sequence was handled by Richard Williams in England. Williams would eventually be instrumental in creating the only other modern, theatrical cartoon superstar, Roger Rabbit!

The Fall of 1976 found THE PINK PANTHER LAUGH & 1/2 HOUR & 1/2 SHOW. It was the first 90 minute Saturday morning series. New to the collection of cartoons were THE TEXAS TOADS, a theatrical series originally titled THE TIJUANA TOADS, and MISTERJAWS, a TV "original" about a German shark. The series lasted only one season.

Once again the Panther headed to the big screen for THE PINK PANTHER STRIKES AGAIN (1976). His animated titles were again handled by Richard Williams and featured a dazzling display of art deco and even more elaborate spoofs of Hollywood. In one shot the audience sees the spectacular opening of THE SOUND OF MUSIC with the image of Julie Andrews on the hilltop. However, as the camera nears and she turns around, the audience finds she has been replaced by the Pink Panther.

THINK PINK PANTHER! was launched as a mid-season replacement show in the Spring of 1978. THE TEXAS TOADS and MISTERJAWS were along for the short ride. It left the airwaves in the Fall of 1978.

THE REVENGE OF THE PINK PANTHER (1978) proved to be the last true film in the series, as Peter Sellers died in 1980. The feature had DePatie-Freleng return to create the animated credits.

ABC picked up the character in 1978 for THE ALL-NEW PINK PANTHER SHOW. This series featured all new cartoons, including a new series, CRAZYLEGS CRANE, a secondary character in THE TEXAS TOADS. Once again, the series lasted only one season. At this point the package of Panther cartoons went into syndication and appeared on numerous local stations.

The Panther received new life that year when NBC broadcast the first Panther prime time special, A PINK CHRISTMAS (1978). The special was directed by Bill Perez and written by Panther regulars John Dunn and Friz Freleng. An oddly dark special, the story, loosely based on O. Henry's "The Cop and the Anthem", featured the Panther in his grimmest predicament. It also removed the Panther from his brightly colored world found in the shorts. For this and other specials, the Panther was surrounded by a realistic looking world and people.

It's Christmas Eve and the Panther is homeless and hungry. Happy scenes of Christmas and new songs written by Doug Goodwin play counterpoint to the Panther and other homeless people. After many attempts to get food fail (including a bread line and trying to go to jail), he locates a donut. He shares it with a hungry dog who follows him back to the park bench the Panther calls home. In an abrupt ending, a full course meal suddenly appears, courtesy of Santa Claus.

The Panther's next gig was the prime time PINK PANTHER IN OLYM-PINKS (1980). Directed by Freleng and written by Freleng, Dunn and David Detiege, the special was more like a Panther short. The Olympics are being held and the Panther competes against a cheater, who as all cartoon watchers can predict, loses.

DePatie-Freleng officially closed in 1980. Freleng went back to Warners where he worked with other characters he'd been involved with including Bugs Bunny, Daffy Duck and Tweety. This put the Panther in different hands.

PINK AT FIRST SIGHT (1981) offered a slightly different Panther in prime time. Based around Valentine's Day, the story featured a lonely, loveless Panther who imagines every (human) woman he sees as a female panther. Lovesick, he even fantasizes that a child's Teddy Bear is a woman and sensually hugs it. He gets a job as a delivery man to raise money, but causes misery and disaster wherever he goes. Just as in the PINK CHRISTMAS special, it ends with him at his park bench when suddenly, out of nowhere, his female panther passes by and drops her handkerchief which has "Be my Valentine" written on it.

This Panther was quite different than the earlier Panther. The humans talked, making it quite clear the Panther is mute. As if to emphasize the point, the only way the Panther can get a job as the delivery person is to mouth the words to songs played on a tape recorder he carries with him!

This new Panther was from Marvel Productions, a studio known for it's TV series including MUPPET BABIES, G.I. JOE, THE TRANSFORMERS and MY LITTLE PONY. The special was directed by Bob Richardson of MUPPET BABIES and written by Owen Crump and D.W. Owen. Marvel also did the titles for the fi-

Ad for the original feature, THE PINK PANTHER.

© United Artists

"...Is again introduced by the marvellous Richard Williams cartoon character who upstages all of the title credits and is, in effect, everything that Clouseau is not — urbane, witty, sly, quick-witted and graceful."

— Vincent Canby's review of THE RETURN OF THE PINK PANTHER in the New York Times

145

nal two Pink Panther movies, TRAIL OF THE PINK PANTHER (1982), which used outtake footage of Sellers and clips to tell a story, and finally, CURSE OF THE PINK PANTHER (1983), which attempted to launch a new bumbling detective.

The Panther strode back into Saturday morning in 1984 with PINK PANTHER AND SONS from Hanna-Barbera on NBC. The series introduced his "sons," Pinky and Panky. Pinky, the elder son, wore a loose sweatshirt, while Panky, the baby, wore diapers. The father wore nothing. No mention was made of their mother.

> "He's amazing. He came over here and spent weeks wiggling his behind backwards and forwards in order to feel the correct movement for that opening shot of the Panther."
>
> — Richard Williams describing animator Ken Harris, who was 77 years old in 1975 when he was doing this action for THE RETURN OF THE PINK PANTHER

Once again, the Panther was seen as mute when other characters, including his sons, talked. In this series, the Panther was mostly a supporting character. The stories primarily revolved around the sons and their gang the "rainbow panthers," a group of young panthers who were all different colors. The show lasted one season.

The Panther attempted another shot at prime time in 1989 when CBS optioned a live action animated pilot. The plot featured the Panther stepping out of a cartoon to assist a journalist caught in a burning theater. Before he can get back into the screen, it burns, trapping the Panther in the "real" world. However, only the journalist can see or hear the Panther. Yes, hear. The show's creators felt that the Panther would have to speak.

Several voices were tested and the one finally chosen was a Jack Nicholson-style, cool character.

The pilot was shot and the animation supervised by the Film Roman studio. Roman's studio is best known for the Emmy Winning Garfield TV specials.

When new CBS head Jeff Sagansky took over control of the network, he viewed the pilot. He loved the idea of mixing the animated Panther with live action. However, he hated the idea of a journalist, he hated the origin story, and he hated the fact that the Panther talked. He did like the animation. Work was begun on a new pilot.

> "The last thing I did for Warner Brothers was the Pink Panther. I didn't especially like the character, but I didn't dislike it. He was kind of hard to animate, with long legs and tail, but it worked out all right. I probably did 60% of the animation on the titles at the beginning."
>
> — Ken Harris

CO-STARS

The Pink Panther was truly a solitary character, never officially having any kind of co-star. He might meet up with anything from an elephant to an irate painter, but these were all one-shot personalities. At times it appeared that he had a standard cast due to the similarity in character designs, especially what seems to be a recurring male character. Generally the people are short and squat, around half the height of the Panther.

In the feature titles, he was teamed with The Inspector. Once again, this was a short, squat character. He was dressed in the typical trench coat and often sported a magnifying glass. Not only did he appear in his own series of cartoons, but he appeared in his own movie title, A SHOT IN THE DARK (1964). This Inspector much more closely resembled a caricature of Clouseau (Peter Sellers) than the Inspector in the TV cartoons did.

OTHER MEDIA

Once the Panther began his own series of shorts, he became a popular character for merchandising. By the end of the Seventies, over 250 companies worldwide held licensing rights. He was found on almost every imaginable object.

From 1971 to 1984, Gold Key published over 80 issues of THE PINK PANTHER comic book. To aid the telling of stories, the Pink Panther spoke and his dialog was written in a very "proper" voice. The Pink Panther also appeared in his own stories in the short-lived THE INSPECTOR comic book series from Gold Key, published from 1974 through 1978.

For many years he was the silent spokesperson for Owens Corning Fiberglass insulation. These commercials were animated by Richard Williams, who did several of the Panther's feature titles. He was also the silent spokesperson for everything from Kodak film developing to Safeco Insurance.

He has even found himself in the food arena. In 1974, Post (General Foods) released Pink Panther Flakes. They were frosted corn flakes, colored pink! The cereal line only lasted through two box designs. More recently, Pink Panther Pink Lemonade has appeared from Natural Choice.

SUPERSTAR QUALITY

The Pink Panther became an international superstar in very little time. Oddly, the fact that he doesn't speak has helped his rise to stardom. At first it was a novelty that attracted attention, later it became an easy way to market the character internationally. However, the Panther's popularity grows from his emphasis on style. The less he spoke, the more popular he became. Similar to Roger Rabbit, he is a living testimony that it is the audience that makes a cartoon star a Superstar.

Though he never speaks a word, his audience speaks in volumes... of laughter.

A: Pink Panther Pink Lemonade

B: Seventies limited edition series of glasses from Sizzler Family Steak House.

C: Pink Panther merchandise.

D: Rare promotional album featuring music from A PINK CHRISTMAS.

© Mirisch-Geoffrey-Depatie/Freleng

A

C

B

D

Superstar Summary

THE STAR: Popeye, the Sailor

YEAR OF DEBUT: 1933 (POPEYE THE SAILOR)

STUDIO OF DEBUT: Fleischer (Paramount)

SIGNATURE: "I yam what I yam!" (close second: "Well, blow me down!")

KEY CREW BEHIND THE STAR: E.C. Segar (comic strip creator), Max and Dave Fleischer (producers), Jack Mercer (voice), Seymour Kneitel (animator/director)

CAREER HIGH: POPEYE THE SAILOR MEETS SINBAD THE SAILOR (1936) — Innovative and entertaining first two-reel color Popeye cartoon.

SELECTED SHORT SUBJECTS: Brotherly Love, Dream Walking, Goonland, Popeye the Sail Meets Sinbad the Sailor, Sea Sick Sailors

For over half a century, schoolchildren have sung some variation of Popeye's theme song. Despite all his popularity as a hero of a newspaper comic strip, Popeye today is best remembered as a Cartoon Superstar.

Popeye is a sailor with no real desire to go into any other occupation even though he frequently is seen temporarily working in other lines of work. His right eye squinches shut causing his left eye to "pop" open wide. His forearms balloon with muscular strength and are decorated with an anchor tattoo. Originally he smoked a corncob pipe, but in recent years, perhaps because of anti-smoking sentiment, it often mysteriously disappears.

Popeye would swallow a can of spinach to gain almost superhuman strength. In his animated cartoons, audiences would wait expectantly for the minute Popeye would pop open a can of the green weed, guaranteeing an exciting climax to the adventure. From 1931 to 1936, the spinach industry officially credited Popeye with increasing the United States consumption of spinach by 33%. One spinach growing town in Texas erected a statue in honor of Popeye. There was even a Popeye brand spinach.

Popeye never initiated a fight and would only resort to his spinach after all other efforts had failed. The recipient of Popeye's powerful punch was often the villainous Bluto, later renamed Brutus, who was usually trying to force his affections on Popeye's skinny girlfriend, Olive Oyl.

POPEYE BECOMES ANIMATED

Popeye was created by cartoonist Elzie (E.C.) Segar in 1929 almost as a throwaway character for his comic strip "Thimble Theater." The ugly, tough-talking, one-eyed sailor was probably the last character anyone would have picked to win the hearts of millions but Popeye's popularity proved phenomenal. Within four years, Popeye was appearing in animated cartoons produced by Fleischer Studios.

Unlike the lighthearted and bright cartoons of the West Coast cartoon studios, the Fleischer Studios in New York caricatured the darker, meaner streets of the Big Apple in black and white tones that seemed as vivid as any color efforts. Story construction was tight because director Dave Fleischer followed a strict graph that showed where the peaks of tension should occur during a cartoon.

This formula had helped make a star of their main character, Betty Boop. On July 14, 1933, a very different Betty Boop short appeared. The name of the cartoon was POPEYE THE SAILOR and Betty only briefly showed up on screen to dance the

SING A SONG OF POPEYE

hula with Popeye. The rest of the cartoon was devoted to Popeye rescuing Olive from Bluto. The cartoon was designed to test the audience's reaction to the familiar comic strip sailor. Popeye passed with flying colors and his own series of cartoons was soon in production.

Songwriter Sammy Lerner, who wrote the theme song "I'm Popeye the Sailor Man," turned out the classic in less than two hours. "I knew the song had to be illiterate and not in the peak of melodic taste to be in character for the subject matter," Lerner remarked in an interview. "But when I saw the first cartoon I wanted to crawl into a corner." Eventually the song was elected to the Songwriters Hall of Fame.

"It was lucky Popeye was a cartoon because I'd have made a pretty poor Popeye in body," claimed Jack Mercer who supplied the voice for Popeye for most of the character's career. "I'm only five feet five inches tall and didn't weigh more than 110 pounds at the time. Besides I don't like Popeye's favorite: spinach. I do like hamburgers, just like Wimpy. In fact, it's about my favorite food."

Mercer became the voice of Popeye after the original voice, William "Red Pepper Sam" Costello was fired by the Fleischers. Fame had quickly gone to Costello's head. Mercer, who was working in the Fleischer animation department at the time, was recruited for the part. He brought a gentleness and humor to the character that was lacking in Costello's interpretation.

The selection of voices was very important because unlike cartoons from the other studios, the Fleischer cartoons were post-synced. The dialog was recorded after the animation was completed rather than before. This method encouraged those under-the-breath ad libs that highlight the series which added a freshness and another dimension of reality.

The first official Popeye cartoon was I YAM WHAT I YAM released in September of 1933 with Dave Fleischer credited as director and Seymour Kneitel as head animator. The Fleischer cartoons, in vivid black and white, were one of the

From THE POPEYE SONG FOLIO published in 1936 by Famous Music.

© *King Features*

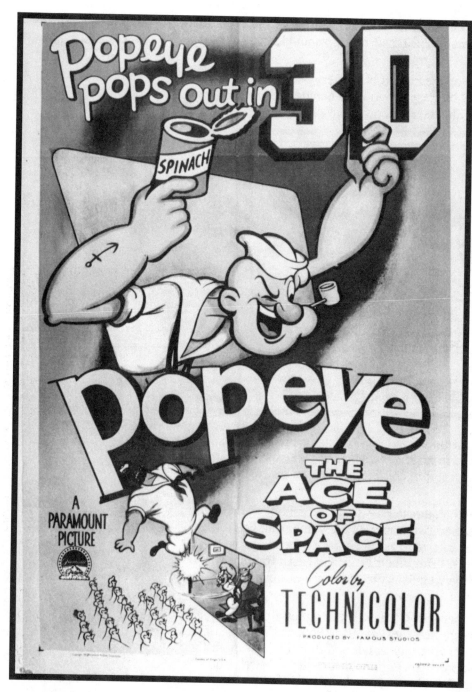

most faithful adaptations ever of a comic strip character to animation. They retained the spirit of the original inspiration, and the series is filled with remarkable variety, well rounded characters, and excellent story construction.

Olive, voiced by Betty Boop's Mae Questel, was often the catalyst for a story. In A DREAM WALKING (1934) both Popeye and Bluto chase a sleepwalking Olive through a construction site hoping to save her from serious injury. Still asleep, she returns unharmed back to her apartment after Popeye and Bluto have exhausted themselves in a wasted effort to be heroes. In CLEAN SHAVEN MAN, Olive's comment that she likes a clean shaven man leads Popeye and Bluto into a grooming battle. At the end, they discover Olive enamored of a bearded stranger.

Certainly the high point of Popeye's career at the Fleischer studios were the three two-reel Color Specials, POPEYE THE SAILOR MEETS SINDBAD THE SAILOR (1936), POPEYE MEETS ALI BABA AND HIS 40 THIEVES (1937) and POPEYE MEETS ALADDIN AND HIS WONDERFUL LAMP (1939). All were filmed in Technicolor. To give more depth to the action, miniature sets were built and the celluloid action was filmed in front of them. In other words, the animated characters had three dimensional foregrounds and backgrounds. Even today the effect is amazing.

"One of my professional pains is that my name doesn't appear on the screen. I feel I've lost a great deal without the public and profession being aware I wrote this song."

— Sammy Lerner, writer of the Popeye theme song

THE FAMOUS POPEYE

For a variety of reasons, the Fleischer studio was taken over by Paramount in 1942. The studio was renamed Famous Studios and the Fleischer family left. Many of their staffers, in particular Seymour Kneitel, stayed on to continue doing the cartoons.

In keeping with the war effort, Popeye changed from his familiar sailor outfit to Navy whites. Along with the white uniform, Popeye began to lose some of the hard edge he exhibited in earlier cartoons. Gradually other changes became evident making these later cartoons less worthy of consideration to some fans.

The films were now pre-synced like other animated cartoons. Even though Jack Mercer was working as a storyman, the amusing ad libs were eliminated. Although color cartoons were common from other studios, it wasn't until 1943 and the release of HER HONOR THE MARE that the Popeye series was produced in color. Backgrounds became simplified

More and more stories seemed to revolve around the cliched situation of Popeye losing Olive to Bluto with the resolution depending upon a fight. The little character touches so effective in the earlier black and whites, such as tanks or volcanoes appearing on Popeye's muscles after he ate spinach, disappeared.

While it is easy for some to dismiss the approximately 120 cartoons that Famous produced from the middle of 1942 (YOU'RE A SAP, MR. JAP) to 1957 (SPOOKY SWABS), the series still has much to recommend it. The color quality was good. Outstanding animation craftsmen including Otto Mesmer, who created Felix the Cat, and Bill Tytla, who animated villains for Disney's early features, worked on several episodes.

Several cartoons are of special interest, including SHE SICK SAILORS (1944), which made fun of the Fleischer Superman cartoons. Olive falls in love with Superman after reading his comic book adventures so Bluto disguises himself as the Man of Steel to win her affections. Soon, it is a test of super-strength between this phony Superman and Popeye.

In 1953, the only 3-D Popeye cartoon was released, THE ACE OF SPACE.

Paramount stopped production on the Popeye series in 1957 and sold the backlog of 234 cartoons to Associated Artists Productions (A.A.P.) for TV distribution. Within the first five years, the series recouped ten times it's cost. The demand for Popeye cartoons was unbelievable. King Features decided to produce a new series of Popeye cartoons for TV with Mercer and Questel returning to do voice work.

POPEYE THE TV MAN

"It took about 30 years to make the first 234 cartoons, but the next 206 were whipped out during 1960 and 1961," recalled Mercer. The cartoons were churned out as quickly as possible using the most limited animation imaginable. The animation work was farmed out to five different companies all over the world and some of the key directors were Seymour Kneitel, Gene Deitch and Jack Kinney.

A major change in these made-for-TV cartoons was renaming Bluto as Brutus. At the time it was rumored the change was to placate the Disney organization which supposedly felt that the name sounded too close to its dog character, Pluto. As might have been predicted, these quickly produced Popeye cartoons did not meet with the same audience appreciation as the earlier efforts.

The stories are static adventures with lots of talking, lots of reused poses, and little action or imagination. Some of the characters from the original comic strip such as the Sea Hag make appearances but this does not compensate for the weak stories. Some stories revolved around a fairy tale theme including LI'L OLIVE RIDING HOOD. HITS AND MISSILES has Popeye, Olive and Wimpy traveling to the moon to discover that not only is it made of cheese, but there are cheese creatures living there as well. POPEYE AND THE DRAGON dealt with the medieval adventures of Sir Popeye.

Opposite: Popeye's only 3-D cartoon, THE ACE OF SPACE.

Below: Movie poster from the early Fifties.

© King Features

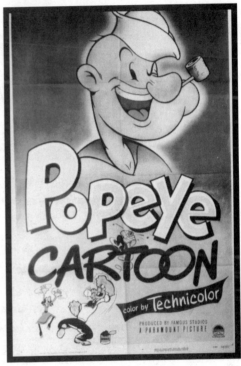

"Popeye is much more than a goofy comic character to me. He represents all of my emotions, and he is an outlet for them... to me Popeye is really a serious person and when a serious person does something funny, it's really funny."

— E.C. Segar, Popeye's creator

The character didn't appear on the screen in a new adventure until 1972 when the ABC SATURDAY MORNING SUPERSTAR MOVIE presented "Popeye Meets the Man Who Hated Laughter." This 60-minute animated adventure, directed by Jack Zander, had Popeye trying to rescue every King Features character from the

Phantom to Beetle Bailey and Blondie from the evil designs of Professor Grimsby. Only Popeye seemed to be strong enough to survive this mishmash.

There was a limited release feature in 1973 entitled THE POPEYE FOLLIES: HIS TIMES AND LIFE. It was a compilation of the early Fleischer shorts.

In 1978, Hanna-Barbera was able to secure the rights to the character for THE ALL NEW POPEYE HOUR on CBS. Once again, Jack Mercer was brought in to do the voice of the character and help with the stories.

Within the limits of Saturday morning kidvid restrictions, Hanna-Barbera tried to recapture the spirit of the earlier Popeye cartoons. Brutus was re-christened Bluto and Popeye got back his old darker shirt, but this time with a blue tint.

Popeye Spinach above, and Popeye's Fried Chicken offers corn on the cob below.

© King Features

The rest of the supporting cast returned but violence was no longer permitted. At best, Popeye and Bluto were now competitors, not only for the love of Olive Oyl but in search for various treasures such as the Dalmonica diamond.

The show was divided into five segments. Three segments featured various adventures of Popeye. One segment focused on the treasure hunting and one segment

was unrelated to the Popeye universe and showcased the misadventures of Dinky Dog, the world's largest puppy. Popeye and his friends were later recruited to do short spots on health and safety to remind young viewers not to play with knives and to wash their hands. The series ran three years.

Several segments from the series became the basis for a 1978 prime time special, THE POPEYE SHOW (or POPEYE CATCHES DISCO FEVER). Hanna-Barbera also produced THE POPEYE VALENTINE SPECIAL (1979) for prime time. Olive Oyl was teamed with Alice the Goon in a series from H-B reportedly inspired by the popular movie PRIVATE BENJAMIN about women in the army.

152

A DIFFERENT POPEYE

1980 saw the release of POPEYE, a live action feature starring Robin Williams as

Popeye and Shelley Duvall as Olive. The actors used heavy make-up to resemble the comic characters. Famed director Robert Altman headed the production, based on a script by Jules Feiffer. Harry Nilsson did a musical score for the film, but the movie ended with the Sammy Lerner classic. The movie was poorly received by the critics and did not do strong business.

Another unusual version of Popeye came years later from Hanna-Barbera. In 1987, POPEYE AND SON premiered. Major changes were made in the spinach-eating hero. He had apparently married Olive and was the proud father of a young son. The son bore no resemblance to either parent but gained strength from spinach just like his old man. Popeye had seemingly abandoned his familiar pipe and now wore a loud, floral Hawaiian shirt. Olive had become a modern woman worried more about her aerobics than the half-hearted disasters that threatened the other members of her family. Bluto, too, had been domesticated and had also produced a son, named Tank, who took after him in the worst way.

"The funnier he looks, the better the cartoon will be."

— Max Fleischer, producer

That same year Ted Turner, the major force behind the colorization of movies, started to work on Popeye. At the cost of over $10,000 per short, he began converting the 120 black and white Popeye shorts to color. Rather than use the computer colorizing system employed in such features as THE MALTESE FALCON and KING KONG, he simply had the cartoons redrawn. This was done by enlarging each frame of the cartoon and having new artists trace the animation and paint new cels and backgrounds.

Almost all the subtlety and charm is missing from these new color Popeye cartoons. Instead of the intricate Fleischer backgrounds, there are simplified designs. Even the animation suffers under the hands of artists merely tracing action and not understanding the art form. Turner took great pains to explain that the black and white negatives were not destroyed so that new prints could be made. Originally only seen on the Turner-owned cable stations, in 1989 these colorized versions began being syndicated to other stations.

Popeye meets a two-headed giant in POPEYE MEETS SINBAD THE SAILOR.

© King Features

Popeye's most recent work is a series of animated commercials in which Popeye abandons his spinach for Quaker Oats cereal. These animated spots are certainly "animated," but it is a bit shocking to hear Popeye proclaim, "can the spinach, I wants me Quaker Instant Oatmeal." The Quakers, a non-violent religious sect, complained about the use of the aggressive Popeye as "the Quaker man" and the advertising campaign was re-designed.

POPEYE'S CO-STARS

In the original shorts, the Fleischers needed a suitable foil for Popeye. "Lower than bilge scum, meaner than Satan and strong as an ox, the only man living who might lick Popeye" is the way Bluto ("the Terrible") was described in the 1933 newspaper strip story "The Eighth Sea." He was the current villain in the strip when the first cartoon was being designed and was thus chosen to be Popeye's animated antagonist. His voice was originally provided by Gus Wickie.

Fleischer's voice for Betty Boop, Mae Questel, became the voice of Popeye's "sweet patootie," Olive Oyl. Olive was an ill-proportioned, strident, vain woman whose figure resembled a toothpick. Yet despite all her flaws, Popeye loved her with all his heart and was completely loyal to her.

Other characters brought from the strip to the series included J. Wellington Wimpy. This overweight moocher was always willing to "pay you Tuesday for a hamburger today." In the comic strip, Wimpy was a pawn of a character who could be working for the villain as well as Popeye. In the cartoons, Wimpy was more of a throwaway joke.

Swee'pea was an orphan baby found by Popeye. This made Popeye a surrogate father, though in the cartoons, Swee' pea tended to be in Olive's care. Later family additions would include the infamous nephews of Popeye, Peepeye, Pipeye, Pupeye and Poopeye, who all physically resembled their uncle.

POPEYE OFF SCREEN

Already a comic strip star when he began, the animated series cemented Popeye's popularity. 1935 saw the start of a Popeye radio show on the NBC network. That same year, the newspaper and movie star moved into comic books where he has had a regular career in both reprints of his classic strips and new stories.

He was a popular merchandising character right from the beginning. A variety of items including toys, watches, records and books have appeared regularly since the Thirties.

Popeye's Fried Chicken is a popular fast food restaurant. For almost a decade it has used images of the Popeye characters to promote everything from "zesty barbecue beans" to "corn on a stick."

Sadly, Popeye is one of the few Cartoon Superstars almost totally neglected by home video. His three Technicolor shorts are available on numerous tapes since they went into public domain. There are a number of tapes that also contain the weaker King Features entries. However almost none of the classic black and white Fleischers are obtainable by the video collector.

SUPERSTAR QUALITY

The spinach-powered sailor is still swinging after all these years despite a life that has been filled with the most harrowing episodes imaginable. By 1934, a poll of theater owners showed Popeye more popular than Mickey Mouse. A similar poll in 1938 of children in the U.S. gave the same result. Over half a century later, many would agree with that evaluation. Popeye is still "strong to the finich."

"I'm strong to the finich, 'cause I eats my spinach. I'm Popeye, the Sailor man. Toot! Toot!"

— Popeye theme song

Publicity art from BROTHERLY LOVE.

Featured in Paramount-Fleischer's Cartoon—"BROTHERLY LOVE"

© King Features

MANY FACES OF POPEYE

Left: The earliest animated Popeyes. Fleischer (left) and Famous (right) Popeyes.

© King Features

Above: Publicity art from A CLEAN SHAVEN MAN.

© King Features

Left: The cast of King Features' animated Popeye of the Sixties.

© King Features

Right: Popeye and son from Hanna-Barbera's series.

© King Features

Superstar Summary

THE STAR: Porky Pig

YEAR OF DEBUT: 1935 (I HAVEN'T GOT A HAT)

STUDIO OF DEBUT: Warner Brothers

SIGNATURE: "Th-th-th-at's all folks!"

KEY CREW BEHIND THE STAR: Friz Freleng (originator), Tex Avery, Bob Clampett, Chuck Jones, Jack King, Frank Tashlin (directors), Michael Maltese, Warren Foster (writers)

CAREER HIGH: WHO FRAMED ROGER RABBIT? (1988) which once again demonstrated that all Porky Pig needs is his one famous line to elicit a smile of recognition and affection from the audience.

SELECTED SHORT SUBJECTS: Claws for Alarm, Deduce You Say, Kitty Kornered, Porky in Wackyland, You Oughta Be in Pictures

P orky Pig was one of Warner's first big Cartoon Superstars. He was the first talking star to really emphasize a speech impediment, stuttering. Donald Duck appeared earlier, but talking like a duck is not a speech impediment for a duck. Porky's declaration of "Th-th-th-at's All Folks" at the end of the Warners cartoons became a universal icon for theatrical cartoons. Spielberg insisted upon using it to end his homage to the animated cartoon, 1988's WHO FRAMED ROGER RABBIT?

Despite his popularity, Porky never seemed to find that one special role or film where he didn't have to share the spotlight. For some reason, Porky was always put into a team. From his earliest days when he was teamed with Ham and/or Beans he went through a number of partners. Gabby the Goat, Daffy Duck, Charlie Dog, Sylvester and others were his partners at various times. Sometimes he got top billing, sometimes he didn't. If it weren't for the fact that he ended a majority of the Warner's shorts with his immortal, "Th-th-th-at's All, Folks," he might not be considered any more important than an Elmer or Yosemite Sam.

The key difference between Porky and other foils is that Porky was not the aggressor. In most instances he was more of an innocent bystander and voyeur. He was the quiet, average, well meaning everyman. The world that Porky lived in was full of wild, crazy characters and happenings. As hotel managers fumed, aliens ran wild and house-hold chores became hazardous, Porky remained the calm center of the raging tornado of events.

Porky was also fairly smart and more often than not realized the futility of the situation. However, he often found himself swept up by fast moving events which didn't allow time for his more deliberate thinking. In many ways he predated the "sane man in an insane world" motif found in such popular characters as the original Captain Marvel, Mary Richards, on THE MARY TYLER MOORE SHOW, and Dick Louden , on NEWHART.

This "average" persona made Porky much more easily domesticated. In fact, he was the most domesticated of the key Warners stars. He was frequently seen as a home owner, often with pets. Porky was often a legitimate business man, beset by the scams and schemes of con men such as Daffy Duck.

This Warner's superstar had a girl friend for a period of time. Petunia Pig appeared in a number of shorts starting with PORKY'S ROMANCE (1937), directed by Frank Tashlin. She disappeared from animation after a few years, but continued on in the comics.

Porky has had a number of character conversions over the years. It might be said that Porky grew up in cartoons. He began his cartoon career as a youth in school.

His next short featured him a grown man with a daughter. A few shorts later, he was young again! He lived on a farm with his father. It was all very rural and domestic. Then once again, he was a grown pig of the world, showing up almost anyplace.

His size ballooned to enormous extremes before settling on his now familiar chubbiness. Although he wore many costumes over the years, he is best remembered as being attired in a bowtie and coat, but no pants.

Like Daffy, Porky might be considered more a cartoon actor than a personality. He could be calm and collected, aggressive and angry, the leader or follower. It almost always depended on who was starring with him at the time.

Without complaint, he endured a great deal of abuse. Like many of the great live action supporting stars of the Thirties and Forties, Porky's presence always added significantly to the films he appeared in.

A page from Warner's 1980 licensing book, used by merchandisers as a guide to drawing the character.

© Warner Brothers

LIFE BEGINS FOR PORKY PIG

In 1935 Warners debuted a short similar to the live action "Our Gang" comedies featuring a cast of young animals, I HAVEN'T GOT A HAT. It was directed by Friz Freleng. The animal kids got up in front of the class to perform. Ham and Ex, a pair of pups, sang the title song. Oliver an owl, played the piano, and so on. The first student was a big, fat, nervous pig. He stuttered as he recited "The Midnight Ride of Paul Revere" which mysteriously transformed into "The Charge of the Light Brigade." Even though he had the least to do through the entire film, several key Warner figures thought this Pig had possibilities. These people included a new director, Tex Avery, and three animators, Robert Cannon, Bob Clampett and Chuck Jones.

Avery was so taken with the character's possibilities, he was able to convince supervisor Leon Schlesinger to approve future work on the Pig. GOLDDIGGERS OF '49 (1935) was Avery's first Porky film. It featured some of the speed characteristic of Avery's work. It still portrayed Porky as an oversized hog willing to trade his daughter in marriage, to Beans, from I HAVEN'T GOT A HAT, for food. Porky remained an adult for BOOM BOOM (1936) where he portrayed a soldier, once again co-starring with Beans. This short was director Jack King's first Porky short. King would later be one of the main directors of Donald Duck shorts.

King, Avery, and later Frank Tashlin took turns on the Porky shorts of 1936 and the Pig's age varied. He's a youth wanting to join the air corp in Avery's PLANE DIPPY (1936) but more adult when he is forced to join a ship's crew in King's

SHANGHAIED SHIPMATES (1936). In Avery's PORKY THE RAINMAKER (1936) he's the young son of Farmer Pig who helps end a drought.

At any age, Porky seemed to inspire the crew. Fourteen Porky Pig shorts were released in 1936 alone! 1937 brought another 16, and 17 films starred Porky in 1938! In these developmental years, Porky's shorts were as varied as his ages.

MILK AND MONEY (1936), a melodrama spoof directed by Avery, has Porky trying to save the farm by entering a horse race. Thanks to a pesky horsefly, Porky wins! PORKY'S DOUBLE TROUBLE (1937), directed by Frank Tashlin, finds Porky, a bank teller, at odds with the law. A gangster, who looks like Porky, kidnaps the famous ham and replaces him at the bank for a robbery. Luckily Petunia Pig can tell the difference by kissing each one. After identifying which one is Porky, she then goes off with the gangster!

PORKY AT THE CROCADERO (1938), directed by Tashlin and written by Lew Landsman, has Porky as a hopeful band leader. He gets a job at a restaurant where the band leaders he idolizes are to play. When the leaders don't show, Porky gets his big break.

Publicity art for
PILGRIM PORKY.

© Warner Brothers

One of the key Porky shorts was 1937's PORKY'S DUCK HUNT. It not only introduced one of his main co-stars, Daffy Duck, it also set the pace for what Warners cartoons would become. Tex Avery directed the film and infused it with the most lunacy seen in a Warners short to that date. It was also somewhat of a beginning of the end for Porky. After two years of popularity, finally beginning to star in shorts on his own, Porky was about to be eclipsed by the second of Warners triumvirate.

PORKY'S HARE HUNT, a year later in 1938, again finds Porky hunting an insane antagonist. It introduced the prototype for Bugs Bunny, who would become the third of Warner's Superstar trio.

PORKY AND DAFFY

Daffy would end up being as important to Porky as any live action comedy team partner. The two seemed a natural team-up no matter who was handling them. Daffy's manic behavior was almost always the perfect foil for Porky's more hesitating, cautious demeanor.

"...Porky was a Boy Scout kind of character... I always felt that Porky Pig was the most subtle of all the characters because he was consciously playing a part."

— Chuck Jones

Many of Porky's best shorts feature Daffy. PORKY PIG'S FEAT (1943), directed by Tashlin and written by Melvin Millar, is a hilarious battle of wits as Porky and Daffy try to sneak out of a hotel room without paying. Poor Porky is stuck in the middle as Daffy's plans become wilder and wilder. For the first time the Warners' Trio appear in the same short as Daffy and Porky phone Bugs Bunny for advice. Amazingly, they find out he's stuck in the same hotel having also tried the same wacky plans.

In fact, it seems as if Porky is always having to share with Daffy. In DAFFY DUCK SLEPT HERE (1948), directed by Robert McKimson and written by Warren Foster, Porky tries to spend the night in the same room with Daffy and his friend "Hymie," an invisible kangaroo. THUMB FUN (1952), directed by McKimson and written by Tedd Pierce, has Daffy the hitchhiker riding with Porky to Miami. Daffy overstuffs the car trunk and eventually gets Porky in trouble with the law.

Then there are the times that Daffy just seems intent on irritating "chubby." YOU OUGHT TO BE IN PICTURES (1940), directed by Friz Freleng and written by Jack Millar, has Daffy convince Porky to quit his job at Warners. As Porky tries to make it in the real world of movies, mixing an animated Porky with live action studio footage, Daffy tries to become top toon at Warners. After several disasters, Porky heads back to the cartoon studio and discovers he is still their top star. In an uncharacteristic burst of physical violence, he then beats Daffy to a pulp. The live action animation mix is incredibly sophisticated, using many of the techniques later used in WHO FRAMED ROGER RABBIT?

In MY FAVORITE DUCK (1942), directed by Chuck Jones and written by Michael Maltese, Daffy is intent on ruining Porky's camping trip. Talent agent Porky is kept from going on vacation by Daffy and his "talented" client in YANKEE DOODLE DAFFY (1943), directed by Freleng and written by Pierce. DAFFY DOODLES, directed by McKimson and written by Foster, has Daffy as a street painter who insists on painting moustaches on every face he sees. Porky stands for law and order as the policepig who brings him to justice.

Daffy tries to steal the picture again in BOOBS IN THE WOODS (1950), by McKimson and Foster, as Porky tries to paint the countryside. Determined to stop Porky's fun, Daffy disguises himself as the land owner and denies Porky the right to paint the land. Daffy erases the land from the painting but tells Porky he can paint the mountains. Porky begins painting the mountains until Daffy, in a different disguise, claims to be the old man of the mountain. Daffy then tells Porky he can't paint the mountains either!

CLAMPETT'S PORK SHORTS

Bob Clampett took a fancy to Porky and between 1938 and 1940 became the man behind the Pig. His shorts featured a wild and crazy world which Porky attempted to make sense of despite all obstacles. Even when other directors and writers took over, Clampett's Porky continued to be a show stopper. Clampett really started the ball rolling with the classic PORKY IN WACKYLAND (1938). This surreal gem features Porky in search of the last DoDo. To locate this rare species, Porky ventures to Wackyland. ("It can happen here" claims a sign.) When Porky first confronts the bird, a strange clump of feathers with a long neck, it states, "Yeah, I'm really the last of the DoDos, do-dodo-do-do..." and begins singing and dancing on Porky's head before running away. Backgrounds

"The audience at the same time laughed at and felt sympathy for Porky Pig. He was our first full-fledged star."

— Bob Clampett

Publicity art for AFRICA SQUEAKS.

© Warner Brothers

"Porky was just an ineffectual comedy relief."

— Bob McKimson

change, perspective is useless, and the DoDo continually baffles Porky until the Pig plays a trick of his own.

Another Clampett high point of this period is PORKY IN EGYPT (1938), written by Ernest Gee, where Porky's caught in the desert with a camel that goes crazy with the heat. Yet another, INJUN TROUBLE (1938) has Porky trying to protect the wagon train from Injun Joe with the help of Sloppy Moe. ("I know something I won't tell!")

Publicity art for PORKY'S PARTY.

© Warner Brothers

As the Forties continued, others handled Porky, but Clampett's shorts still created some of the wildest moments in any character's career.

1943's CORNY CONCERTO, written by Frank Tashlin, is Clampett's satire of Disney's FANTASIA. To the sounds of "A Tale of the Vienna Woods," Porky hunts Bugs Bunny, one of the rare times Porky hunts the rabbit.

BABY BOTTLENECK (1946), written by Foster, features Porky and Daffy in charge of delivering babies with expected disastrous results. Also from 1946 is the daffy KITTY KORNERED in which Porky tries to put out his four cats. One is Sylvester, one of Porky's first teamings with the popular puss. As Porky resorts to shadow dogs and brute force, the cats try hiding in fishbowls and disguising themselves as men from Mars.

SECOND BANANA PORKY

When Chuck Jones began overhauling Daffy in the late Forties into a selfish, conniving character, he also began fiddling with Porky. Jones seemed to see Porky as the ultimate "straight" man whose patience and good manners would be continually tested to their limits. There were three main series in which Jones used Porky.

First was a witty set of satires teaming him with Daffy. Writer Michael Maltese was able to create some of the funniest shorts during this period by polarizing Daffy and Porky to the maximum. Previous directors and writers had always played Porky as a foil to Daffy's wild action. However, in these shorts, Porky is a quiet but much more effective assistant to the prideful, out of control Daffy. Clampett and Warren Foster had given Porky a similar role, albeit via cameo, in the 1946 Daffy classic THE GREAT PIGGY BANK ROBBERY.

Jones and Maltese had a special talent for parodying a genre. Pulp space heroes, Sherlock Holmes, cowboy heroes, Robin Hood and even DRAGNET all got their comeuppance in such classics as ROCKET SQUAD (1950), DRIP ALONG DAFFY (1951), DUCK DODGERS IN THE 24-1/2 CENTURY (1953), DEDUCE YOU SAY (1956) and ROBIN HOOD DAFFY (1958).

Publicity art for
NOTES TO YOU.

© *Warner Brothers*

Daffy is supposedly the hero although his confidence and effectiveness is constantly eroded by increasingly desperate acts. On the other hand, the true hero is usually his willing assistant, Porky, in the guise of Friar Tuck or "Dr. Watkins" or an eager young Space Cadet. Porky demonstrated an ability to save the situation no matter how badly Daffy had messed it up.

Then Jones brought Porky and Charlie Dog together. LITTLE ORPHAN AIREDALE (1947), co-scripted by Maltese and Tedd Pierce, began the series. This set of shorts consisted of the efforts of Charlie to get adopted by Porky. Charlie kept trying in such shorts as AWFUL ORPHAN (1949) and OFTEN AN ORPHAN (1949). Similar to his personality in the the Forties, Porky is the stooge for a domineering, loud-mouthed partner. Porky has little luck controlling the series of events.

Jones and Maltese also re-teamed Porky with Sylvester. It was these shorts that feature Sylvester desperately trying to warn Porky of unnatural danger to no avail. These shorts featured a Porky so oblivious to the unusual that he doesn't seem to realize anything is wrong. It began in 1948's SCAREDY CAT when Porky takes Sylvester to their new home. Once there, the mice in the house try to eliminate the owners. Only at the end, when he's tied up and headed towards the gallows, does Porky realize there is a problem. Similar to Jones' Road Runner series, these shorts are all the same basic plot repeated with variations. In CLAWS FOR ALARM (1954) Porky and Sylvester spend a night in an abandoned hotel. As Porky sleeps, Sylvester fights a desperate battle against murderous mice. All Porky ever seems to realize is that Sylvester is causing problems.

"I played Porky pretty square... I liked him."

— Chuck Jones

JUMPIN' JUPITER (1950) adds an other worldly atmosphere as Porky and Sylvester's campsite is stolen by aliens. Only Sylvester realizes that they are no longer on Earth and being watched by aliens. Between Porky's bumbling and Sylvester's hysterics their campsite is dropped by the spaceship and lands safely on the Moon. Porky blissfully drives across the lunar terrain with a mentally exhausted Sylvester. Jones' Sylvester in these shorts features the same expressions of shock and horror as found in the female cats pursued by Pepe LePew.

There were other key directors who handled Porky in the Forties and Fifties. The often forgotten Art Davis offered PEST THAT CAME TO DINNER (1948), written by George Hill, in which Porky battles a termite. PORKY CHIPS (1949), written by Bill Scott and Lloyd Turner, has a hip squirrel interfering with lumberjack Porky.

"All the directors liked working with Porky Pig but he was never a star, never really a big star. We directors preferred working with Bugs and with Daffy."

— Friz Freleng

Robert McKimson, a former animator under Bob Clampett, and the artist who drew the definitive Bugs Bunny model sheet, was one of Warners busiest directors. He offered DAFFY DUCK HUNT (1949), written by Warren Foster, in which Porky again goes after Daffy only to discover the duck can't be opened until Christmas! In FOOL COVERAGE (1952), written by Tedd Pierce, Daffy tries to sell Porky insurance.

THE SIXTIES AND TV

As with the other Warners stars, Porky saw limited theatrical activity in the Sixties. His last theatrical short, CORN ON THE COP (1965), had policeman Porky Pig teamed with Sgt. Daffy O'Duck trying to capture a crook who looks like Granny.

TV opened many doors. Porky's shorts were released to syndication in the Fifties and found a ready audience. The early Sixties brought him a regular role on the prime time THE BUGS BUNNY SHOW (1961-63). 1964 found him receiving his own Saturday morning series, THE PORKY PIG SHOW (1964-67). In 1971, PORKY PIG AND FRIENDS went into syndication. It featured a snappy theme song played over new animation of farm animals carrying Porky dressed as a farmer.

Most of Porky's work in the Seventies came via appearances in the various Warners TV specials and features that contained clips of classic Warner shorts. Being one of the top three Warners' toons, he almost always had a role, though never a starring one.

1980 began with Porky reprising his co-starring role from DUCK DODGERS IN THE 24-1/2 CENTURY in the sequel DUCK DODGERS AND THE RETURN OF THE 24-1/2 CENTURY. The short was meant to be released theatrically, but only got wide viewing aired as part of the DAFFY DUCK THANKS-FOR-GIVING SPECIAL in 1981.

Porky continued appearing in bits and pieces either via new or classic footage in the string of Warners specials and features.

A number of Porky Pig shorts were compiled into a feature length show by Films Incorporated in 1986. PORKY PIG IN HOLLYWOOD played at art, revival and campus theaters. The feature included 16 of his best shorts including YOU OUGHTA BE IN PICTURES and PORKY PIG'S FEAT.

1988 gave Porky his newest boost when Steven Spielberg insisted the Pig close out his live action-animation spectacular, WHO FRAMED ROGER RABBIT? Porky appears at the very end as a policepig trying to break up the band of toons. As he scurries them out, he casually mentions, "Th-th-th-at's all folks." He stops and says he likes the sound of that as the Warner's ring drops down over him for a typical Warners-style finish. The image is "poofed" away by Disney's Tinkerbell and her wand.

Being one of Warner's trio, Porky will undoubtedly turn up in the future. Oddly, one thing holding the Pig back from more use is the item that has made him a popular mimicked voice for years... his stuttering. Current sensibilities are sensitive about creating the illusion that Warners, Porky, or his many co-stars are possibly ridiculing stuttering. Even though famous stutterers such as singer Mel Tillis come to Porky's defense, the studio is very cautious about Porky's use. Such caution has sadly made him under-used for many years.

PORKY'S CO-STARS

Porky's first co-stars were such now forgotten characters as Beans, a cat that looked somewhat like Felix, and Gabby, a feisty goat. However, as their main star, he often helped other key characters debut. Both Daffy Duck and Bugs Bunny had their first screen appearances with the Pig. (Daffy was more developed than Bugs at the time.)

Sylvester, the lisping black "puthy" cat with an enormously long tail, appeared with Porky on and off for many years. This relationship was almost always as Porky's pet. As a result, he was mute in these adventures. Another of Porky's "pets" was Charlie Dog. This fast talking mutt (of various breeds) was perpetually trying to get Porky to officially adopt him as a pet.

Porky Pig merchandise from many eras.

© Warner Brothers

PORKY PIG'S FEATS OFF SCREEN

Porky Pig along with Bugs and Daffy first appeared in comic books in Dell's *Looney Tunes Merrie Melodies Comics* #1 (1941) and his adventures continued there for over 200 issues. After a number of one-shot appearances in Dell's Four Color series beginning in 1942, Porky eventually was given his own title which lasted until 1984. Porky made appearances in a number of other comic books featuring Warners' cartoon stars.

In the comics, Porky maintained his screen persona as a middle class conservative citizen. Along the way, he inherited a sailor-hatted, little pig nephew named Cicero. Petunia, his girl friend, was redesigned to be more physically appealing to a pig and nicer. She appeared frequently.

Porky was also seen in countless children's books. He was also a regular, along with Petunia, in the Bugs Bunny comic strip, though he hasn't appeared much lately.

Of course Porky was popular in merchandise and his image has appeared on countless toys and premiums. While there are some examples of Warner merchandise featuring just Porky, including a wristwatch from 1949, he most often appeared along with a host of other Warner cartoon stars on game boxes, clocks and drawing sets.

SUPERSTAR QUALITY

A star who has lasted over five decades, Porky shows no signs of diminishing in popularity. He's had a long, solid career adding just the right stuff that made other cartoon actors look good. Being a good straight man is a difficult and often overlooked skill. Porky is still one of the best and has outlasted flashier characters. Concerning Porky's future, that's not all folks!

Superstar Summary

THE STAR: Rocky and Bullwinkle

YEAR OF DEBUT: 1959 (ROCKY AND HIS FRIENDS)

STUDIO OF DEBUT: Jay Ward

SIGNATURE: "Watch me pull a rabbit out of this hat."

KEY CREW BEHIND THE STAR: Jay Ward (producer), Bill Scott (writer, voices), June Foray, Paul Frees (voices), Bill Hurtz, Ted Parmelee, Pete Burness, Gerry Ray (directors), Allen Burns (writers)

CAREER HIGH: THE BULLWINKLE SHOW (1961), a prime time show that focussed massive media attention on the moose and squirrel.

R ocket J. Squirrel was an All-American Boy Scout hero. Bullwinkle J. Moose was a "smart goof." Together this odd couple of animation won the hearts of millions. Even though their actual screen career was quite brief, they have become a fixture in the media consciousness of numerous generations.

Rocket J. Squirrel wore an unfastened pilot's helmet with goggles. Especially when he was launched by the powerful arm of his friend, Bullwinkle, Rocky was able to travel very far, very fast and very high. Real flying squirrels, of course, can only glide for short distances.

Rocky shared a simple house in Frostbite Falls, Minnesota, with Bullwinkle. It was never clear whether he owned the house, although he never seemed to worry about paying the rent. In fact, Rocky didn't have a job. It was probably just as well because he was constantly globe-trotting to save mankind from a variety of disasters.

Rocky was much smarter than Bullwinkle but in some ways, much more naive. Each time recurring bad guy Boris Badenov would appear in a hokey disguise, Rocky would comment that the character looked awfully familiar, but go along with the deceit. Although he was cautious, he believed in the goodness of people and never denied anyone who needed help.

His friendship with Bullwinkle was unquestioned. Even though he usually knew better, he frequently went along with Bullwinkle. No matter how odd Bullwinkle acted, Rocky stood by him.

Bullwinkle J. Moose was a tall brown moose with antlers who sometimes wore clothes and sometimes didn't. It took Bullwinkle a lot of effort to think but that never stopped him. Unlike Rocky, he could get angry, but he never used his physical strength to intimidate anyone.

Bullwinkle also never had a job. He was certainly a lucky moose, frequently avoiding fantastic death traps and injuries though stupidity. He had an eye for the ladies and could fall in love at the drop of a handkerchief.

Bullwinkle often thought he was smarter than he actually was which led to trouble. His strong friendship for Rocky sometimes propelled him into action to save his little buddy. Bullwinkle was incredibly stubborn and once he had made up his mind would refuse to change it.

TWO BROKEN LEGS AND A RABBIT: PREHISTORY OF THE TEAM

Jay Ward and Alex Anderson had become friends while attending the University of California at Berkeley. After college, Anderson worked for a brief time with his uncle, Paul Terry, who owned the Terrytoons animation studio. Ward went to Harvard and got a Masters Degree in Business. He returned to Berkeley to open a real estate office. On his first day of business, a runaway truck crashed into the office, breaking both of Ward's legs.

Anderson visited Ward in the hospital and talked to him about his idea of producing a low budget animated series for TV. Ward was intrigued and became Anderson's partner in the new company, Televisions Arts Productions, Inc (TAP). In 1948, TAP presented three proposals to NBC: Crusader Rabbit, Dudley DoRight and Hamhock Jones, a private eye whose enemy was a Siamese twin. NBC rejected two of the proposals but approved Crusader Rabbit.

The cast of THE BULLWINKLE SHOW.

© Jay Ward

Working together in a makeshift studio set up in Anderson's mother's garage in Berkeley, the two men produced what many historians consider the first limited animation series made for TV. It was done in serial format. There were five four-minute cliff-hanging installments for each story so that it could be strung out over an entire week or stripped together for one episode. Crusader Rabbit lived in Galahad Glen with his friend, Ragland ("Rags") T. Tiger. Crusader was a small but quick-witted and aggressive hero. Rags looked ferocious but was actually the more passive and dumb of the duo.

To compensate for the limited animation, Ward and Anderson emphasized clever writing. When Crusader asks Rags to whistle a chorus of the song "Dixie," the tiger hesitated and responded, "Is it in public domain?" Villains included Dudley Nightshade, Babyface Baracuda, Achilles the Heel and a two headed dragon named Arson and Sterno.

The series started production in 1949 but because of difficulty in selling the show, it didn't officially premiere until August 1, 1950, almost a year after advertisements promoting it appeared in trade magazines. Ward and Anderson moved the studio to Los Angeles but production on the series stopped in 1950 because of a lawsuit concerning the ownership of the show. To avoid further legal battles, Anderson and Ward sold their company but were able to retain the rights to other characters and pilots that the company had been developing.

One of those projects was THE FROSTBITE FALLS REVIEW. It was about a group of anthropomorphic animals running a television station in the North Woods. Among the characters were Oski Bear (the cameraman), Blackstone Crow (a fiery director), Sylvester Fox (an egotistical actor), and Flora Fauna (Fox's leading lady). There were also two other characters: Rocky, the flying squirrel, and Bullwinkle, the "French-Canadian moose."

"How long can a grown man keep writing for squirrels and mooses?"
— Alan Burns, writer for Bullwinkle and creator of THE MARY TYLER MOORE SHOW

MENU

Really Good Food!

Bullwinkle's®
Family Food 'n Fun

Bullwinkle had been named after a local used car dealer because Ward thought the name was funny.

The proposal for the show was to parody TV programs.

After the selling of TAP, Anderson went into advertising and Ward returned to real estate. Creston Studios, under Shull Bonsall, produced a new color series of Crusader Rabbit adventures in 1957-58. In 1958, Ward decided to return to animation but Anderson was too busy with a successful advertising career. So, Ward joined with Bill Scott, a prominent animation storyman who had worked at Warners, UPA and with Bob Clampett.

ROCKY AND HIS FRIENDS

Their first project was ROCKY AND HIS FRIENDS, using two of the characters created for THE FROSTBITE FALLS REVIEW. Reportedly, Anderson was a consultant to Scott at the start of the series but soon dropped out of the picture.

June Foray was a talented voice artist who had supplied voices for animated cartoons at Warners and Disney. Ward had used a female voice, Lucille Bliss, for Crusader Rabbit and felt that Foray might provide a similar boyish voice for Rocky. Over a lunch of drinks, Ward was finally able to get Foray to commit to doing a flying squirrel.

Bill Scott unexpectedly found himself cast as Bullwinkle. He had been reading the lines for the moose during rehearsals. One day he asked Ward who was going to be hired to do the voice for the pilot. Ward replied he always thought Scott was going to do it because he seemed to understand the character so well. The rest of the voice cast included famous voice actor Paul Frees as the villain Boris Badenov and William Conrad, well known radio and TV performer, as the narrator. Foray did double duty as Natasha, the female companion to Boris.

ROCKY AND HIS FRIENDS was similar in format and style to CRUSADER RABBIT. The series was about a diminutive but sharp hero and his large, bumbling companion. Rocky and Bullwinkle lived in Frostbite Falls, Minnesota but that didn't prevent them from having adventures all over the world. Complications usually came from two villains from Pottsylvania, Boris Badenov and Natasha Fatale.

Each half hour featured two cliff-hanging episodes in the adventures of Rocky and Bullwinkle. Much as with CRUSADER RABBIT, the limited animation was overshadowed by the slapstick action, wild puns and satire. In particular, each episode ended with two funny possible titles for the following installment. An example was an episode that ended with two characters tied to a log speeding toward a circular saw. The following installment would supposedly be called "Two for the Ripsaw or Goodbye, Mr. Chips."

"Goodbye Mr. Chips" was a famous book and film, and "Two for The Sea Saw" a famous play.

The rest of the half hour was filled with segments including "Fractured Fairy Tales" which were twisted versions of famous fairy tales narrated by Edward Everett Horton. For instance, Aladdin didn't have a magic lamp but a magic lump on his head that granted wishes. The prince didn't wake Sleeping Beauty but built a theme park around her.

An even more popular segment was "Peabody's Improbable History." Mr. Peabody, a highly intelligent dog who walked upright, had a pet boy, Sherman. In order to help Sherman understand history better, Mr. Peabody built a time machine called the "Wayback Machine." Each episode the pair would journey back in time to find out the real story behind a historical event. Usually, it depended upon Mr. Peabody to come up with the proper guidance to help these events occur.

Another segment that often appeared was "Aesop and Son." The famous philosopher would tell his son a fable. At the end of the story, Aesop provided a moral while his son offered a punish moral as well.

Occasionally there was a short segment entitled "Mr. Know It All." Bullwinkle would be the expert who gave foolish advice. Another short segment was "Bullwinkle's Corner" where Bullwinkle attempted to read famous poems but with a Jay Ward twist.

AND NOW HERE'S SOMETHING WE HOPE YOU'LL REALLY LIKE

ROCKY AND HIS FRIENDS premiered November 19, 1959. The first season, on ABC, offered two storylines for the moose and squirrel. The first story lasted 40 episodes and is generally known as "Jet Fuel Formula." Rocky and Bullwinkle use Grandma Moose's cake recipe and accidentally discover a rocket fuel powerful enough to propel a stove to the moon.

The secret ingredient is mooseberries and the government wants Bullwinkle to duplicate the formula. Trying to prevent this from happening are Boris and Natasha as well as two moon men, Gidney and Cloyd, who have a "scrooch" gun and don't want tourists on the moon.

The second story that first season was "Box Top Robbery" which only lasted a dozen installments. The global economy is threatened by counterfeit cereal box

ROCKY

Opposite: Cover to the menu from Bullwinkle's, a short-lived family restaurant.

Below: The menu.

© Jay Ward

"The combination of innovative direction, writing and voice talent made classic cartoons that entertained adults as well as kids."

— Jim Henson, creator of the Muppets

167

tops. It was a satirical jab at General Mills and its cereals who were sponsoring the show.

ROCKY AND HIS FRIENDS was one of the first examples of "runaway animation." This is a term used to describe an American animated series where the majority of the work is done outside the country, usually to save money.

"In an effort to reduce costs, the advertising agency that had the General Mills account invested in an animation studio in Mexico," recalled director Bill Hurtz. "Then they made a contract with Jay which agreed that we'd write the stories, direct them, design them, and assemble them, but that the animation was...the backgrounds and inks...would be done in Mexico.... This was nothing that Jay was particularly fond of."

Even though some of the Ward staff, including Hurtz, were periodically sent down to Mexico for quality control, problems arose. "We found out very quickly that we could not depend on Mexican studios to produce anything of quality," remembered Bill Scott. "They were turning out the work very quickly and there were all kinds of mistakes and flaws and booboos. They would never check. Moustaches popped on and off Boris, Bullwinkle's antlers would change, colors would change, costumes would disappear. By the time we finally saw it, it was on the air. It went directly from Mexico to airing. As a result, we tried to pull as much of the work as possible up North." Reportedly, at one point to avoid customs problems, people would bring some of the completed episodes back across the border in their suitcases as home movies.

"We feel it's adult humor but NBC can't understand the jokes so they think it's a children's show."

— Jay Ward

That first season, 26 shows were produced. The next season 52 shows were produced. Those adventures included Bullwinkle inheriting a mine full of "upsidaisium," the anti-gravity metal. Also memorable from that season were the terrifying metal munching mice from the Moon who under the direction of Boris were eating TV antennas; the bad TV reception was throwing the nation into chaos.

With the success of THE FLINTSTONES in prime time, networks were looking for similar shows that could appeal to both adults and children. ROCKY AND HIS FRIENDS, because of its humor, had become a cult favorite. NBC decided to take a chance and transfer the show to prime time. The show was retitled THE BULL-WINKLE SHOW since the Moose had captured the hearts of America. This also kept it from being confused with ABC's ROCKY AND HIS FRIENDS.

"These cartoons weren't for children and they weren't for adults. They were for everyone."

— June Foray

BULLWINKLE'S NIGHT LIFE

The show premiered Sunday, September 24, 1961 on NBC at 7:00pm. In the beginning, the programs were introduced by a Bullwinkle puppet voiced by Bill Scott. The puppet was just the head and neck and looked like it was made out of a soft, fuzzy terrycloth material. One time it suggested to the kids in the audience to pull the knobs off their TV sets. "In that way, we'll be sure to be with you next week," reasoned Bullwinkle.

"NBC was furious," Ward stated. "Seems about 20,000 kids *did* pull the knobs off their sets. Well we fixed it. We had Bullwinkle come on and say, "Remember, kids, a couple of weeks ago we asked you to pull the knobs off your sets? Well, you can put them back on now. Use glue — make it stick.'"

While for the most part the puppet said less outrageous things such as "What other show has a host with antlers? On this network, anyway," NBC requested that the puppet be removed and it became just a vague memory for those people fortunate enough to see those first run programs.

THE BULLWINKLE SHOW was similar in format to ROCKY AND HIS FRIENDS. There were two cliff-hanging installments of the adventures of Rocky and Bullwinkle. These episodes included "Missouri Mish Mash" which was the story of the Kirward Derby which made its wearer the smartest man in the world. When asked if the famous hat was named after Durwood Kirby, a comedian on THE GARRY MOORE SHOW, Ward replied, "Of course not. But what else would you name a derby? They've already used 'Kentucky.'" The explanation did not prevent the comedian from expressing his dissatisfaction.

Other memorable series include the "Goof Gas Attack" with the Pottsylvanian secret weapon that caused stupidity but had no effect on Bullwinkle. "Wossamotta U." ("What's-a-matter-you") had Bullwinkle become a football star at Wossamotta University where he had to face the Mud City Manglers, vicious crooks disguised as an all girl football team. During the three seasons on NBC, THE BULL-WINKLE SHOW introduced the swampy little island of Moosylvania which Ward would use in a big publicity push later.

The rest of the show was filled with some of the same additional segments that appeared on ROCKY AND HIS FRIENDS. One new segment was "Dudley Do-Right of the Mounties." Based on the pilot concept developed earlier by Ward and Anderson, Dudley inherited a hyphen for his last name. Dudley was a member of the Royal Canadian Mounted Police, and while his heart was in the right place, he was a bit thick-headed. His arch enemy was Snidely Whiplash, a classic melodrama villain with black cape and stovepipe hat. It was a satire of the old Nelson Eddy movies.

To help this new prime time show succeed, and just for the fun of it, Ward staged many Bullwinkle publicity stunts. In 1961, he roped off a section on Sunset Boulevard where his studio was located. He hired an 18-piece "Bullwinkle Philharmonic" orchestra to play and issued 500 invitations. Jayne Mansfield unveiled a 14-foot revolving statue of Bullwinkle Moose. Actually 5,000 people showed up! "It had all the elements of a riot," Ward observed.

Opposite: The backside of the gigantic Macy's Thanksgiving Day Parade Bullwinkle balloon.

© Jay Ward

Ward offered substantial cash to anyone who would go over Niagara Falls in a Bullwinkle costume or who would smash into Lenin's Tomb in a 1938 Hudson Terraplane, marked "The Bullwinkle Special." He had beautiful girls dressed in Salvation Army uniforms parade down Madison Avenue carrying signs reading: "Repent! Watch THE BULLWINKLE SHOW!"

Ward also owned The Bullwinkle Stables which at one time housed 27 of his race horses. Ward's jockeys wore yellow and orange silks, with Bullwinkle's head on the back.

The most amazing Bullwinkle-related stunt was the "Statehood for Moosylvania" campaign. Ward purchased a small obscure island in the Minnesota lake region and dubbed it "Moosylvania" just like its cartoon counterpart. Then he had a van converted into a circus wagon with a calliope and a "Wossamatto U." logo. Ward dressed up in an Admiral Nelson outfit and his publicist, Howard Brandy, dressed as Dudley Do-Right. They traveled the country and got 50,000 legitimate signatures on their petition for statehood. The stunt climaxed with Ward driving the van, calliope blaring, onto the White House lawn. He arrived just as news of the Cuban Missile Crisis was breaking and armed guards escorted him off the White House premises.

> "We're often asked why we made Bullwinkle a moose. The best answer we can give is, 'Why not?'"
>
> — Bill Scott

THAT TRICK NEVER WORKS

At the time, NBC Vice President Sydney Eiges told the press, "I thought the whole thing was in bad taste." NBC press representatives somehow mysteriously failed to show at certain Bullwinkle functions even after being reminded by the ad agency handling the General Mills account. In fact, though the agency and the sponsor had originally contracted for THE BULLWINKLE SHOW to be show at 6:30 pm EST, the network pushed it back to 7:00 where it had to battle the popular LASSIE.

When renewal time came up, the sponsor began talks with CBS but NBC reluctantly agreed to an earlier and cheaper time slot at 5:30pm. However, when the time switch was made, NBC announced that ENSIGN O'TOOLE would fill THE BULLWINKLE SHOW time slot but made no mention of the new time for BULLWINKLE. This action led many to believe that BULLWINKLE was canceled and in fact one newspaper quoted "network sources" that BULLWINKLE "definitely will not return next fall." Later, NBC denied it had made such a statement.

Ward countered by issuing the following announcement: "It is with great ennui and profound personal apathy that the National Broadcasting Company announces the renewal of THE BULLWINKLE SHOW for the 1962-63 TV season. THE BULLWINKLE SHOW will air at 5:30pm on Sundays, a time slot once occupied by OMNIBUS. Oh, well, it's in color." These were new episodes.

THE BULLWINKLE SHOW lasted until September 1963 on NBC Sunday night and moved to Saturday morning for one season. ABC picked up the reruns and presented them on Sunday from 1964 through 1973.

While Ward and Scott went on to other projects such as THE GEORGE OF THE JUNGLE SHOW, they still retained an affection for the Moose and Squirrel. Bullwinkle, who had become the spokesmoose for Cheerios cereal, would appear in animated commercials and print ads for many years.

"We toyed with the idea of other projects for Bullwinkle," remembered Scott. "We had a Bullwinkle's Valentine Day special planned. A couple of things like that." The project that got the farthest along was THE STUPORBOWL, a parody of the Superbowl football game. "We went ahead and did the pilot, shot straight storyboards. Animatics, I guess it's called. We heard that the network was pretty high on it until they checked with the NFL and found out they didn't think it was so funny." Supposedly, the project was rejected because the storyline had Boris attempting to fix the outcome of the game and the show harshly parodied actual team owners including Georgia Frontiere.

In the Seventies, Clem Williams Films, Inc., packaged a 90-minute compilation show for the college circuit. Entitled AN EVENING WITH BULLWINKLE AND HIS FRIENDS (aka THE JAY WARD CARTOON FESTIVAL), it had the complete "Wossamotta U" story as well as other Ward cartoon segments such as Dudley Do-Right.

At one time it was announced former Warner's director Friz Freleng had acquired the rights to Rocky and Bullwinkle and was going to produce a new series. "Jay had said he might be interested in having Friz produce the cartoons if we could write the stuff and keep the creative control. But that's as far as it went. It never got to rights. It never got into any commitment," stated Bill Scott.

The last appearance so far of Rocky and Bullwinkle was a commercial for Hershey's kisses. Bullwinkle attempts to perform his famous hat trick and pulls out a bag of the chocolates.

In 1986, the New York Museum of Broadcasting paid tribute to Ward and his crew with a festival that ran for several months. That same year saw the founding of THE FROSTBITE FALLS Far-Flung Flier, a newsletter dedicated to the thousands of Ward fans around the world. In 1987, a tribute, entitled "Rocky and Bullwinkle and Friends: A Tribute to Jay Ward," was presented at the Los Angeles Museum of Broadcasting.

In 1988 Walt Disney Home Video purchased the video rights to the entire Rocky and Bullwinkle library for around $1 million. Also in the package were the other elements of the show including "Fractured Fairy Tales," "Mr. Peabody," and so on. Disney Home Video were planning on beginning releasing tapes featuring the stars sometime in the 1990s.

With the death of Bill Scott in 1985 and Jay Ward in 1989, the rights to the characters may go to other hands. That may mean new adventures of Rocky and Bullwinkle sometime in the future.

SUPPORTING CAST

Boris Badenov was a spy from Pottsylvania. He was short and dressed completely in black, including his hat. He had a white complexion with a thin black mustache. In the early episodes his pupils were blood red but they eventually evolved into white. His heavy Slavic accent could have easily been Russian. He was an unrepentant comic villain. His superior was Fearless Leader, a scarfaced, monocled nasty fellow who resembled a World War II Nazi officer. Badenov was completely inept when it came to dealing with the Moose and Squirrel. He often donned a series of disguises that totally fooled Rocky and Bullwinkle. Yet he was still unable to win no matter what dirty tricks he tried. Boris really enjoyed being a villain and admired nasty attitudes in others.

"Every recording session was like going to a party. We laughed, we told jokes, we asked about the family life."

— June Foray

171

Natasha Fatale was Boris' companion. She was tall and well built, often wearing a slinky black dress. Her complexion was white and she had long black hair. She also had a thick accent which was more of a purr associated with a femme fatale. As did her partner Boris, she donned a series of disguises that usually evoked sympathy and affection from the Moose and Squirrel. It was obvious that Natasha cared about Boris and stood by him no matter how badly he failed.

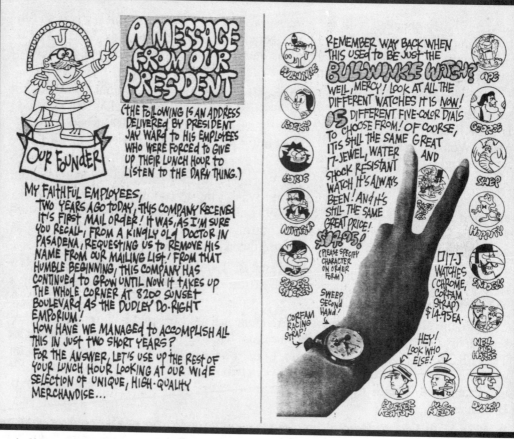

A live action film, starring Dave Thomas and Sally Kellerman as BORIS AND NATASHA, has been completed and New Line Cinema announced it would be released in 1990.

Captain Peter "Wrong Way" Peachfuzz was based on Peter Piech, the executive producer. Both Bill Scott and Paul Frees at different times provided the voice for the character in an imitation of Ed Wynn. A Navy man who was continually confused, Peachfuzz was involved in government business and usually got Rocky and Bullwinkle involved.

Gidney and Cloyd were two Moon men who often journeyed to Earth. Physically, they were similar to the Ward commercial character, Quisp.

OFF THE TUBE

Of all of the Ward characters, Rocky and Bullwinkle were the ones who were most merchandised. They appeared on the usual items from Soaky (bubble bath) bottles to coloring books to bendable figures. Some Rocky and Bullwinkle items were released as cereal premiums in the Sixties as a result of their close association with General Mills and, in particular, Cheerios.

"Boris Badenov is our villain and he's all bad. Rocky, our other hero, plays it straight and is all good. It's all a take-off and satire on melodrama."

— Bill Scott

Al Kilgore was responsible for writing and drawing a short lived and little seen comic strip, between 1962 and '64, that captured the spirit of the show and was greatly admired. There were several ROCKY AND HIS FRIENDS comic books published by Dell and Gold Key as well as numerous issues of a BULLWINKLE comic book published at various times by Dell, Gold Key and Charlton. Star (Marvel) began a series of BULLWINKLE comics in 1987 that was discontinued in 1989. Blackthorne Publishing

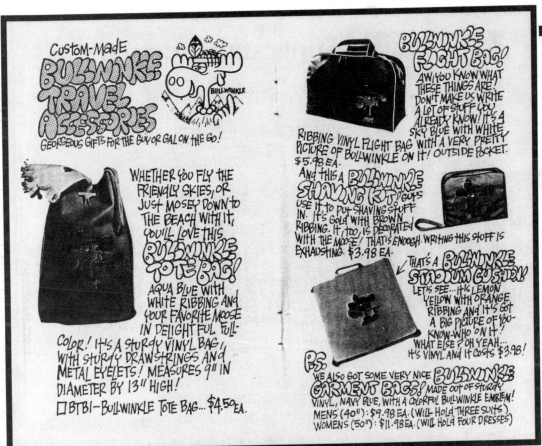

Custom-Made **BULLWINKLE TRAVEL ACCESSORIES** GORGEOUS GIFTS FOR THE GUY OR GAL ON THE GO!

WHETHER YOU FLY THE FRIENDLY SKIES, OR JUST MOSEY DOWN TO THE BEACH WITH IT, YOU'LL LOVE THIS **BULLWINKLE TOTE BAG!** AQUA BLUE WITH WHITE RIBBING AND YOUR FAVORITE MOOSE IN DELIGHTFUL FULL COLOR! IT'S A STURDY VINYL BAG, WITH STURDY DRAWSTRINGS AND METAL EYELETS! MEASURES 9" IN DIAMETER BY 13" HIGH!

☐ BTB1-BULLWINKLE TOTE BAG... $4.50 EA.

BULLWINKLE FLIGHT BAG! AW, YOU KNOW WHAT THESE THINGS ARE! DON'T MAKE US WRITE A LOT OF STUFF YOU ALREADY KNOW! IT'S A SKY BLUE WITH WHITE RIBBING VINYL FLIGHT BAG WITH A VERY PRETTY PICTURE OF BULLWINKLE ON IT! OUTSIDE POCKET. $5.98 EA.

AND THIS A **BULLWINKLE SHAVING KIT!** GUYS USE IT TO PUT SHAVING STUFF IN. IT'S GOLD WITH BROWN RIBBING. IT, TOO, IS DECORATED WITH THE MOOSE! THAT'S ENOUGH. WRITING THIS STUFF IS EXHAUSTING. $3.98 EA.

← THAT'S A **BULLWINKLE STADIUM CUSHION!** LET'S SEE... IT'S LEMON YELLOW WITH ORANGE RIBBING AND IT'S GOT A BIG PICTURE OF YOU-KNOW-WHO ON IT! WHAT ELSE? OH YEAH... IT'S VINYL AND IT COSTS $3.98!

P.S. WE ALSO GOT SOME VERY NICE **BULLWINKLE GARMENT BAGS!** MADE OUT OF STURDY VINYL, NAVY BLUE, WITH A COLORFUL BULLWINKLE EMBLEM! MENS (40"): $9.98 EA. (WILL HOLD THREE SUITS) WOMENS (50"): $11.98 EA. (WILL HOLD FOUR DRESSES)

Opposite and this page: From the Dudley Do-Right Emporium.

© Jay Ward

even issued a BULLWINKLE AND ROCKY comic book in 3-D.

In 1983 a series of Bullwinkle Family Restaurants opened in which customers watched audio-animatronic versions of Rocky, Bullwinkle and other Ward characters while they ate. These shows were written by Scott and featured the actual voices of Scott and Foray. Food items included Bullwinkle's Famoose Pizza and Rocky's Remarkable Burgers. Desserts such as Rocky's Road, Frostbite Falls and Bullwinkle's Mousse rounded out the meal. The gift shop had a wide range of Bullwinkle merchandise not available elsewhere, and there was even a large game room and a booth where people could get their pictures taken with the characters. Most of the locations had closed by the end of the Eighties.

Jay Ward, himself, opened one of the first cartoon character merchandise stores in 1971. Called The Dudley Do-Right Emporium, it was located right next door to Ward's studio and was often run by his wife. It carried an array of souvenirs including watches and sweatshirts and cels which all featured Ward's characters.

SUPERSTAR QUALITY

Though this team only worked for a few years, their impact on the animation industry and generations of viewers is enormous. Dozens of catch phrases, from "Bullwinkle is a dope," to "All on this itty-bitty card," to "Fan mail from some flounder" are still used today. The free-wheeling humor of the Jay Ward studio is a marker by which many modern cartoonists are measured. Many cartoon characters still being produced and promoted today are less visible in our society than this mighty Moose and Squirrel. Much as Marilyn Monroe, James Dean and other cult stars, Rocky and Bullwinkle's career ended far too early... but their legacy of films and laughs will last forever.

"(Ward) wanted Rocky the squirrel to be an All-American boy with a derring-do voice. Rocky was an idealist."
— June Foray

ROGER RABBIT

SELECTED SHORT SUBJECTS: *A Hare in My Soup, Herman's Shermans, The Little Injun That Could, The Wet Nurse, What's Cookin'*

Superstar Summary

THE STAR: Roger Rabbit

YEAR OF DEBUT: 1988 (WHO FRAMED ROGER RABBIT?)

STUDIO OF DEBUT: Walt Disney (Touchstone/Amblin')

SIGNATURE: "P-p-p-p-p-lease"

KEY CREW BEHIND THE STAR: Gary Wolf (creator), Steven Spielberg (producer), Robert Zemeckis (director), Richard Williams (animation director), Charles Fleischer (voice)

CAREER HIGH: WHO FRAMED ROGER RABBIT? (1988) — His debut where he sometimes got to be more than a supporting character.

When Roger Rabbit tore across movie screens in 1988 he created one of the biggest commotions in animation since Mickey Mouse worked a steamboat. This most modern Cartoon Superstar is the epitome of an Eighties hero — instant success, instant gratification and instant immortality.

Roger is one of the few animated superstars to come from a feature film. Most achieved fame in short cartoons or TV series. Though many features contain beloved characters, few attain much of a life outside of their feature. The Pink Panther is a bit of a peculiarity, having only appeared in title sequences not as part of the main story. However Roger Rabbit seemed to burst forth from his big screen debut into a completely separate lifeform.

Roger is visually a somewhat typical white rabbit cartoon character. He sports a big red nose, and a shuck of red hair on top of his head. His normal dress is a pair of baggy red pants, with suspenders that button in the front, yellow gloves and a polka dot bow tie.

A grab bag of characteristics, the animated Roger has little real personality of his own. He features the traits of many great cartoon characters: there's a bit of Goofy, a dash of Screwy Squirrel, some of the Mad Hare from Disney's ALICE IN WONDERLAND, a touch of Bugs Bunny and probably a drop of dozens of other key cartoon characters.

Richard Williams, animation director on WHO FRAMED ROGER RABBIT? has stated, "The Rabbit is a Frankenstein job. A bit from this, a bit from that." The character had to look familiar enough so that audiences would think they'd seen him before. "So it's a series of cliches pushed into new forms," he continued.

This mixture of personalities has made Roger a bit of a split personality. In different situations and with different characters he acts quite differently. It is impossible to really guess how he may act. He may be brash and coherent or a bumbling clown. His wit could be quick or slow. There may be compassion or coldness. There is no consistency in his behavior.

Unlike many of his fellow toons, Roger does not act as a star in his films. Any cartoon superstar worth his weight in cels is always in command of his film. He may face a dangerous adversary. Things may even look dark at times. However, the character always maintains a certain calm and control of the action. Whether it's Bugs' "What's Up, Doc," or Donald's "Oh, yeah?" or Heckle (or Jeckle) stating "hello, ol' bean," these toon superstars are in charge of their destiny. Roger is not.

Roger is more of a reactionary character than a toon of action, similar to an Elmer Fudd or Yosemite Sam. These characters must always react and defend themselves from the onslaught of Bugs. In Roger's films, he is not controlling the events, merely trying to survive them. One might classify him as a second banana who made it big, another typical aspect of the Eighties live action superstar.

What has given Roger his superstar status is this mish mash of toon elements. Roger is almost an "Everytoon." He encompasses all the things that adults remember and love about cartoons. He is violent, yet somewhat cute. He is quick, yet full of expression. He creates numerous disasters, but wants to help. It's as if some giant computer threw all the cartoon characters in the world into a database to create the ultimate toon... and succeeded.

Roger and Judge Doom in the original WHO FRAMED ROGER RABBIT.

WHO CREATED ROGER RABBIT?

One way in which Roger is similar to many Cartoon Superstars is that a number of different creators contributed to his development. However Roger is somewhat unique in that he was inspired by a character in a book.

Who Censored Roger Rabbit, written by Gary Wolf, was published in 1981. Wolf's book was meant to be a surreal spoof of the hard-boiled detective novel, a mixture of Raymond Chandler, Lewis Carroll and Warner Brothers. Roger Rabbit was a six-foot tall rabbit (a height which included his 18-inch ears) who worked for the DeGreasy Brothers. He wore a baggy pair of shorts held up by brightly colored suspenders. His white stomach, nose, toes and palms on a light brown body made him resemble someone who had just walked face first into a freshly painted wall.

Within the first fourth of the book, he is killed. However, earlier that evening he mentally created a duplicate to go out and buy some red suspenders. Toons could create these doppelgangers to perform the dangerous stunts in cartoons. Roger put a large jolt of mental energy into his duplicate so that it will last awhile before it falls apart. The book then becomes a race against time as detective Eddie Valiant and the Roger duplicate try to find out who shot Roger and why, clear Roger of charges in Rocco DeGreasy's murder, and figure out how Jessica fits into the scheme.

Roger was more a comic strip character than an animated star, although he was still a foil to Baby Herman. When toons talked, dialog balloons physically appeared over their head with the words spelled out, and these balloons eventually disintegrated, leaving fine dust. The motivations and personalities of the major characters such as Roger, Jessica and Baby Herman are significantly different than the final feature film versions.

TUMMY TROUBLE

© Walt Disney Company & Amblin Entertainment

In 1981, the Walt Disney studio optioned the book and put it into production. The talent behind this first attempt was Tom Wilhite, (then) currently head of production, Marc Stirdivant, a studio producer; and Darrell Van Citters, one of Disney's top animation directors. All three were key in developing much of the early Roger material, along with a new member, character designer Mike Giaimo.

This team worked on the project for a few years. It was mentioned as an "upcoming" feature for several years in the Disney company stockholders report. The title changed slightly as the years progressed. Titles mentioned included WHO CENSORED ROGER RABBIT?, WHO FRAMED ROGER RABBIT? and simply, ROGER RABBIT. It was allegedly reported that Disney management felt "censored" was too strong a word and held negative connotations.

> ### "We violated every rule that these stupid animators developed for working with live action"
>
> ### — Richard Williams

As the Eighties moved forward, the Disney studio went through several rough years as executives came and went and various financiers tried to buy the company.

When the dust settled in 1984, Michael Eisner and Frank Wells were in the driver's seat. Work on Roger had continued under Van Citters, now working on the special project SPORTS GOOFY, which would never see its intended theatrical release. Roger Rabbit was no longer an active project.

SPIELBERG STEPS IN

Eisner tried to interest outside talent in various co-productions. One such "talent" was Stephen Spielberg. Looking over a list of properties, Spielberg eyed Roger and requested the film. Suddenly Spielberg was more involved with the feature than Disney. Disney had still planned to do the animation, but Spielberg's Amblin' Productions would be handling the majority of work. This marriage of studios makes Roger one of the few Cartoon Superstars to be "joint" property, a situation that greatly influences where and how Roger is allowed to perform.

For a director, Spielberg chose Robert Zemeckis, who had just finished work on his BACK TO THE FUTURE. As fate often works, Zemeckis had been offered the director's job in 1982 by Wilhite. At the time he turned it down feeling the Disney studio wasn't willing to put the necessary money behind the project. However the new management and Spielberg indicated they now were.

Spielberg also decided the Disney staff of classical animators couldn't meet the frantic needs of Roger. A search began for an animation director. This activity took some time as they looked at any animation director who had done live action and animation. They talked with talents as diverse as Don Bluth (AN AMERICAN TAIL) and Phil Roman (Garfield commercials). There was even some discussion of setting up a new animation studio in Northern California under the direction of Lucasfilms, which was already set to do the special effects work.

Finally, all parties agreed upon award-winning director Richard Williams. Known for his many classic commercials in Europe and the U.S., Williams had also directed the RAGGEDY ANN AND ANDY (1977) feature.

Disney set Williams up in a new studio in London called Disney Animation, Ltd.

Unlike the first team working on the film, Williams was not a major factor in developing the feature. He was only involved with producing the animation. He told Zemeckis, "I am your pencil," and proceeded to follow the live action director's lead.

Production began on the live action sequences in 1987. The live cast included Bob Hoskins, Joanna Cassidy, Christopher Lloyd and Stubby Kaye. Also on hand was the man behind the rabbit, Charles Fleischer. Fleischer, a stand-up comic and TV sitcom actor was chosen for the voice of Roger.

Zemeckis and his team of effects men utilized many techniques to enhance the appearance of animated characters reacting with live actors. These included everything from elaborate mechanical puppets to human stand-ins. Once this shooting was complete, Williams began to work on his "special effect."

> "Unlike most films, ROGER must be viewed several times to really comprehend all that's going on."
> — Charles Fleischer

Zemeckis, who thought his work was now done, discovered he would be spending more time watching over the animation. "What I realized," recalled Zemeckis, "was that animators are like actors, and they shouldn't be expected to be directors."

THE ANIMATION OF ROGER RABBIT

Williams' crew worked for six months on the production utilizing animators from around the world. Such talents as James Baxter, Al Gaivoto, Russell Hall (the key artist behind Jessica), Phil Nibbelink, David Spafford and Simon Wells were part of Williams large staff of animators. Williams spent most of his time directing, but did do some animation for the opening Maroon Cartoon. The other artists spent their time animating over the various props, devices, and people. Some of the shadows of those items can still be seen in the final film.

As the deadline neared, it became apparent that the London studio could not handle all the work. To assist production, Disney hired the Baer Animation Studio, headed up by former Disney animator Dale Baer. The small studio had done a number of animated films for the Disney organization in the past. Baer quickly expanded his staff to include such top animators as Mark Kausler (who had worked with Spielberg, Zemeckis and Williams on storyboards for the film) and Matt O'Callahan and background artists Ron Dias and Michael Humphries. This U.S. crew was responsible for 11 minutes of animation in the feature. This included the entire Toon Town section and the chase with Benny the Cab. They also pitched in and picked up odd scenes throughout the film.

"Essentially, Bob (Hoskins) and I had to create an entirely new style of acting on ROGER."

— Charles Fleischer

Finally, the 56 minutes of animation were done and Lucasfilm began work on integrating the live action, the animation and computerized shadowing. During the final moments of editing, a number of sequences were cut, including one where Eddie Valiant (Bob Hoskins) is given a "toon" pig head. This one cut required a few seconds of new animation to be completed only weeks before the debut of the film!

Original artist's conception for Roger Rabbit, prior to Spielberg's involvement. Art by Mike Giamo.

© Walt Disney Productions

ROGER ARRIVES!

WHO FRAMED ROGER RABBIT? opened with one of the fastest, most violent animated sequences in film history; a cartoon called WHAT'S COOKIN'?. The cartoon was more similar to an MGM Tom and Jerry or Warner Brothers cartoon than the traditional Disney efforts. Roger, in his attempt to babysit Baby Herman, was treated to more danger and destruction than in a dozen other cartoons. An entire kitchen became a deadly battlefield. After this breath-taking display of animation, the film suddenly shifted. The animation camera pulled back to find that the cartoon was being shot on a live sound stage. Cartoon characters were real and worked at movie studios just as any live action star.

Taking place in 1947, the film told the story of Roger who is framed for the murder of Marvin Acme, the gag king. Roger goes to detective Eddie Valient (Bob Hoskins) who reluctantly gets mixed up in the mystery that involves the Los Angeles Red Car, more murder, Judge Doom (Christopher Lloyd), freeways, seductive toons (Roger's wife!), and the destruction of Toon Town, where all toons live.

Much of the story doesn't ring true, and there are a number of historical slips. However the film offers a variety of astounding effects sequences, lively animation—sometimes over-animated— and general fun. Considering the mixed history of the film, it's no wonder many Disney studio executives felt the feature was turning into another HOWARD THE DUCK up until the premiere.

Originally budgeted at around $12 million in the early Eighties, the film finally came in with a cost estimated at over $40 million. However, unlike some top dollar films of the Eighties, every dollar seemed visible on the screen in WHO FRAMED ROGER RABBIT? Reviews were mixed, but generally positive. They were astounded by the technology, but found story and character deficiencies. Audiences fell in love with the feature. The film toppled almost every Disney record.

ROGER broke theater records around the world. It became the top grossing film that year, with over $150 million in the U.S. alone, and one of the top money-making features of all time.

WHO FRAMED ROGER RABBIT? received a number of prominent nominations. The Golden Globes nominated it for Best Picture and Best Actor (Hoskins). The script was nominated for best script based on material from another medium by the

Writers Guild of America. The Directors Guild nominated Zemeckis for best director. Even Charles Fleischer, the voice of Roger, was nominated for best supporting male by the American Comedy Awards. Though it didn't win any of these awards, this was a sign of how well received the film was in the professional community.

Roger did better at the Oscars. Nominated in a number of categories, it went on to win three Oscars for its technical work. Additionally, an Honorary Oscar for special achievement went to Richard Williams for the "creation" of Roger Rabbit. This makes Roger the second "Oscar winning Rabbit," an honor he shares with Bugs Bunny.

Originally, Roger was scheduled to appear at the Oscar ceremony via animation but was unable to do so due to last minute production problems.

Eddie and Roger in WHO FRAMED ROGER RABBIT.

© Touchstone Pictures & Amblin Entertainment

A NEW STAR IS BORN

Disney, seeing the impact the film was having, instantly began promoting the "star" of the film as their newest superstar. The Roger Rabbit costume character began to appear at every major Disney event. He was immediately added to the then-in-production Mickey Mouse 60th birthday special (1988). Charles Fleischer, the voice of Roger, became Disney's newest corporate voice.

The feature had given high exposure to the lost form of the animated short film. Disney decided to try cashing in by producing a series of shorts starring Roger. For this, the studio created a new shorts division within their animation studio. The director chosen for the first new Disney short in almost 30 years was one of their newer talents, Rob Minkoff.

"You see that he's a well meaning disaster, and you like him."

— Richard Williams

179

Minkoff and crew began work on the first short, TUMMY TROUBLE in late 1988. The final product was released with the live action HONEY, I SHRUNK THE KIDS in 1989. Once again, Roger was connected with a critically-acclaimed, top-grossing feature film. Only this time he wasn't part of the film.

TUMMY TROUBLE is largely a remake of the first Maroon Cartoon WHAT'S COOKIN'? which was never completed in WHO FRAMED ROGER RABBIT? due to Roger always blowing his lines. Once again Roger is baby sitting Baby Herman, only this time Roger is somewhat responsible for the predicaments when he hands the baby a rattle. Herman quickly swallows the toy and Roger rushes the tyke to a hospital. True to form, Roger becomes the target for confused doctors, sharp objects and mechanical devices.

Critics were much less impressed with Roger's second outing. His first appearance was meant to remind adults *about* violent, free-wheeling cartoons of the Forties. This second short *was* a violent, free-wheeling cartoon aimed at young children.

A short such as TUMMY TROUBLE would never have been allowed on Saturday morning TV. Animators on the film became angered in 1990 when the short failed to be nominated for an Oscar. However, Disney and Minkoff had already nearly finished the next short, ROLLER COASTER RABBIT.

ROLLER COASTER RABBIT was released in June 1990 with the feature film DICK TRACY. Roger is once again reluctantly assigned to babysit Baby Herman. This time it is at an amusement park and Baby Herman's quest for a red balloon puts Roger in a variety of perils. One memorable incident involves an anatomically suggestive gag involving a bull. The main action takes place on a roller coaster and the sequence is a combination of drawn and computer animation. The story structure is similar to the two previous Maroon Cartoons.

ROGER ON TV!

Though still young in his career, Roger has not missed out on TV exposure. His enormous success in theaters was followed by a number of TV appearances. These were largely done to keep his face before the public.

In September of 1988 CBS aired ROGER RABBIT AND THE SECRETS OF TOONTOWN. The one-hour special was hosted by Joanna Cassidy, Eddie's girlfriend Dolores in the feature. It showed how several of the special effects were done, including how the animation was used to cover up the props. There was no new animation created for the show, but Fleischer did some new voice overs to footage from the feature.

"I believe we are the only company that could and would do this."
— Jeffrey Katzenberg, chairman of Disney Studios

The Rabbit's next appearance was on an episode of the Disney TV show which celebrated Mickey's 60th birthday (1988). Roger had a cameo as a bumbling stage hand. Also featured in cameo was Charles Fleischer. In the show, Mickey disappears and a harried Roger tries to help locate the missing mouse. Roger also became part of the opening credits to NBC's WONDERFUL WORLD OF DISNEY.

CO-STARS

In WHO FRAMED ROGER RABBIT? Roger has the opportunity to co-star with some of the biggest names in cartoons: Bugs Bunny, Mickey Mouse, Betty Boop, Donald Duck, Droopy and more. However, in his regular life, Roger really only has two key co-stars: Jessica and Baby Herman.

Jessica Rabbit, his wife, is one of the sexiest human cartoon characters ever to slink across the screen. She isn't bad, as she declares in the feature, "I'm just drawn that way." Her sultry voice (Kathleen Turner) can coo to her "bunny" or deliver a double entendre with equal ease. In the short subjects she is mainly seen as window dressing, appearing briefly to maintain the relationship. She loves Roger because, "He makes me laugh."

Baby Herman (voice by Lou Hirsch) on screen is an adorable little tyke who baby talks his way to everyone's heart. In reality, he is a cigar smoking, dirty middle-age man. In the feature, he is seen much harsher than in the shorts. However, in much of the merchandise, he is often treated as if he were a real baby. At times, it almost seems as if he were Jessica's and Roger's child!

Disney began developing a prime time pilot around Herman as a possible series for 1991.

OUT OF TOON TOWN

Roger, as do many new properties and stars, received the full backing of licensed merchandise. Roger was available on just about every conceivable item. In 1989, the movie was released on videotape at the sell-through price of $22.95. It sold over 7.9 million copies, a gross of nearly $182 million!

He appeared in several special comic book projects. One was a graphic novel from Marvel comics which told of "The Resurrection of [Judge] Doom." Another offered the story of TUMMY TROUBLE via frame blow-ups from the film! With the start-up of Disney's own line of comic books, Roger was given his own title starting in the Spring of 1990.

The costume character has become one of the most visible at the Disney theme parks. He stars in most of the stage shows as well as appearing in the TV ads for the parks. When Disneyland celebrated their 35th anniversary, Roger was one of only a half dozen characters chosen to be the model for gigantic parade balloons. A new Roger Rabbit ride is planned for the Disney-MGM Studios.

Roger also broke ground by being one of the first animated features to be the subject of an art auction. In June of 1989 Disney held a special auction at Sotheby's in New York. The gallery is famous for its auctions of classic animation art from the golden era of animation that often set new records in value. This sale brought in over $1.65 million. One piece, alone brought a bid of $46,000.

SUPERSTAR QUALITY

Roger's ability to immediately cross the line between children and adults has made him virtually unique among superstars. Few people today "grew up" with Roger Rabbit. But his multiple personalities give a familiarity that few cartoon characters have achieved.

As the ideal toon, Roger will remain the focus of laughter, enjoyment and collectors for a long time. Roger may have been innocent of the murder of Marvin Acme, but he definitely killed 'em in the theaters.

"I really don't know how to do just a voice. I have to find the character; know about who he, she or in the case of Roger, it is."

— Charles Fleischer

ROLLER COASTER RABBIT promotional art.

SCOOBY-DOO

Superstar Summary

THE STAR: Scooby-Doo

YEAR OF DEBUT: 1969 (SCOOBY-DOO, WHERE ARE YOU?)

STUDIO OF DEBUT: Hanna-Barbera

SIGNATURE: "Rooby-roo!"

KEY CREW BEHIND THE STAR: Fred Silverman (network executive), Ken Ruby and Joe Spears (writers)

CAREER HIGH: A PUP NAMED SCOOBY-DOO (1988) demonstrates that all the formula elements of the series can be parodied and still keep the basic show entertaining and Scooby lovable.

Scooby-Doo is the first Cartoon Superstar to come from Saturday morning. He is also one of the longest-running characters on Saturday Morning. Whether solving mysteries with the gang, participating in sports, locating missing ghosts, or playing detective as a puppy, Scooby's career is long and varied.

Scooby-Doo is a Great Dane with long gangly legs, a large head and whiskers that give him a scruffy look. He doesn't talk, but his barks, supplied by Don Messick, are clearly understood by almost anyone. Mostly these barks begin with an "r" sound like "Rahhh!"—which means "yeah".

His main goal in life seems to be eating and the reward of Scooby Snacks, a type of dog biscuit tempting enough to send him into danger against his better judgment. The Scooby Snack was a variation on a gag that probably first appeared in Quick Draw McGraw where a dog would do a job if offered a dog biscuit, then often float in the air with joy after receiving his reward.

Relaxing also seems to rate high in his desires. A cowardly cur, Scooby seems afraid of just about anything. However, he overcomes his fear to save his friends. Most of the time, though his help is largely unintentional. Also unintentional is his continual dealing with ghosts and mysteries. He is a coward, but his friends are mystery solvers, hence Scooby is frequently right in the middle of the ghost-busting action.

Though the title star of all his shows, Scooby is actually a team player. His major teammate is Shaggy, a beatnik or early "hippie" type of character. These two are part of another group that includes, at various times, Fred, Daphne and Velma. Together, they solve mysteries.

When Scooby and his crew burst upon the Saturday morning scene they became such tremendous hits they spawned multiple imitations and a second studio! This crazy canine and his mystery loving menagerie brought fun back to Saturday morning.

SCOOBY-DOO? WHERE ARE YOU?

Saturday morning was in trouble. For several years, the networks had done well in the ratings with such action shows as SPACE GHOST, SUPERMAN, THE HERCULOIDS and others. The trouble was parent groups were getting upset about the violence on TV. Soon the networks were switching over to softer shows that toned down all violence, even slapstick. Cartoons now had to be safe. Unfortunately, safe cartoons are seldom very entertaining.

Hanna-Barbera had begun to move away from their hero shows. In their place were attempts at more literary shows including THE ADVENTURES OF GULLIVER and zany humor entries such as THE WACKY RACERS. None seemed to catch on, though. CBS's head of children's programming, Fred Silverman, who had created the superhero sensation a few years earlier, wanted to bring a new look to Saturday morning. He suggested Hanna-Barbera develop a mystery show featuring screwy teenagers. Allegedly he envisioned it as a mix between I LOVE A MYSTERY, a popular radio show in the Forties and Fifties, and THE MANY LOVES OF DOBIE GILLIS, a sitcom from the Fifties and Sixties. Many of these elements survived into the final product. Most prominently, the character of Shaggy with a goatee, a variation of beatnik Maynard G. Krebs from DOBIE GILLIS.

1974 Promotional art.

© Hanna-Barbera

Writers Joe Ruby and Ken Spears were asked to come up with something. They developed an idea of four teenagers and a dog traveling the country solving mysteries that featured monsters. Their success on this series eventually allowed Ruby and Spears to start their own studio.

The presentation was full of haunted houses, monsters, and eerie locales. Silverman planned to use the show as the centerpiece for the new Fall schedule. When it was presented to the network brass, they gave it a thumbs down. The show was considered too scary!

Silverman was now stuck with a schedule with no centerpiece. He desperately tried to think of what to do. According to him, he was inspired by the Frank Sinatra song "Strangers in the Night" where Sinatra improvised the refrain, "Scooby-dooby-doo." That was Silverman's answer. Call the dog "Scooby-Doo." Make the dog funny. Make the dog the star. Suddenly the series became more comedy than mystery and the network bought it.

SCOOBY-DOO, WHERE ARE YOU? debuted in the Fall of 1969 and became an almost instant hit. The combination of humor and mystery, long a staple in films and TV, proved equally enjoyable to the young audience. In fact, it seemed the perfect combination. There were "neat," scary monsters, funny characters, silly gags and real clues to solve the mystery. The series also seemed to have started the concept of massive repetition which children love. The format was so popular that studios, including Hanna-Barbera, tried to recycle it many times over the years in other series such as GOOBER AND THE GHOST CHASERS, CLUE CLUB, BUTCH CASSIDY and THE BUFORD FILES.

Every episode of SCOOBY-DOO, WHERE ARE YOU? is basically the same. The team in their van, the Mystery Machine, arrive at a location. There is a ghost or monster, sometimes the result of a curse, ruining the local trade and atmosphere. The team splits up with Fred and Velma finding clues, Daphne finding trouble, and Shaggy and Scooby finding food and the monster. There is a lot of chasing through doors, hallways, stairways, alleys, and the like. Never is there any hitting, or hurting. By the end, Fred and Velma have uncovered that the ghost/monster/curse is actually a real person creating the problem. Almost inevitably, the villain states he would have succeeded "if it weren't for those kids and that dog."

"... It's been my experience that it's almost always the original characters (like Yogi, Huck, Top Cat and Scooby-Doo) who rise to the level of perennial superstar."

— Joe Barbera

Many mystery series ranging from Charlie Chan to the current MURDER SHE WROTE feature repetitious plots. This allows them to spend more time playing with characters and action. SCOOBY DOO, WHERE ARE YOU? was no different. Since viewers didn't need to follow the plot carefully, they could try to catch the one or two clues. They could squeal at the "scary" monster. They could laugh as Scooby and Shaggy try to get a decent meal without having the monster bother them.

1977 Scooby-Doo model sheet.

© Hanna-Barbera

The first episode, WHAT A NIGHT FOR A KNIGHT, opens with a pick-up truck driving down a dark road. In the back is a crate. Unbeknownst to the driver, the crate opens and a medieval knight in armor appears. The knight reaches for the driver as the scene ends. Shaggy and Scooby, while returning from a late night movie, come across the truck. The only occupant is the suit of armor in the drivers seat. The pair get spooked and head back for the rest of the gang.

They find that the suit was being delivered to the local museum, so they notify authorities. At the museum, the curator tells them that the armor has a curse on it and the missing driver was a British archaeologist. As the crew exit, Scooby picks up a pair of glasses. In the van, they discover Scooby's glasses and visit a library to identify them. The glasses are used by British archaeologists and jewelers. They decide to return to the museum.

Back inside, they begin looking for clues. Shaggy notices a missing painting that reappears later. The rest of the gang discovers wet paint and a secret room. Meanwhile, the knight is on a rampage. There is much chasing and hiding until Shaggy and Scooby hide in a plane. Scooby accidentally starts the craft and begins chasing the knight. After destroying much of the museum, they capture the menace.

Upon pulling off the armor, it is revealed to be the curator. Fred, Daphne and Velma then explain that all the clues pointed to the curator who was forging paintings. The only one who could spot the forgeries was the new British archaeologist. The police thank the kids and the criminal is taken away. However, there is still time for Scooby to scare everyone by dressing up in the armor again.

This first episode features all of the key elements that would become standards in the series. First is the stumbling onto a mystery. Second is Shaggy's continual attempts at humor. As the gang tries to figure out why only the armor is in the truck, Shag offers, "Maybe he went out for the (k)night." Next, in the middle of the chase Velma loses her glasses. Without them she is practically blind. Hearing the Knight struggling, she thinks it is Shaggy with a cold. When they want something done, all they need do is offer Scooby a "Scooby Snack" and he'll volunteer.

Finally, when apparently trapped by the menace, Scooby resorts to costume play. As the Knight nears the pair, Shaggy yells for Scooby to "do something!" Scooby zips off-screen then back on-screen in a painter's smock with an easel. He begins painting the Knight and treating the menace as a model. In the plane, when the motor suddenly starts, Scooby reaches down and pulls out aviator goggles.

Some of the throw-away lines are not followed up in later episodes. Shag is mentioned as being the school's best gymnast. He also claims to be a talented ventriloquist. Both talents are demonstrated within the show. The first episode also featured an intrusive laugh track. It even laughs at things that aren't jokes. When Freddy looks at the truck and armor, he states it looks like "another mystery." This piece of dialogue features a mysterious musical sting, and a huge laugh! The laugh track would come and go through the years and different series.

Unlike most of the other Cartoon Superstars, Scooby was able to arrive fully created because of the logistics of Saturday morning TV. Whereas the older stars had time to evolve into the personalities they have today through years of shorts, Scooby had to be created, written and produced into 26 episodes immediately for TV. For this process, most studios create a "Bible" of the show which gives character descriptions of all the characters and even sample storylines.

Scooby's first season kept true to the rules used in the debut episode with pun-ish, sing-song titles that gave large hints to the "mystery menace." SCOOBY-DOO AND A MUMMY TOO, THAT'S SNOW GHOST, NEVER APE AN APE MAN, MINE YOUR OWN BUSINESS, and SPOOKY SPACE KOOK all indicated either the menace or location of the problem. These variations kept the show at the top of the ratings for three years.

"I've loved Scooby from the inception, and so has everyone else."
— Don Messick, voice of Scooby

CARTOON SHOW OF THE RICH AND FAMOUS

In 1972, it was decided to expand the premise and add some spice. THE NEW SCOOBY-DOO COMEDY MOVIES was an hour-long series. The storylines were similar, but to help fill out the newer length, guest stars were brought in. These guests could be in the form of cartoon versions of live people such as Davy Jones of the Monkees, Don Knotts or Sonny and Cher. These stars provided their own voices. Also used were "classic" stars such as Laurel and Hardy and the Three Stooges (without the real voices). Even fictional guests were used including Batman and Jeannie, from the I DREAM OF JEANNIE series. It was in the Jeannie episode that the first actual supernatural villain, who wasn't a real person in disguise, appeared.

The series even featured guests from other Saturday morning series such as JOSIE AND THE PUSSYCATS and SPEED BUGGY. The series began to become broader and broader. Scooby could easily walk around on two legs when the story needed him to do so, and his face become more elastic.

The COMEDY MOVIES ran only two years. They were later cut into half hour two-parters for the syndicated series.

A youthful Scooby and Shaggy.

© Hanna-Barbera

Meanwhile, the original SCOOBY-DOO, WHERE ARE YOU continued running in repeats on the network.

1976 saw Scooby move over to ABC in a new show, THE SCOOBY-DOO/ DYNOMUTT HOUR. This series began to introduce new members to the Scooby family. Scooby-Dum was a less intelligent, country cousin, type relation to Scooby-Doo. He spoke in a Mortimer Snerd-type voice. More sophisticated was Scooby-Dee, a pretty, white female who stole Scooby's heart. The new stories remained the same, though. Titles such as NO FACE ZOMBIE CHASE CASE, WHATTA SHOCKING GHOST, SCARED A LOT IN CAMELOT and THE HARUM SCARUM SANITARIUM show the same humor and monsters at work. By this time the catch phrase about getting away "if it weren't for these meddling kids" had seemingly become encased in stone.

"You know, people are always ripping things off, but they've never been able to touch Scooby. He's there and he's riding."

— Joe Barbera

The other recurring element of this series was stories starring DYNOMUTT, a robotic dog. He was the clutzy sidekick of The Blue Falcon in this satire of superhero cliches. (Dynomutt and the Blue Falcon would be repeated in their own series later.) The series was expanded the next year to 90 minutes and thus re-titled THE SCOOBY-DOO/DYNOMUTT SHOW.

Scooby continued his popular run, so he was given more time—two-hours to be exact. In 1977 he premiered his SCOOBY'S ALL-STAR LAFF-A-LYMPICS. This mega show was actually a number of smaller series under one umbrella title. Scooby appeared in repeats from the SCOOBY/DYNOMUTT show and in new segments called LAFF-A-LYMPICS. This series set several teams against each other in a satire of the Olympics and BATTLE OF THE NETWORK STARS.

Over 45 Hanna-Barbera cartoon celebrities competed for the Laff-a-Lympics Gold Medallion. The competition took place all over the world. Scooby's "The Scooby Doobys" where in competition with "The Yogi Yahooeys", headed by Yogi Bear, and "The Really Rottens", headed by Dread Baron. Surprisingly, despite their cheating, the Really Rottens actually won the competition occasionally. Mildew Wolf and Snagglepuss were play-by-play announcers for this jam-packed half-hour.

The Scooby-Doo team included Scooby, Shaggy, Scooby-Dum, Dynomutt, Blue Falcon, Speed Buggy and Tinker, Captain Caveman and the Teen Angels, Hong Kong Phooey and Babu the genie. Ads for the LAFF-A-LYMPICS also showed Josie and the Pussycats and Babu's companion, Jeannie, but last minute legal problems kept them off the air.

"I started with them 17 years ago as Shaggy. That was the same year we started 'America's Top 40' ... Shaggy has been the longest acting job I've ever had."

— Casey Kasem, voice of Shaggy

The incredibly large number of cast members in this segment didn't give any character much of a chance to do anything.

Next came SCOOBY AND SCRAPPY-DOO (1979) with the introduction of a new character, Scrappy-Doo. Scrappy was a pint-sized edition of Scooby who could talk clearly and was fearless. He was originally voiced by Lennie Weinrib. In recent years Don Messick has taken over the task. The addition of Scrappy eliminated the majority of the regular cast. It was now mostly Shaggy, Scooby and Scrappy in the adventures, though the others showed up from time to time.

Scooby's wild takes from A PUP NAMED SCOOBY-DOO.

© Hanna-Barbera

For example, in WIZARDS AND WARLOCKS, Daphne joins the trio as they go to a gaming convention where the wizards really are magical. The stories weren't all mysteries either. Shaggy, Scooby and Scrappy just cause trouble for a temperamental chef in SCOOBY GUMBO.

This same year, Scooby appeared in his first prime time venture, SCOOBY-DOO IN HOLLYWOOD. This musical satire of TV told the tale of Scooby's desire to get away from his Saturday morning series. Shaggy and Scooby produced a number of pilots including SCOOBY DAYS, parodying HAPPY DAYS, with Scooby as the "Fonz", SUPER SCOOBY and SCOOBY'S ANGELS. However, when he fails to sell any prime time shows, and hears the kids calling for him, Scooby decides to return to his Saturday morning series, "ror the rids."

On Saturday morning, it seemed as if the magic was beginning to wear out. The 1980 season saw him star in THE RICHIE RICH/SCOOBY-DOO SHOW. He was now given second billing! This series only lasted one season and only featured re-

A PUP NAMED ...
SCOOBY DOO.. Main Models (31)

MAY 13 1988

MISC.
SCOOBY and SHAGGY
Takes

REVISED
MAY 18 1988

TAKES

**Sample takes from
A PUP NAMED
SCOOBY-DOO.**

© Hanna-Barbera

peats of the SCOOBY AND SCRAPPY-DOO show.

SCOOBY, SCRAPPY AND YABBA-DOO debuted in 1982 and brought a new member to the Scooby clan, Yabba-Doo. Yabba was Scooby's country-western cousin. His cry was "Yippidy Yabbadie Doooo!" This series featured two Scooby stories. Each featured Scooby, Scrappy and Shaggy travelling the world in search of fun and food. The Yabba-Doo segments featured Scrappy and Yabba helping Deputy Dusty out West.

1983 saw a new SCOOBY AND SCRAPPY-DOO series. These stories featured Scooby, Scrappy and Shaggy assisting Daphne. She was now an investigative reporter for a teen magazine. Almost false advertising, THE NEW SCOOBY-DOO MYSTERIES debuted in 1984. The series was actually repeats of earlier series' segments.

SCOOBY CHANGES HIS IMAGE

THE THIRTEEN GHOSTS OF SCOOBY-DOO (1985-86) attempted to take the series in a new, more serious direction. A permanent guest star was added in the guise of Vincent Price. It seems that Scooby, Shaggy and Scrappy had somehow opened a box releasing the 13 most evil spirits. Price, the guardian of the box, assisted them week after week as they continued to capture the ghosts. Though it was a clever concept, the new direction didn't work. The Fall of 1986 was the first season since his debut in 1969 that Scooby wasn't featured on a network's Saturday morning schedule.

In 1987, Hanna-Barbera began a series of ten made-for-TV features. Three of them featured the popular Scooby. SCOOBY AND THE BOO BROTHERS had Scooby, Shaggy and Scrappy working with three goofy ghosts to find a hidden treasure. SCOOBY-DOO AND THE GHOUL SCHOOL found the trio discovering their students are young monsters. SCOOBY AND THE RELUCTANT WEREWOLF had Dracula turn Shaggy into a werewolf causing Scooby, Scrappy, Shaggy and Googie, Scooby's girl friend, to go to Transylvania for a cure.

Scooby was re-born, so to speak in 1988 when Hanna-Barbera and ABC offered A PUP NAMED SCOOBY-DOO. This new series took the characters back to 1963, when they were kids and Scooby was a pup. The storylines were still pretty similar to the original series, with the group always solving a mystery, but this was a hipper Scooby. Producer Tom Ruegger strove to put new life into the concept.

Placing it in the Sixties was one way, allowing the artists and writers to jab a bit of fun at the time period. They also parodied some of the familiar icons of the original series such as the mindless chases, Velma's brilliance and final discussion of suspects.

The art style was changed allowing the characters to do extreme takes when seeing ghosts. For example, its not unusual to see the young Scooby's nose and legs fly off when confronted with a spooky object.

This new version of Scooby seems to have hit a nerve with modern audiences. In its first two seasons, the series has proven to be a popular show in the ratings. It was also nominated both years for an Emmy as best animated program. However, it was not renewed for a third season in 1990 by ABC.

SCOOBY'S CO-STARS

Scooby's key co-stars were his fellow sleuths. Of course his closest friend was Shaggy, who looked a little like Scooby. They were both unkempt, hedonistic and passive rebels. He communicated easily with Scooby and sometimes seemed less intelligent. He also shared Scooby's love of food, rest and safety. The two obviously loved each other, and it could be presumed that Scooby was Shaggy's dog. Shaggy's source of income was never revealed. It has been suggested that he was a college drop-out during the hippie era of the Sixties.

The other sleuths included Fred, a clean cut, blond youth. He was the force behind the group, generally giving out the orders and finally revealing the criminal. Velma was probably second in command. This heavy-set brunette female with glasses was the stereotypical "bookworm." However her pleasant personality probably made her the most friendly, and normal, of the group. Daphne was saddled with the "dumb blonde" persona, even though she was red-headed. She was pretty and showed intelligence, but she seemed more like Fred's date than part of the group.

Next in line for co-star status would be Scooby-Dum and Scrappy-Doo. Dum was a country bumpkin version of Scooby-Doo. Dimwitted, slow and generally a loose end in stories, he seemed only along for the ride. Scrappy, on the other hand was a key force. He seemed to be a replacement for Fred, Velma and Daphne. It was Scrappy who generally gave the orders to Shaggy and Scooby and always showed curiosity at the slightest unusual event. Seemingly enamored by his Uncle, Scooby, he would cheer him on. However when things looked bad, he would jump up and shout, "Puppy Power" and head into the fray.

SCOOBY-DOO OFF THE TUBE

Scooby has been as popular out of the box as in. He has appeared in a number of comic book titles, beginning in 1970, as well as toys, children's books and records. A costume version of Scooby resides at Great America in Northern California and appears at Universal Studios, Florida. As are many H-B characters, he was employed to do educational work such as the film strip THE SCOOBY-DOO GANG IN SKIN DEEP which dealt with acne problems.

SUPERSTAR QUALITY

Scooby-Doo, became the favorite cartoon star of a generation of children. Since his debut over two decades ago, dozens of mystery-solving kids have worked with an equal number of dogs and other critters. However, only the original, Scooby-Doo is still fondly remembered by those who grew up with him. When it comes to solving mysteries, Scooby-Doo is top dog!

"Along came Scooby-Doo. That was something I couldn't predict... the dog became the star... we worked so hard on his personality."

— Joe Barbera

THE SMURFS

Superstar Summary

THE STAR: The Smurfs

YEAR OF DEBUT: 1981

STUDIO OF DEBUT: Hanna-Barbera

SIGNATURE: Smurf-speak ("I smurf, you smurf, he smurfs")

KEY CREW BEHIND THE STAR: Peyo (creator), Gerard Baldwin (producer, story editor), Al Gmuir (background stylist), Hoyt Curtin (music).

CAREER HIGH: Series debut (1981), receiving the highest rating of an animated series in over eight years, and saving Saturday morning animation on NBC.

T hree apples high and blue, the Smurfs revitalized a studio, put a network in first place and changed the way everyone looked at Saturday morning. They also became the source for endless animation jokes. However these little blue folks Smurfed all the way to the bank.

The Smurfs are small blue elves in simple white clothing. At first glance all Smurfs look alike. Closer inspection shows that each one is an individual. Similar to the Seven Dwarfs, each Smurf seems to have been named for one major personality characteristic. They include Hefty, Brainy, Clumsy, Handy, Jokey, Vanity, Lazy, Greedy, Grouchy and Dreamy to name a few. Some Smurfs were named for their trade. These include Farmer, Barber and Tailor. There are also Smurflings and a Baby Smurf. All of these are watched over by their leader, Papa Smurf.

All 103 Smurfs live in a village in the middle of a medieval forest. The village, comprised mostly of mushroom houses, is near the River Smurf. They live a communal existence, deriving all their needs from nature. The most common need is the Smurfberry, a source of food and drink—and many plotlines. Living off the land, away from the world of man, they have little need for gold or money.

Their world exists in a classic, fantasy medieval time when knights roamed the countryside, dragons really breathed fire and witches and sorcerers cast spells. The humans of this world are largely unaware of the Smurfs. As a rule, the Smurfs have always avoided humans. To aid in this, Papa Smurf placed a spell that insures no one can find the Smurfs' village unless a Smurf leads them to it.

This magical village is home to several key areas. There is the Village Square with a well. It is here the group sometimes meets to discuss a situation. Papa Smurf's lab is full of books and equipment which he uses for creating his magic. Greedy's kitchen is where the food is prepared. Handy's workshop is full of practical gadgets made out of natural elements. Then there is a dining hall where they all meet and a theater where they can perform. Located at various edges of the village are the Smurfling's bunkhouse, a farm, a bridge and a dam, both of these on River Smurf.

Perhaps the most famous aspect of these little blue folk is their language. In "Smurf-speak," one can substitute the word "Smurf" for almost any adjective, verb or adverb. "What a Smurfy day." "Have you Smurfed those trees yet?" "He's eating Smurfy fast." It is this feature that has caused the Smurfs to become a popular joke topic. Comedians were quick to put "Smurf-speak" to work in a number of adult humor routines.

The Smurfs are generally pleasant, positive characters who spend a lot of time singing and having fun. At least this is the image most people have of these characters. Even Hanna-Barbera took a swipe at that image in one of their other series, YOGI'S TREASURE HUNT. Dick Dastardly and Muttley disguise themselves as purple "Smirks" who wear white caps. Watching them on TV, Blabber Mouse tells his partner, "Gosh, Snoop, they're so sweet, it's sickening." In actuality, the characters and series are a bit better than they are often given credit for being.

In 1984 one critic was able to see through the TV comics' jokes and snide remarks to state that the Smurfs are actually well done. As *Daily Variety* said in their review of one of the Smurfs'

The Smurfs and Smurfette.

© Hanna-Barbera

prime time specials, "The truth is, the Smurfs are anything but the unrelentingly and unbelievably sweet characters many believe them to be. As this special shows, they're a thoroughly human bunch of tiny blue people, and they're capable of every bit as much unpleasantness as the rest of us."

The TV show won numerous awards for its daring use of unusual topics for Saturday morning. These included shows about physically handicapped characters, substance abuse and death. Few other Saturday morning shows can Smurf those accomplishments.

THE ORIGINS OF THE SMURFS

The Smurfs were developed from the comics, just as Popeye was decades before. The main difference is that the comics didn't appear in the U.S. until after the animated series.

Created in 1957 by the Belgium cartoonist Peyo (Pierre Culliford) in a children's book, the Schtroumpf (the Flemish word for "watchamacallit") quickly became one of Europe's most popular comic characters. Peyo had been writing a weekly comic series about the adventures of two medieval characters named Johan and Peewit (later named Pee Wee) that appeared in SPIROU. In one adventure, he introduced a tribe of little blue elves named after an inside joke with fellow cartoonist Franquin about the word "schtroumpf." These characters are really quite similar to what eventually came to animation.

As with many supporting characters, their success eventually eclipsed the original stars of the strip. "Schtroumpf" became the more familiar "Smurf" when the strips were translated into English. Each Smurf is named after his personality or trade. The Smurfs work together, play together and have any number of wild adventures.

They were featured in a number of top-selling comic albums reprinted in America with such titles as "The Smurfic Games" (1975), "King Smurf" (1977) and "The Astrosmurf" (1978). By the Seventies they were heavily merchandised throughout the continent.

It wasn't until 1979 that these characters began coming over to the U.S. via the Wallace Beerie company. Fred Silverman, then president of NBC, saw his daughter playing with some of the toys. He commissioned Hanna-Barbera to develop a series, even though NBC had earlier rejected a proposal for a Smurf series. This led many people to initially believe that the Smurfs were originally a toy converted to animation, which was often done in the mid-Eighties with such titles as HE-MAN, MY LITTLE PONY and GI JOE.

Smurf model sheet.

© Hanna-Barbera

For the American market, though, some changes had to be made. The biggest change was the addition of a new character, Smurfette. Peyo's creation was a totally male universe. There were no females with the exception of some humans. To explain the presence of a single woman, the story crew devised a story where the Smurfs main nemesis, a generally inept sorcerer named Gargamel, creates a female Smurf to trap the blue creatures. However Papa Smurf uses his magic and turns the scheming vixen into the friendly and helpful, Smurfette. Actually, Peyo used a similar story to introduce a Smurfette in one of his comic adventures, but she did not remain as a regular character.

This change, along with all the writing and drawing, was under the continual supervision of Peyo. Hanna-Barbera held regular meetings with the creator in Europe where they would show sketches and talk over story ideas. Peyo also visited the studio several times a year. He had veto power over any storyline, character design, or drawing he didn't like. In fact, this became somewhat of a problem during the first few shows. Peyo would look at a frame of film and state that the drawing was wrong and out of proportion. The studio had to explain that in animation, the characters would stretch and squash in single drawings, but that it was necessary for the movement to look natural. Peyo had to use an interpreter to communicate with the U.S. studio.

Hanna-Barbera put a special staff in charge of the production headed up by Gerard Baldwin. Baldwin had begun directing on Jay Ward's THE BULLWINKLE SHOW and later directed on THE FAMOUS ADVENTURES OF MR. MAGOO as well as a number of Dr. Seuss TV specials. In the initial years of the show, Baldwin was both producer and story editor. In 1985 Baldwin left the series and several other hands have handled it since. Key writers in the first years were Peyo, Baldwin, Yvan Delporte, Len Janson and Chuck Menville. Al Gmuir was in charge of creating the background styles while Phyllis Craig was key colorist.

To voice the head Smurf (Papa Smurf), Hanna-Barbera brought in one of their most reliable veterans, Don Messick. Messick had provided voices for some of H-B's biggest stars including Scooby Doo and Boo Boo. Messick's multiple voices also speak for Azrael, Dreamy, Sleepy and many others. For the continuing villain Gargamel, and others such as Nosey and Baby, Paul Winchell (Jerry Mahoney and Disney's Tigger) loaned his tones. Master voice man Frank Welker (Dynomutt, Slimer, Foofur) spoke for Hefty, Poet, Peewit, Clockwork and others. Other animation greats included Lucille Bliss (the original Crusader Rabbit) as Smurfette and June Foray (Rocky the Flying Squirrel) as Jokey, Mother Nature, and others. Other voices for Smurfs over the years include Arte Johnson (LAUGH-IN), Allan

Young (Disney's Scrooge McDuck), Avery Schrieber, Janet Waldo (Judy Jetson) and Ed Begley, Jr.

THE SMURFS HIT THE SCREEN

The series debuted as a one hour show in 1981 and quickly became the top rated show on Saturday morning. Though some critics cringed at the soft cuteness in the show, kids couldn't get enough of these little blue friends. The show was getting 44 shares, meaning 44 out of every 100 TVs turned on were tuned into the Smurfs. By comparison, today's top-rated Saturday morning shows generally receive shares of around 20.

The series took NBC from the number three spot to the top-rated network for the year. This promptly cancelled NBC's plans to replace animated shows on Saturdays with a new weekend edition of the TODAY show.

"Without the villain, The Smurfs' world would be too ideal. The children can take delight in his (Gargamel's) failures."

— Gerard Baldwin, Producer

NBC retained the top spot for almost the rest of the decade, thanks to the continuing strength of the Smurfs.

Hanna-Barbera gained a new prominence in the animation community due to the quality of the series. Though aimed at young children, the series was well done with generally strong stories, good graphics, a distinctive, classical music score and competent animation.

1981 also saw the Smurfs in their first prime time special. The hour show aired on Sunday night and was really only one of the Saturday morning shows broadcast in prime time. However the added exposure helped boost the ratings on Saturdays. NBC advertised the Smurfs as "The 'biggest' little sensations since Charlie Brown!"

1982 saw the Smurfs expand to 90 minutes. To help fill the time, two new characters were introduced, Pee Wee and Johan, the humans whose comic series had spawned the Smurfs. The year also saw the series win its first Emmy for Outstanding Children's Entertainment Series.

Smurf model sheet.

© *Hanna-Barbera*

To keep the Smurfs fresh, the studio made sure each new season had something new to offer. 1983's offering was Baby Smurf. Such an event, according to Smurf legend, occurs only once in a blue moon. The third season also won Smurfs their second Emmy.

The 1985-86 season introduced the Smurflings. This group of young Smurfs included Nat, Slouch, and Snappy. They were adult Smurfs reverted to childhood when they fell into a backwards clock in Father Time's cave. The Smurflings felt sorry for Smurfette, being the only female, and created Sassette using Gargamel's original formula. However, they didn't use enough blue clay so Sassette was an adolescent tomboy. Also added was Puppy, a full sized puppy who easily towered over the tiny Smurfs.

Grandpa Smurf, voiced by Jonathan Winters, is around 1,000 years old. He debuted in the 1986-87 season. Gargamel also received some help this year in the form of wizard school dropout, Scruple. 1987 introduced Wild Smurf, who was raised by forest animals.

In 1988 four new characters arrived. One was a Smurf (Nanny Smurf), one was her pet (Smoogle), one was an evil wizard (Nemesis) and the other was a wizard's human niece (Denisa).

1989 found the first major change in the direction of the series as the little blue folk began extensive travels through time. The season contained the 400th episode aired! This was also the last season for the Smurfs on NBC's Saturday morning schedule. They were not renewed for the Fall of 1990.

PRIME TIME AND THE BIG SCREEN

Along with the Saturday morning show, the Smurfs continued appearing in prime time via more specials. THE SMURFS SPRINGTIME SPECIAL (1982) was their second prime time special, but the first developed strictly as a special. The story took place around Easter and featured a baby duck. It was nominated for an Emmy.

"Even though they're a happy little group of Smurfs, they have problems too. That's what life is all about."

— Joe Barbera (1982)

The Smurfs' third prime time special, THE SMURFS' CHRISTMAS SPECIAL (1982) proved to be another rating and critical success. It won an Emmy nomination and its time slot for the evening. *Daily Variety* found, "THE SMURFS CHRISTMAS SPECIAL deals strongly in the power of good over evil, and it's done with charm."

1983 saw the Smurfs' fourth special, MY SMURFY VALENTINE. In it, the Smurfs save the world from darkness.

The U.S. theatrical release of THE SMURFS AND THE MAGIC FLUTE from Atlantic pictures in 1983 brought more attention to the little blue folk. This film was not done by Hanna-Barbera. The feature was actually a European feature from the Seventies, based on Peyo's book of the same name, published in 1975. Like the original comic album, the story featured Johan and Peewit and only had the Smurfs in a supporting role stopping a villain who had a flute that caused uncontrollable dancing. It still grossed over $20 million; about as much as most Disney features of the time.

1984 found the Smurfs fifth prime time special tied to the Olympics. The actual Olympics were held in Los Angeles that year and THE SMURFIC GAMES had Papa Smurf organize the first "Smurfic Games" to shape up the blue folk.

Critics found the special entertaining. *Daily Variety* said, "As usual, strong storylines and vivid characters, hallmarks of the Smurfs series and spex [sic] insured that THE SMURFIC GAMES finished ahead of most of today's network animation programming."

The Smurfs sixth prime time special, SMURFILY EVER AFTER (1985), had Smurfette try to turn a simple ceremony between two wood elves, one of them mute, into a major production. It featured the unusual aspect of having the bride and groom exchange their vows in sign language.

In 1986 the series began to run in syndication. Titled SMURFS ADVENTURES, it ran a half hour. It was one of the first animated TV series to appear both on Saturday Morning and daily in syndication.

1987 found their seventh special, and second based on Christmas, 'TIS THE SEASON TO BE SMURFY. It was not as well received by the critics. *Daily Variety* cited its "weak production values." This was somewhat surprising since Hanna-Barbera had used the special to highlight their new computerized camera system. This new system allowed them to use over 100 different levels, bringing additional depth to the animation.

MEET THE SMURFS

Though it would be impossible to describe all 103 of the Smurfs, the majority of stories focus on a small group. The leader of the Smurfs, Papa Smurf, is also the oldest. He is approximately 542 years old and has a white beard. An alchemist by trade, he can whip up any number of magic potions and spells. However, this is usually as a last resort. A paternal figure, he always refers to the group as, "my little Smurfs." The majority of the other Smurfs seem about the same age.

Smurfette, originally created by Gargamel, is the first female Smurf. Though she spends a great deal of time working with flowers, she is not a helpless sterotypical female. Next to Papa Smurf she is generally the most level headed.

The pompous, know-it-all, Brainy has self appointed himself in charge whenever Papa Smurf is not around. He wears glasses, often has a book and is conceited about his intelligence. Clumsy is not only clumsy, but also a bit more simpleminded than the average Smurf. Hefty is the group's strongman and has a rough voice and tattoo. Greedy wears a chef's hat and is the chef and key consumer of his own desserts. Handy is the no-nonsense handyman who can fix or build anything. He frequently has a pencil behind his ear, ready to work.

Jokey just spends time giving people packages that explode which he finds very amusing. Vanity carries a mirror and is usually looking into it because he loves how he looks. Lazy's droopy eyelids help identify him and his naturally "relaxed" attitude. Grouchy hates everything, and often voices his opposing view to anyone else's opinion. Weepy is very emotional and constantly cries into his ready handkerchief. Harmony carries a horn, but seldom a tune. Poet has a quill always ready to capture his rhyme. Painter keeps palette at hand, wears a beret and speaks with a French accent. Others who make occasional appearances include the day dreamer, Dreamy, the Tailor, the Farmer and the Miner.

A number of Smurfs appeared only once for a particular episode. These include such characters as Nosey, who's curious, Dabbler, who never finishes anything, and Sweepy, a chimney sweep.

THE CO-STARS

Gargamel is the main recurring character outside of the Smurf village. Living in a dilapidated cottage with his cat Azrael, this second rate wizard is always trying to get the Smurfs. His reason: They're good to eat. There's also the fact that if he can get six of them he can create a formula that makes gold. Gargamel sometime gets (no) help from Scruple, a youngster who got kicked out of Wizard's School.

The Smurfs must also worry about Hogatha, an ugly witch constantly seeking to become beautiful. This redheaded character became so popular that a spin-off series was developed for her, but it never made it on the air. Chlorhydris was another sorceress. She hates love. Several of the other villains are directly related to Gargamel. There is the overweight Balthazar. He is Gargamel's godfather. Ma Gargamel also gets into the act frequently.

> "The Smurfs is unquestionably the most original program currently on Saturday morning and arguably the best kidvid program in several years."
> — Charles Solomon, Los Angeles Times (1983)

Helping the Smurfs are a large number of regular characters. Homnibus is a human alchemist and friend of Papa Smurf. He gave the Smurfs Puppy. Peewit (also called Pee Wee) is another human. He's a young squire and hopeful ladies man. Clockwork Smurf is actually a robot Smurf made out of wood. Also dropping in on the Smurfs are such reliable fantasy figures as Mother Nature, Cupid, The Tooth Fairy and Father Time.

CARTOON SUPERSTARS

OUTSIDE THE VILLAGE

Since the Smurfs first landed in the U.S. via merchandise, they were no stranger to it once animated. In fact they were one of the creations instrumental in the merchandising avalanche that has yet to subside. Found on almost every product imaginable, the Smurfs continual presence no doubt added to their irritation factor among some critics.

There were three issues of an original Marvel Comics comic book series in 1982-83 that were later repackaged in a variety of different formats. There were even Smurf video games, although the most popular items seemed to be the little plastic figures which pre-dated similar cartoon figures.

"The days of showing little elves playing around a mushroom are gone forever."

— Joe Barbera (1964)

The Eighties saw the founding of the Official Smurf Fan Club, and the founding of the Smurf Collector's Club in 1986. 1984 saw the Smurfs licensed to the Taft amusement parks for ten years. Costumed versions of the characters wandered the park greeting visitors. In Northern California's Great America, there is a Smurf Village consisting of small mushroom houses that children can go into.

SUPERSTAR QUALITY

For over three decades the Smurfs have amused and entertained the world. When these little blue creatures invaded America, they charmed a whole new generation. There are those who balk at their simplistic stories or "Smurf speak", but they are forgetting the audience these characters were created for. In the eyes of young children, the Smurfs' fantasies are as elegant as those of Oz and Toyland. When well written and directed, they offer some of the best children's programming seen on Saturday morning. For a long time, things will continue to be just Smurfy.

Smurf figures.

© *Peyo*

"Our job as adaptors has been to preserve the qualities that make Peyo's Smurfs so special, while also using our abilities and experience to allow the animated Smurfs to stand on their own as cartoon stars."

— Joe Barbera

Ad for the US release of THE SMURFS AND THE MAGIC FLUTE.

© Peyo

TOM & JERRY

SELECTED SHORT SUBJECTS: *Cat Concerto, Mouse Cleaning, Posse Cat, Solid Serenade, The Two Mouseketeers*

Superstar Summary

THE STARS: Tom Cat & Jerry Mouse

YEAR OF DEBUT: 1940 (PUSS GETS THE BOOT)

STUDIO OF DEBUT: MGM

SIGNATURE: "Yeow-ow-w!" (Tom's scream)

KEY CREW BEHIND THE STAR: William (Bill) Hanna & Joseph (Joe) Barbera (directors and writers)

CAREER HIGH: The team stars in the Oscar winning (their 6th) THE TWO MOUSEKETEERS (1951) where they fight for food and honor. Jerry gets the food; Tom gets the guillotine.

Tom and Jerry are the ultimate cat and mouse team, and the most honored cartoon characters in motion pictures. This long-running pair have won a total of seven Oscars for Best Animated Short Subject. Only a handful of live film-makers have won more Oscar statuettes than Tom and Jerry. The only other multiple Oscar-winning cartoon characters are Tweety (Pie) and Mr. Magoo, both with two each.

Tom and Jerry's life as Cartoon Superstars has been as hectic off-screen as on. Starting at MGM under the team of Bill Hanna and Joe Barbera, they were then assigned to foreign director Gene Deitch, Warners' Chuck Jones and then back to Hanna-Barbera for TV work before doing a stint at Filmation and finally resting once again at Hanna-Barbera. More than most Cartoon Superstars, Tom and Jerry have had a varied career due to changes in directors, studios and mediums. Their characters have been developed and redeveloped over the past 50 years.

In their classic shorts, of the 1940s and 1950s, Tom and Jerry were some of the most violent of all cartoon stars. In an almost sadistic way, the animators found joy at bringing the most pain possible to Tom. The creators were not content to fall back upon the standard jokes of hitting the characters with heavy objects. Sharp objects ranging from forks and knives to guillotines as well as fire and exploding mice were all part of the arsenal used on Tom. Few 'toons have suffered as much as Tom did. Unless, of course, it is Roger Rabbit, found elsewhere in this book, whose animated adventures can be traced almost directly to the violence found in the MGM Tom and Jerry shorts.

Tom and Jerry are more than a violent, one-joke, cat-chases-mouse cartoon series. The natural cat and mouse conflict inspired many studios, leading to Paramount's Herman and Katnip, Paul Terry's Little Roquefort and Percy and even Hanna-Barbera's Pixie and Dixie battling Mr. Jinks. None of these series have achieved the status of Tom and Jerry.

Tom and Jerry having distinctive, if not firm personalities. Similar to Mickey Mouse, Tom and Jerry are actors who are able to assume roles. They can appear in any situation. Their most common locale is a modern home. But they have appeared in many lands and many different time periods. They've chased each other everywhere from the Wild West (in POSSE CAT) to the Hollywood Bowl (TOM AND JERRY IN THE HOLLYWOOD BOWL). Traveling in time, they've lived as French King's "Mouseketeers" (THE TWO MOUSEKETEERS) and classical composer Johann Strauss' pets (JOHANN MOUSE). They even appeared in several classic MGM musicals opposite such live actors as Gene Kelly and Esther Williams.

A key factor to their personalities is their relationship. Unlike such other chase series as the Coyote and Road Runner, there is a mutual admiration between Tom and Jerry. One even gets the sense that these characters could be friends in a different life.

The Coyote shorts are similar to Tom and Jerry in that the key characters don't speak... generally. Though the rule was for silence, Tom, like the Coyote, did give voice occasionally. Jerry seldom spoke in the shorts, though he did talk and sing with Gene Kelly in the feature ANCHORS AWEIGH.

Tom's voice was always a surprise. There seemed to be no consensus for his sound, so each time he spoke it was different. In fact in SOLID SERENADE (1946) he speaks in four distinctly different voices! A standard, nondescript male voice is used when he's tempting the dog with a stick. He uses a deep French-accent when talking with the female cat. He be-bops a song in a throaty soul style. The final one is a low, growling laugh when he thinks he has cornered Jerry for good.

Still from the Oscar-winning CAT CONCERTO.

© MGM

On top of these voices was the classic Tom scream. This was allegedly done by taking a scream and cutting off the start and finish so only the ultimate force is heard.

Tom is always put in the position of villain. He tries to stop Jerry from getting food. In THE MIDNIGHT SNACK (1941) Tom catches Jerry in the act of stealing food. Tom holds the mouse captive while he, himself, samples the goodies. He throws parties in the house when the humans are gone. He shows off in front of other characters by humiliating Jerry. He is also a very competent mouser. In fact, Tom is a self-confident character. Like Bugs Bunny, he tries to maintain control of any situation.

Jerry is often the foil. At the beginning of each short, he is often seen getting the worst of it. This is a clue to the power of Tom. A trusting character, Jerry is willing to believe Tom when the cat pretends to be friendly. However Jerry is not above taking full advantage of a situation to seek revenge on Tom. In QUIET PLEASE (1945) a dog threatens Tom's life if the house isn't kept quiet. Jerry immediately attempts to wake the dog with any variety of objects from a shotgun to falling dishes. Jerry also enjoys stirring up things between Tom and other characters.

Even though Jerry is the smaller of the two, he is definitely not innocent. In fact some people feel that Tom is a hero in the shorts, representing the everyman trying to put up with little annoyances that continue getting bigger. Even when Tom has obviously lost the battle, Jerry cannot resist creating one more painful moment for Tom.

A GAME OF CAT AND MOUSE BEGINS

Tom and Jerry have gone through many creative hands. The Tom and Jerry everyone knows and loves were created during the golden days of animation at MGM. Bill Hanna and Joe Barbera had just joined the studio and had worked on several pictures when they were teamed on a cartoon featuring the old cat and mouse story. PUSS GETS THE BOOT (1940) featured a very round and shaggy looking Jasper (cat) and an even more rounded mouse.

In this cartoon, the standard set up of the cat trying to catch the mouse is utilized. Jasper ultimately fails and is kicked out for the night. The art style was still similar to the cuter Disney look. The pacing was good, but not noticeably different from other MGM cartoons.

At just this time, Tex Avery had joined the MGM staff. Whether his wild humor and bizarre takes, as in his Droopy highlighted elsewhere in this book, had any direct effect on Bill and Joe is unknown. However, it did show MGM that cartoons didn't have to look like Disney to be successful. Bill and Joe quickly built Tom and Jerry into one of the fastest, most violent, yet loving cartoon series ever created.

During their early years, Tom and Jerry slowly evolved into a true team. The artwork became more and more slick and stylized. Together Bill and Joe created a team not unlike Laurel and Hardy. More than mere adversaries, there is a camaraderie about them. This underlying, at times completely submerged, feeling of friendship, admiration and even concern is apparent in numerous of the classic shorts.

A year after their debut, Tom and Jerry received their first Oscar nomination for THE NIGHT BEFORE CHRISTMAS (1941). It was their third film. Then in 1943 they won the first of their seven Oscars with YANKEE DOODLE MOUSE. The short features them in an explosive (thanks to fireworks) battle

in a basement.

"Some citizens for the protection of children of the world have decided cartoons are evil, that they're violent and full of mayhem. We showed the network folks five of the old Tom and Jerrys and they laughed so hard they had tears in their eyes. Then they said, 'We can't use them. If we put those on we'll get killed.'"

— Joe Barbera

Sensing Tom and Jerry were a hot team, MGM had Bill and Joe crank them out almost as fast as Tom and Jerry battled. By the mid-1940s, they were releasing four to five shorts per year! This rapid release schedule no doubt figured in the ever increasing world of locales and co-stars. This pace continued into the 1950s.

Bill and Joe were assisted in the shorts by a number of top animation talents including Ed Barge, Ken Muse, Ray Patterson, Irv Spence and Jack Zander. Also key to the success of the shorts was the jazzy music orchestrated by Scott Bradley.

For almost 20 years Bill and Joe continued on this one series of fast-paced, still loved cartoons. Seven Oscars later, Bill and Joe were released from the studio in 1957 due to a lessening interest in the studio producing cartoons. Hanna and Barbera then established their own company and began producing shows for TV.

TOM AND JERRY IN PRAGUE

With animation becoming popular on TV, studios began rethinking theatrical shorts. MGM decided to get back into the shorts business. They hired European director Gene Deitch in 1961. Deitch, who had done numerous cartoons including the popular Tom Terrific series, produced over a dozen Tom and Jerry cartoons overseas.

Gene Deitch's Tom and Jerry are definitely different than the classic shorts by Hanna and Barbera. Deitch allegedly only had a few of the classic shorts to show his foreign crew as examples. For that reason, these don't always follow much of the Tom and Jerry legend. They created their own additions to the legend.

Although the shorts were never as funny as the classics, they did have a quirky style all their own. Deitch was able to maintain the inner side of the characters by having them show occasional feelings. One of the more bizarre examples is in MOUSE INTO SPACE (1962) when Tom feels he's caused Jerry to leave. Tom is so full of despair, he takes to the bottle!

Deitch also did some experimentation with the team. Though THE TOM AND JERRY CARTOON KIT (1962) was not really successful, it is an amusing idea and sometimes has gags that pay off.

1962 saw the release of THE TOM AND JERRY FESTIVAL OF FUN. This was a theatrical feature created by editing together a number of the classic shorts of the Hanna and Barbera era. This and the new Deitch shorts proved somewhat successful, so MGM decided to move ahead.

TOM AND JERRY AND CHUCK JONES

MGM then decided to continue making cartoons in the U.S. In 1962 they hired famed Warner Brothers director Chuck Jones. Tom and Jerry were probably the first cartoon characters Chuck Jones ever inherited fully grown. All of his Warners characters were either developed by him (Pepe LePew, Road Runner & Coyote) or still early in their development (Bugs Bunny, Daffy Duck, Porky Pig) when he began working with them.

Jones later said about the series, "I couldn't really draw Tom very well; I had to turn him into a different cat really. So I purposefully said 'The hell with him.' And I tried to keep Jerry attractive personally, more like the Road Runner, in that he never really hurt Tom in my version."

The new team tried to make the concept work, but they never seemed to find the right combination of elements. Jones tried to use some of his Coyote and Road Runner themes, but they failed because Tom and Jerry operate under different desires.

No one can fault Jones for failing to come up to the high standards set over a decade before he took on the characters. Jones does deserve credit for creating some of the most graphically interesting Tom and Jerry shorts with the help of layout man Maurice Noble.

Jones' crew was also the team that removed "Mammy Two Shoes" from the cartoons. Mammy was the maid of the house that Tom lived in. She was generally only seen from the knees down and often shuffled through her scenes. When Jerry frightened her, everything from dice to switchblades might fall from her bloomers. When MGM became sensitive to the issue of racial stereotypes, they had Jones and company animate white legs over the previously black ones.

THE OSCAR WINNERS
(1943)
YANKEE DOODLE MOUSE
(1944)
MOUSE TROUBLE
(1945)
QUIET PLEASE
(1946)
THE CAT CONCERTO
(1948)
THE LITTLE ORPHAN
(1951)
THE TWO MOUSEKETEERS
(1952)
JOHANN MOUSE

Opposite: Poster for THE TWO MOUSEKETEERS.

© MGM

"For example, Jerry might drive a golf ball right through Tom's teeth and all of Tom's teeth would break and fall out. To me, that's pretty painful."

— Chuck Jones

Phil Roman, one of those who did the new legs, remembers the task, "We were brought in and spent days rotoscoping and re-animating the legs so that they would be thin and white; not thick and black. When we asked what they would do about the Black accent, they told us they were going to put a funny Irish voice in. We guessed it was all right to make fun of the Irish!"

MGM again closed their animation studio. It was 1967.

TOM AND JERRY COME TO TV

In 1965, the Hanna and Barbera Tom and Jerry cartoons were put on CBS's Saturday morning schedule. They ran on the network until 1972. Though they were well received in the ratings, parent groups criticized the highly violent nature of the shorts.

> "Hanna-Barbera handled the characters beautifully, much better than I did."
>
> — Chuck Jones

1975 saw the team revived when Hanna-Barbera, now one of the most successful TV animation studios, acquired the rights to produce new Tom and Jerry cartoons for Saturday Morning. Sadly, times had changed... and so had the creators. The team debuted in THE NEW TOM AND JERRY/GRAPE APE SHOW (1975) very much in tune with TV standards.

What Hanna-Barbera did was re-create Tom and Jerry for TV. The pair were changed into a sort of a silent Yogi Bear and Boo Boo. Jerry even ended up wearing a bow tie.

Early Tom and Jerry merchandise.

© MGM

Always buddies, the team wandered around the world. Tom and Jerry would often stare at each other, puzzled, as talking characters babbled on around them. No doubt old Tom and Jerry fans were equally puzzled, if not a little disappointed. Even Joe Barbera commented that he yearned for a return to the old days so that "when a cat chases a mouse, he doesn't have to stop and teach him how to blow glass or weave a basket."

Next to acquire the team was Filmation. They produced THE TOM AND JERRY COMEDY SHOW (1980). This series returned Tom and Jerry to being adversaries, but that was about the only saving grace. Tom and Jerry without speed and violence are not Tom and Jerry. It was like the Marx Brothers without Groucho.

In 1987, Turner Entertainment Company and Hanna-Barbera Productions announced a full length feature animated Tom and Jerry film. During pre-production, the studio admitted they were having difficulty developing a lengthy story for two characters who didn't speak. In late 1989, it was announced that Hanna-Barbera and Turner had put the project on the "back burner."

New for 1990 are TOM AND JERRY KIDS from Ted Turner and Hanna-Barbera. The team seems to have been to the same fountain of youth that the Muppets, the Flintstones and other characters have visited. How audiences will react to them is still not known.

TOM AND JERRY'S CO-STARS

Even though Tom and Jerry were the series stars, their co-stars sometimes garnered as much screen time as the team. Some even went on to their own shorts. The most recognized of their co-stars would be Spike and Tyke. Spike, a bulldog, menaced Tom almost from the start. Originally given a number of names including "Killer," he ended up with the moniker Spike and acquired a son, Tyke. A single parent, Spike was overly protective and proud of his young boy. This pair even starred in a few of their own shorts as well as series of stories in the Tom and Jerry comic books.

Jerry obtained a nephew called Nibbles or Tuffy, depending on the short. This tiny mouse was generally always hungry and frequently spoke. He was more prominent in the comic books as it gave Jerry someone to talk to.

Both characters had a series of relatives who would visit, and who were usually the opposite of their own personality. Tom's relations were often weak-kneed scaredy cats, while Jerry's family tree seemed to be largely made up of tough cat fighters. The notable exception was the almost infant-like Nibbles.

Another semi-regular role was Tom's romantic interest. There was no consistency here. Tom, living up to the Tom cat reputation, was always looking for new ladies.

THE ORIGINAL "TOM AND JERRY"

Actually, Tom and Jerry didn't start out as a cat and mouse. From 1931 to 1933 there was a series of cartoons featuring two humans called "Tom" and "Jerry." This series was produced by the Van Beuren studio in New York. The shorts were filled with wild surreal humor similar to the early Fleischer cartoons such as Betty Boop and Popeye, and silent Felix the Cat cartoons. When the cartoons were later sold to TV, the characters were renamed "Dick and Larry" to avoid confusion with the now famous cat and mouse. Of some interest was one of the writers on that old series... Joe Barbera.

TOM & JERRY

A variety of modern Tom and Jerry merchandise.

© MGM

OTHER LIVES

Tom and Jerry have recently seen a rebirth in the merchandising field, but this cat and mouse have always been around in one form or another. In the 1940s and 1950s there were a number of toys produced of the pair. Today, MGM/Turner is beginning a whole new push to merchandise the characters. To attract new customers, they are updating the characters by dressing them in modern clothes.

They debuted in comic books in the first issue of *Our Gang Comics* (1942). By 1949 they had taken over the title and continued on with it up through 1982. The pair also appeared in a wide variety of children's books. Tom and Jerry also appeal to adults as evidenced by the ceramic figures, music boxes and a very expensive French book devoted to the duo.

SUPERSTAR QUALITY

Luckily, the best of Tom and Jerry are still available to viewers through constant repeats and a growing number of videocassettes. In a way, videocassettes are the best way to view the team nowadays. That way every ax, every live wire, every gruesome action will be found intact. They were the ultimate cat-and-mouse pairing that set standards unreached by most other cartoon characters.

"We asked ourselves what would be a normal conflict between characters provoking comedy while retaining a basic situation from which we could continue to generate fresh plots and stories. We almost decided on a dog and a fox before we hit on the idea of using a cat and mouse."

— William Hanna

WOODY WOOD PECKER

SELECTED SHORT SUBJECTS: *Barber of Seville, Beach Nut, Knock Knock, Musical Moments from Chopin, Wet Blanket Policy*

Superstar Summary

THE STAR: Woody Woodpecker

YEAR OF DEBUT: 1940 (KNOCK KNOCK)

STUDIO OF DEBUT: Walter Lantz (distributed by Universal)

SIGNATURE: "Ha-ha-ha-ha-ha" (Woody's laugh)

KEY CREW BEHIND THE STAR: Walter Lantz (producer/director), Ben Hardaway (writer), Mel Blanc (voice), Grace Stafford Lantz (voice), Shamus Culhane, Dick Lundy & Paul J. Smith (directors)

CAREER HIGH: WET BLANKET POLICY (1948) which introduced the "Woody Woodpecker" song, a phenomenal pop hit and Oscar nominated tune.

oody Woodpecker literally exploded from the screen in his first appearance. Some Cartoon Superstars took several cartoon appearances to develop their personality. Woody immediately established himself as an aggressive, self-confident and wildly funny character. Though he mellowed over the years, his debut showcased the basic elements that made him a star.

That first cartoon (1940's KNOCK KNOCK) introduced probably the greatest distinguishing characteristic of Woody, his maniacal laugh. Its machine-gun-like rapidity was unmatched by any other character. It was the key item that propelled the "Woody Woodpecker" song to such heights of popularity. Walter Lantz often pointed out that even though Woody's cartoons had been shown in over 72 countries, the famous laugh was the only part that is not dubbed. The laugh was a cry of triumph as well as a confirmation of an energetic and unrestrained craziness.

Woody's original coloring was a hodgepodge of bright primary and secondary colors making him a vibrant rainbow when compared with other characters. Later, even limiting his design to the familiar white, blue, gold and fire-engine red still made him stand out. The colors matched his brash, raucous character.

There was never any shyness or hesitancy about Woody. He knew what he wanted and nothing and no one prevented him from trying to get it. He had the supreme self-confidence that he deserved the best simply because he was who he was. The emotional and physical costs to other characters were not even a passing concern to him. If Woody needed gas for his car or food or lodging or the love of a girl, he was unstoppable.

Rarely was Woody the victim who had to retaliate against the machinations of other characters such as crooked insurance salesmen or sadistic shopkeepers. Especially in the early cartoons, it was Woody who instigated the problem and then continued to aggravate the situation. In such conflicts, his moods could swing from hysterical joy to explosive anger. There was the implication that he personally enjoyed these often violent conflicts.

Despite model sheets, there never seemed to be a consensus of agreement on the size of Woody. In some cartoons, he might be as small as a real woodpecker and easily held in a hand. In other cartoons, he would be about three or four feet tall, probably comparable to a Donald Duck. There were even times where his size varied within the same cartoon. However, in the majority of cartoons, he was usually the smallest character constantly challenging physically more imposing antagonists including Wally Walrus and Buzz Buzzard.

He seemed more clever than intelligent and often won because his opponents were slower than he was or less persistent. His attitude never allowed him to admit defeat.

In the early cartoons, Woody was extremely violent and hyperactive, almost a blur of constant movement. Seemingly without bones at times, he was a hard bird to contain as his head could pop out from the smallest opening whether it was a radiator cap or a knothole.

Much as did his long-lived cartoon counterparts, including Mickey Mouse, Woody eventually became domesticated in the Fifties. The wild-eyed, ill-proportioned nuisance of the Forties had his top notch moved forward, bill shortened and body made squatter in an attempt to make him cuter and easier to draw.

Again, similar to other characters, he was cast in the role of surrogate father to young relatives, Knothead and Splinter. Despite his softening, he was still a mischief-maker and irritant to his supporting cast. However, his days of wild extremes were over as he became as much a symbol for Lantz's studio as Mickey Mouse was for Disney's studio. In a medium overloaded with animated mice, dogs, cats, bears and ducks, Woody was the only woodpecker. He overcame poor stories, limited animation and often unimaginative direction to become an instantly recognizable and loved personality.

WOODY WOODPECKER

Woody and Walter Lantz from THE WOODY WOODPECKER SHOW.

© Walter Lantz

THE BIRTH OF WOODY

Before Woody, probably the most popular character developed by Walter Lantz was Andy Panda. Andy was created in 1939 to take advantage of the publicity surrounding the donation of a panda to the Chicago Zoo. In the beginning, Andy was a bright young boy panda bear with a large, gruff, slow father. Andy would have become Lantz's main star if not for a happy accident.

According to legend, while Lantz was on his honeymoon at a cabin at Sherwood Lake, California, his bliss was interrupted repeatedly by an annoying woodpecker. At the worst times, the bird would tap away on the roof.

"I threw rocks at the bird and he would not go away," remembered Lantz. "I was going to shoot him, but there was a law against it."

The legend continues that upon returning to the studio, Lantz regaled his staff with his misadventures. It was decided to use Lantz's experience as the basis of a new Andy Panda cartoon, KNOCK KNOCK (1940). Some version of this story has often been told, usually by Lantz himself to describe the creation of Woody Woodpecker. While a similar incident may have happened to Lantz, the cartoon was released in 1940 and Lantz got married almost a year later, in 1941. Like many character creation stories, it simplifies for the general audience what might have been a complicated process over a long period of time.

There had been four previous Andy Panda cartoons before KNOCK KNOCK. One of the elements that made this cartoon different was the contributions of storyman Ben "Bugs" Hardaway. Hardaway had recently come from Warners where he had been involved in the development of two wild and crazy characters, the early Bugs Bunny and Daffy Duck. In fact, Bugs Bunny inherited his first name from Hardaway's nickname.

There are similarities between the unrestrained but generally good-natured looniness of the early Warners characters and Woody. One example might be the tendency towards quick, erratic, but almost constant character movement.

"After awhile, these characters become no longer characters to me. They're real."

— Walter Lantz

Another connection was Woody's voice. It was supplied by Mel Blanc who had done similar work on Bugs and Daffy. Some people have even suggested that a beginning version of Woody's laugh was heard in an early Bugs Bunny laugh. Blanc had been doing a version of the laugh since his high school days. In a broader sense, Woody's voice, a frantic yet self-assured gurgle punctuated by that 'rat-a-tat-tat' laugh, was unique. The visual and the vocal blended immediately to create a memorable character.

Early Woody designs.

© Walter Lantz

KNOCK KNOCK was to be just another typical Andy Panda installment, capitalizing on Papa Panda's mounting frustration to a problem. Supposedly just like Lantz, Papa Panda's work is disturbed by an unknown pounding sound. The source of the disturbance is a grotesque looking woodpecker who apparently has tormented the father previously. The father's escalating attempts at violence continually backfire on him, leaving the bird unharmed. On the other hand, little Andy, in an attempt to discover whether it is possible to capture a bird by putting salt on its tail, ends up trapping the wacky woodpecker. However, the bird still gets the last laugh.

The lovable but hopelessly middle-class Pandas never stood a chance against this insanity. Woody's brightness made him the star of the cartoon, a fact reinforced by early audience reaction and distributors asking for sequels. Lantz had directed this first cartoon himself, as well as the first solo Woody cartoon entitled WOODY WOODPECKER (1941). (It's also known as THE CRACKED NUT). Woody's forest friends, concerned about his sanity, guide him to a psychiatrist who by the end of the cartoon has been driven crazy by Woody.

WOODY AS A STAR

Director Alex Lovy took over the character for a short while starting in 1942 with ACE IN THE HOLE. A wartime effort, it had janitor Woody becoming a pilot who takes an airplane on an outrageous joyride and ends up back as a janitor. Despite the possibilities of the premise, it lacked the intensity of some of the earlier cartoons.

That frenetic energy was recaptured in 1944 when Shamus Culhane inherited the directing assignment. Culhane's first outing was BARBER OF SEVILLE, considered by many people to be a cartoon classic. It is filled with a fast-paced succession of physical gags as Woody's barber skills are practiced on a pair of unsuspecting patrons. It is with this cartoon that the redesigning of Woody's appearance begins. His color scheme becomes limited and his body modified to be more appealing.

Culhane's work emphasized violent action but the exaggeration of that action reaffirmed the humor in the character. THE BEACH NUT (1944) had Woody destroying Wally Walrus's peace-of-mind and his seaside amusement park. THE RECKLESS DRIVER (1946) finds Woody attempting to renew his driver's license and, after a wild car ride with examiner Wally Walrus, deciding he really wants a pilot's license instead.

In 1946, ex-Disney director Dick Lundy was phased in as Woody's director. Lundy felt that Culhane's work was too wild, even though in retrospect they may have been some of the funniest cartoons of Woody's career. Lundy brought to the series a Disney timing and an almost fanatical concern for lush, soft quality animation.

Lundy still made the woodpecker a bird of action. One of the major differences was there was now a reason behind Woody's behavior. When Woody destroyed an apartment in BATHING BUDDIES (1946), it was because he wanted to retrieve his dime.

MUSICAL MOMENTS FROM CHOPIN (1947) was definitely a memorable Lundy effort. This Oscar-nominated cartoon had Woody and Andy Panda playing piano duets in a barn for an appreciative barnyard crowd. Interestingly, MGM's THE CAT CONCERTO and Warners' RHAPSODY RABBIT explored similar themes during this same year.

Andy is a more dignified performer while Woody pounds away on the keys with nearly every part of his body. An accidental fire on stage forces the performers to rush to finish their concert before their pianos are consumed by the flames.

Woody is a softer character in this film, as he is in most of Lundy's episodes. Even WET BLANKET POLICY (1948) softens such extreme violence as Buzz Buzzard chasing Woody with a huge ax and trying to toss the bird into a pit of alligators. In this cartoon, Woody is atypically the victim rather than the perpetrator.

Special hardcover book showing "The Easy Way to Draw."

© Walter Lantz

"Color's done a lot to make Woody. They hit a red that I've never seen anywhere else."

— Walter Lantz

1950 AND A NEW WOODPECKER

1950 was a year of change for Woody. Lantz closed his studio for a year due to problems with Universal, his distributor. When he reopened, he took over directing chores again. Only Woody cartoons would be released in 1951 and 1952 and would remain the primary releases from the studio for the next two decades.

In 1950, Woody appeared in a short animated segment in the feature film, DESTINATION MOON. It was Woody's function to explain the principles of rocket propulsion, an unfamiliar concept to audiences in those days. This was the first time that Lantz's wife, Grace Stafford, did the famous voice.

She had been doing voices for Lantz's cartoons, primarily the female characters, but wanted to do Woody. When Lantz was auditioning for a new voice actor for the bothersome bird, Grace anonymously slipped in her own taped tryout and an unsuspecting Lantz picked his wife.

Grace's influence on the character was immediately noticeable. She had always felt the character was too extreme and she toned down her vocal interpretation. LaVerne Harding, one of the few female animators at the time, redesigned the character as well. As early as Alex Lovy's tenure, Harding had been assigned the "cute" scenes. In an interview, she confessed she always had more of a feeling for "cuteness than goofiness."

The brash aggressiveness of the Forties was giving way to a calmer, more domesticated attitude in the Fifties and the new Woody reflected this shift. Certainly budget restrictions also contributed to the lessening of non-stop action that had been an important aspect of the character.

By 1953, a new director took over Woody's career. Paul J. Smith would continue directing Woody until Lantz closed his studio in 1972. It is Smith's version of the woodpecker that is perhaps best known to today's audience thanks to their almost continual exposure on TV. At best, Smith was a competent but unexciting director who was always able to complete his cartoons within their small budget. He was not noted for adding character touches to Woody as had earlier directors.

Other than brief periods when such directors as Jack Hannah, who introduced Gabby Gator, Sid Marcus and Alex Lovy did a handful of cartoons, Smith was the primary director of Woody. After 1966, he became the sole director.

Woody's cartoons of the Fifties spoofed popular topics including Westerns (HOT NOON, SLINGSHOT 6-7/8) and science fiction (TERMITES FROM MARS). SCALP TREATMENT (1951) has Woody and Buzz as Indian braves battling for the love of the same Indian princess and Buzz trying to scalp Woody with a lawn mower. WOODPECKER FROM MARS (1956) has Woody mistaken for a Martian when he is scooped up by a flying hubcap from an auto accident while wearing a space helmet to visit a kiddie TV show.

WW ON TV

TV gave Woody a new life reaching a new audience. THE WOODY WOODPECKER SHOW first appeared in 1957. Three of Lantz's theatrical cartoons were surrounded by some new animation and a live action introduction by Lantz, himself. In some ways, it was reminiscent of the format established by Walt Disney with his DISNEYLAND TV series but on a much smaller scale. Jack Hannah directed the live action segments. After a year on ABC, the show's 26 episodes were syndicated for many years.

"Woody was a little wild at the beginning and he was really raucous and loud in all his actions. But he was never as wild as Daffy Duck."

— Walter Lantz

On September 12, 1970, Woody invaded Saturday morning with an NBC show featuring post-1948 cartoons. Due to network restrictions, these episodes were heavily edited. While Lantz vocally maintained that "there's a difference between violence and slapstick," he made the cuts. "We took out all the pointing guns and some of the whacks on the head," he recalled. The show lasted for two years and was revived again for a year in 1976.

In the late Seventies, MGM's financial success in rereleasing Tom and Jerry to the syndicated market encouraged Universal to package the 185 Lantz cartoons for the same market. These cartoons spanned the entire range of Woody's career.

Woody lasted until 1972, an uncommon feat since most studios stopped producing theatrical shorts in the Fifties. In 1972, the last eight new Woody Woodpecker cartoons were released. They were indistinguishable from the shorts of previous years.

In 1979, at the 51st Academy Awards, comedian Robin Williams presented Walter Lantz with an honorary Oscar. An animated Woody, done by Virgil Ross, appeared on the screen to share the honor and thank Lantz.

> **"(Woody) does things you would like to do, but just don't have the nerve."**
> **— Walter Lantz**

WOODY WOODPECKER.®

© *Walter Lantz* PRODUCTIONS, INC.

Studio art.

© *Walter Lantz*

It was an animated event that would later be duplicated by Mickey Mouse and Bugs Bunny many years later.

During the Eighties, Woody and Lantz parted ways. In 1985, Lantz sold his library to MCA/Universal, the studio that had contracted with him for cartoons since 1927. MCA began to fully exploit their new property. 1988 saw a new syndicated Woody show debut on TV. It featured a new title as well as new animation, graphics and music between the cartoons. Woody got his own "900" number so that children could phone in and enjoy an adventure story. He has also appeared in a number of public service spots. He joined many other superstars in WHO FRAMED ROGER RABBIT? (1988).

"Walter once laughed and told me he was one of the luckiest producers in the business. He was always able to pick up top talent who were in-between studios."

— Jack Hannah, director on Woody and other Lantz characters

SUPPORTING CAST

Wally Walrus is a big, fat, bald walrus who spoke in a thick Swedish accent. Wally was the authority figure who was the primary target for Woody's wild antics. Originally, he had two tusks, one of which was broken, protruding from beneath his bushy white mustache. Later, when animation became more simplified in the series, these tusks were eliminated. Wally was usually cast in a role where he was a man of property or prominence, such as an apartment owner or a sheriff. Woody would then proceed to endanger if not destroy this safe little world. Wally's strictness generally prompted Woody to ever escalating extremes.

Buzz Buzzard was introduced in the late Forties to be the recurring villain. He was obviously meant to be tougher and of lower class than Wally. He is best remembered from the Western-oriented cartoons where his bad guy image as an outlaw gunslinger stands out. His crooked neck and large beak gave him a naturally foreboding appearance. Even when he was given such lighter roles as a sailor or a bellboy, there was never any doubt that he was a nasty character.

Woody merchandise.

© *Walter Lantz*

Knothead and Splinter were the bland nephew and niece introduced into Woody's life to create a pseudo-family. They were much more interesting in the comic book adventures.

OTHER MEDIA

Surprisingly, Woody is one of the most merchandised of the Cartoon Superstars, approaching or matching the Disney characters. Woody appears on games, records, books, toys, masquerade costumes and even his own telephone. The

Macy's Thanksgiving Day Parade has had a 75 foot Woody balloon for years. Woody also appears in "Happy Art," a series of oil paintings done by Lantz.

Woody began appearing in comic books in 1942 and received his own comic book in 1947 that ran for over 200 issues. Woody has appeared in giveaway comics and special annuals. He was even more popular in Sweden where original comic book stories with Woody rivaled some of the fabled work of Carl Barks on Donald Duck.

He is popular all over the world. Japan even has a small theme park devoted to him. Woody's image was responsible for taking a low-selling Mexican popcorn and turning it into a best-seller.

Woody model sheet.

© Walter Lantz

There have been many exhibits of Woody including ones at the California Museum of Science and Industry, the Smithsonian in Washington and Universal Studios in California which now has a special store devoted to selling Woody merchandise.

MCA, who now owns the property, promised a new wave of merchandise to tie in with Woody's 50th anniversary in 1990. In June of 1990, it was announced that Woody would receive a star on Hollywood's Walk of Fame during the 1990-1991 season.

SUPERSTAR QUALITY

Though most of Woody's cartoon career doesn't seem to have the boffo laughs associated with other superstars, his energetic personality has won him millions of fans. His large smiling beak is known around the world. His laugh is perhaps the most infectious of all screen legends. Many a slow afternoon has been brightened by the visual of that knotted piece of wood from which Woody pops his head out to ask, "Guess who?"

"I directed several Woody Woodpeckers but it was like following in someone else's footsteps."

— Jack Hannah, director

Superstar Summary

THE STAR: Yogi Bear

YEAR OF DEBUT: 1958 (THE HUCKLE-BERRY HOUND SHOW)

STUDIO OF DEBUT: Hanna-Barbera

SIGNATURE: "I'm smarter than the average bear!"

KEY CREW BEHIND THE STAR: Daws Butler (voice), William Hanna and Joseph Barbera (directors), Warren Foster and Michael Maltese (writers)

CAREER HIGH: HEY THERE, IT'S YOGI BEAR! (1964) — Yogi is chosen to star in Hanna-Barbera's first theatrical full-length feature.

SELECTED SHORT SUBJECTS: *Droop A-Long Yogi, Hey There It's Yogi Bear (feature), Hoodwinked Bear, Show Biz Bear, Snow White Bear*

ogi Bear was smarter than the average bear and certainly more popular as well. While many animated bears have appeared over the years, Yogi stands out as a favorite for all age groups.

Yogi was a big brown bear who wore a hat with the brim upturned in the front. He also wore a white shirt collar with a long, wide green tie. This suggestion of clothing immediately made him highly distinctive and established that he was more human than bear.

Despite this distinction, Yogi definitely did "bear"-like things. He lived in a cave, usually with his smaller friend, Boo Boo—although it had items such as a bed, sheets, and lamps that could be found in a simple home. He tried to hibernate, but was often interrupted by anything from the shooting of a TV Western to the arrival of the seven dwarfs.

He was intelligent and was able to talk, not only to other animals but to people. Yogi often talked in a sort of rhyming pattern. "I think I spy a pizza pie!" or "I have a hunch, here comes my lunch" are two examples of this pattern.

Yogi lived in Jellystone National Park. Although supposedly confined to the park, Yogi would make occasional trips outside the boundaries usually resulting in major problems. There was the time Yogi mistook a sports page headline about a baseball battle between the Chicago Bears and Giants, and so headed to Chicago to even up the score.

When Yogi went to Paris, he was mistaken for an Ambassador and declared war on the country after an outraged chef kicked the catsup loving bruin out of an elegant restaurant.

In the beginning, Yogi's primary motivation was food. Unlike other bears, Yogi didn't like "nuts and berries." He had a taste for the goodies that visiting tourists would bring to the park. He prided himself on actually stealing these picnic baskets until parent groups expressed concern that such a demonstration of thievery might be a bad influence on young viewers. Judging by Yogi's stomach, he was highly successful in his goal as a glutton.

Yogi's not a bad bear. He just believes he can interpret the rules liberally if they happen to interfere with his activities or his appetite. Yogi realizes the rules are for his own protection. He's just not sure he wants to be that protected. Yogi is even sometimes patronizing to authority. Yogi's challenging of Ranger Smith is seen more as a game than an actual act of rebellion. He is genuinely fond of people, especially Ranger Smith who is almost a father figure.

Yogi was not always successful in his many schemes yet always seemed to be the winner no matter what the final outcome. He was actually the first of many good guy "con men" created by Hanna-Barbera. Yogi certainly was the most successful and effective. He performed his cons without malice and never hurt or deprived another character intentionally. Yogi was a very positive and upbeat character who rarely if ever admitted defeat. Generally, he was happy and enjoyed his life which really had few complications.

Although he is not the most law-abiding of bears, he seems to follow his own code of ethics. However, his impish spirit and pride sometimes get in the way of his making a good decision. In some ways, although he enjoys the fringe benefits of being a ward of the government, he feels that he has certain inherited rights that supersede everything else. In the early days, the term most often used to describe Yogi was "nonconformist." Perhaps it was that independence that made him such an audience favorite at a time when most people had to conform.

Yogi and Boo Boo in HEY THERE, IT'S YOGI BEAR.

© *Hanna-Barbera*

HANNA-BARBERA PUT ON THE DOG: THE BIRTH OF YOGI

William Hanna and Joseph Barbera had been working at MGM since 1938 when they turned out the first Tom and Jerry short. In the mid-Fifties movie studios closed their animation units and phased out theatrical shorts. Hanna and Barbera left MGM and decided to start up their own studio.

"The movie cartoon business was dead," recalled William Hanna in a 1961 inter-

view. "The only alternative was television. But everyone we talked to told us we were out of our minds. No one could afford good animation on television!"

In desperation, Hanna and Barbera created a process they called "planned animation," and which today is known as "limited animation." When a character spoke, only his mouth moved. When he walked, only his legs moved. Working with former Warner Brothers animation storymen Warren Foster and Michael Maltese, they tried to create stories that depended more on dialog than action.

Their first success was THE RUFF AND REDDY SHOW. It debuted on NBC as a series for Saturday morning. At that time, Saturday morning had not yet become an animation battlefield. THE RUFF AND REDDY SHOW was treated like the reruns of old movie cartoons that were being aired at the time. A live host sold products, talked to the audience and showed cartoons.

Hanna-Barbera had proved they could produce new cartoons for TV in a cost effective manner. Their next series established a major change in TV animation. The format of the show was three separate cartoons, each starring a different character. Instead of a live host, such as other cartoon shows employed, the show was "hosted" by the animated characters via opening and closing animation. These animated stars even hawked the sponsor's product.

THE HUCKLEBERRY HOUND SHOW officially premiered on October 2, 1958. It was sponsored by Kellogg's Cereals and syndicated to local stations by Screen Gems. It became Hanna-Barbera's first big hit, garnering an Emmy award for its first season. The star of the show was a blue, slow talking dog known as Huckleberry Hound, who was often a hero in spite of himself. The second of the three cartoon segments featured the adventures of two Southern accented mice, named Pixie and Dixie, who battled a cat named Mr. Jinks. The third segment introduced a character who would quickly eclipse the

"Hanna and Barbera are creating children's visual shows and adult radio shows. Turn off the sound and children will enjoy what they see. Turn off the picture, and adults will enjoy what they hear."

— Buffalo Bob Smith, creator of Howdy Doody

main star of the show, Yogi Bear.

INTRODUCING YOGI BEAR

The character of Yogi was born out of many elements. The name Yogi Bear was most likely inspired by the name of the popular baseball player, Yogi Berra. Many of Hanna-Barbera's early series are "pun" heavy. However, there were several other names considered, including "Yo-Yo Bear." In Yogi, there's a bit of Art Carney's sewer worker Ed Norton, from the highly popular THE HONEYMOONERS. Voice artist Daws Butler, who supplied Yogi's voice, captured a similar tone and rhythm pattern to the Norton character when he did Yogi's voice. Even Ed Norton's upturned hat made it on to Yogi's head. But Yogi's personality is far different from that of Ed Norton. In fact, Yogi had more in common with Norton's fat friend, Ralph Kramden, who was always scheming unsuccessfully to improve his lot in life.

Whatever his inspirations, Yogi transcended these beginnings to become a recognizable and loved character on his own. Audiences loved the character whose only goal in life seemed to be getting as many goodies as he could from the "pic-a-nic" baskets that tourists would bring into the park. Feeding the bears, or rather *not* feeding the bears, was a concept familiar to many Americans who had vacationed in national parks.

The first year of the series found the writers and artists still developing the character. The most visible change in Yogi came in his face coloring. Yogi's color separation between the brown and light tan sometimes occurred on only his muzzle, while other times it included his entire face. However Yogi's character was nailed down fairly fast.

Yogi didn't like being cooped up. In the first short produced, YOGI'S BIG BREAK, he is seen trying to escape from the park because he feels trapped. Once outside, though he discovers it is hunting season and desperately tries to get back in. In this very first short, he tells already faithful Boo Boo that he is "smarter than the average ranger." (He would substitute "bears" to that line later.) Yogi is always interrupted in his napping. SLUMBER PARTY SMARTY (short #2) has his winter nap disturbed by an annoying duck. (The debut of a character to be eventually called Yakky Doodle.) Yogi constantly craved food. In PIE PIRATES (short #3) Yogi attempts to get a huckleberry pie out of a house guarded by a dog. He and Boo Boo end up eating inner tube minestrone. Yogi can do anything. BIG BRAVE BEAR (short #6) features gangsters hiding out in Yogi's cave and making Yogi drive the getaway car. He ends up driving over an erupting geyser.

Though Boo Boo appears in these early shorts, their relationship varies. Sometimes he lives with Yogi, other times he visits Yogi's cave. However, Boo Boo is always playing the part of Yogi's conscience. Boo Boo frequently reminds Yogi that "the ranger isn't going to like this." He also finds the ranger when Yogi needs rescuing because a plan has gone wrong.

The success of the cartoons in THE HUCKLEBERRY HOUND SHOW was due to the fact that they were double-leveled. Children enjoyed the slapstick action while adults chuckled over the clever lines. When Yogi pulled Boo-Boo aside to talk about the birds and bees, Boo Boo asked, "Sure, Yogi, what do you want to know?" When awakened by a continual pounding on the door, Yogi states, "It can't be opportunity; opportunity only knocks twice." Shortly before he is shot by

"It's been my experience that it's almost always the original characters who rise to the level of perennial superstar.... (Huck and Yogi) are superstars who never grow old, whose continuing popularity makes possible the creation of starring vehicles for them decades after they first appeared."

— Joe Barbera

Opposite: YOGI'S GANG breaks into the Seventies.

© Hanna-Barbera

"Yogi bear lives better than a million-aire. That's because he's smarter than the average bear."

— Yogi Bear theme song

Souvenir of Jellystone Park.

© Hanna-Barbera

Cupid's arrow, Yogi tells Boo Boo, "Do you think for one moment they would let a curly-headed kid in short shorts run around and shoot people with arrows?" When he and Ranger Smith talk their way into bit parts of a TV western, one of the crew worries until the director tells the staff "who could ruin a TV Western!"

"Our dialog," explained Joseph Barbera at the time, "explains why our animal cartoons have a 40 percent adult audience." That clever dialogue was supplied by two of the top storymen who had worked at Warner Brothers, Warren Foster and Michael Maltese. These writers even recreated variations on some of their classic shorts. For example, Yogi's OINKS AND BOINKS is almost a remake of Bugs Bunny's THE WIND-BLOWN HARE (1949), both written by Foster.

Yogi's popularity was so great that there was a national campaign to nominate him for President of the United States. In some areas, he actually became a write-in candidate. Yogi Bear clubs spouted on college campuses. He became an official mascot for numerous military bases.

YOGI ON HIS OWN AND THE BIG SCREEN

So successful was Yogi that it was decided to give him his own show. THE YOGI BEAR SHOW premiered on January 30, 1961, frequently playing in early evening time slots. It followed the same format as THE HUCKLEBERRY HOUND SHOW and 1959's QUICK DRAW McGRAW SHOW. There were three separate cartoons with animated hosts. To fill out the half hour, two new series were developed. Yakky Doodle, an irritatingly talkative duck, first seen in a Yogi cartoon, was always being protected from Fibber Fox by Chopper, the bulldog. Snagglepuss, the thespian mountain lion, often had to "exit stage left" in order to avoid his nemesis. He also had appeared earlier, in a Quick Draw McGraw cartoon as a sheep-stealing lion.

New titles for this season included BEARS AND BEES which found Yogi selling honey to raise money. Yogi caught crooks disguised as old ladies in DISGUISE AND GALS. In TOUCH AND GO-GO-GO, Yogi's fairy godmother gives him the power to turn anything he touches into a picnic basket... even Boo Boo!

THE YOGI BEAR SHOW lasted until 1963.

By 1962, Hanna-Barbera was receiving at least $1 million a year from its licensing contracts of Yogi and friends. Over $40 million worth of Yogi merchandise was sold each year. Yogi was the spokesbear, and cover feature, of Kellogg's OK cereal. With Yogi being perhaps the major reason for H-B's merchandising success story, plans were made to expand his career.

HEY THERE, IT'S YOGI BEAR was released in 1964. It was the first full-length animated cartoon produced by Hanna-Barbera. Patterned after the highly successful Disney features, the film offered lusher animation than the regular YOGI BEAR TV series. A number of songs were written by Ray Gilbert (who had contributed to a number of Disney features) and Doug Goodwin (who did the songs for a number of top Christmas specials) including the catchy "Whistle Your Way Back Home."

Rather than follow the TV formula of simple situations and gags, the feature was a somewhat complicated string of plot twists. It begins in the Spring as Cindy tries to lure Yogi into her clutches. However, Yogi is too busy stealing picnic baskets. When he's caught and tagged to be shipped to the St. Louis Zoo, Yogi tricks another bear to go in his place.

Yogi becomes a masked bandit and steals more picnic baskets than ever. Cindy, missing Yogi, confesses to the crimes hoping to be sent to the zoo. Once on the train though, she discovers she is headed for a different zoo and is heartbroken. That night her cage falls off the train and she is freed. However it doesn't last long as she gets kidnapped by the mean Chizzling Brothers Circus.

Yogi, feeling lonely and missing Cindy, decides to come out of hiding. He reveals himself to Boo Boo and the pair go to the Ranger station in time to learn that Cindy has been lost on the way to the Zoo. Yogi and Boo Boo break out and track Cindy to the Circus from which they manage to escape, but end up in New York. It's up to the Ranger to rescue them from the top of a skyscraper under construction.

YOGI'S REBORN ON SATURDAY MORN

Despite Yogi's popularity, it was almost a decade before he again appeared in new adventures on TV. His debut on Saturday morning would open a new career for Yogi. No longer would he be the solitary bear at odds with authority. From this time forward he would be mostly seen as a team leader for other classic characters in the Hanna-Barbera library.

In 1972, he appeared in an hour special entitled YOGI'S ARK LARK. It appeared on ABC's SATURDAY SUPERSTAR MOVIE and of all the films shown in this catch-all program, only Yogi's was developed into a TV series. The movie was eventually re-edited into two episodes for a new series called YOGI'S GANG.

The series debuted on ABC in 1973. Yogi had commissioned Noah Smith to construct a huge balloon ship named the "Ark Lark." Yogi rounded up many of his animal friends to join him as he journeyed across the world to fight for environmental and moral issues. Joining Yogi was Huck Hound, Snagglepuss, Quick Draw McGraw, Peter Potamus, Wally Gator, Magilla Gorilla and other Hanna-Barbera characters. Yogi no longer stole picnic baskets. Now he battled foes with names such as Mr. Bigot, Mr. Waste, Mr. Vandal, Mr. Smog and Mr. Cheater. This series also included an element missing from the previous Yogi series: a laugh track so that people would know what was supposed to be funny. Only 17 episodes were made but they were repeated the following year in an earlier time slot.

Yogi didn't need to wait long for his next revival. In 1977, the first two-hour Sat-

Ad for *HEY THERE, IT'S YOGI BEAR.*

© Hanna-Barbera

"Because of the overwhelming acceptance of Yogi Bear, we feel that we're witnessing the making of a modern day legend... we're confident a bear named Yogi will take his place alongside of Rip Van Winkle, Johnny Appleseed and even Robin Hood!"

— William Hanna

217

urday morning cartoon show premiered: SCOOBY'S ALL-STAR LAFF-A-LYMPICS. The series was composed of different segments with a separate half hour devoted to a comedic athletic competition between the Yogi Yahooeys, the Scooby-Doobys and the Really Rottens. The Yogi Yahooeys were composed of Yogi as team leader, Boo Boo, Cindy, Huckleberry Hound, Quick Draw McGraw, Pixie, Dixie, Mr. Jinks, Auggie Doggie, Doggy Daddy, Yakky Doodle, Hokey Wolf, Snooper, Blabber, Wally Gator and Grape Ape. Other than the large purple gorilla, all of these characters were from the early Hanna-Barbera hits and were a nostalgia team competing against the more modern characters in the Scooby-Doobys and some even newer characters created especially for the Really Rottens. As might be suspected with all these characters crammed into 30 minutes, even Yogi could barely get a brief moment in the spotlight. Later, in 1978, these episodes became part of SCOOBY'S ALL-STARS and were still later, in 1980, rerun under SCOOBY'S LAFF-A-LYMPICS.

The Scooby show was an experiment in "umbrella" packaging where a strong character would appear in a segment or two and the remaining segments would introduce the adventures of other characters. This type of "umbrella" format was used in Yogi's next TV outing, YOGI'S SPACE RACE. This series premiered on NBC in 1978 in a 90 minute format. One 30 minute segment was devoted to the race itself, as five teams competed for an all expense paid vacation to Mars. Yogi was teamed not with Boo Boo, but with a new character, Scare Bear, who had frizzy, stuck-out hair and was a coward. Their interplanetary craft was dubbed the "Supercharged Galactic Leader." The premiere episode pitted the teams against each other in a five hundred lap race around the rings of Saturn.

Another segment of YOGI'S SPACE RACE was a 30 minute episode devoted to "The Galaxy Goof-Ups" which featured Yogi, Huckleberry Hound, Scare Bear and Quack-Up, a Daffy Duck inspired character, as a bumbling squad of outer space policemen. They were under the command of Captain Snerdley and did their best to earn their reputation as goof-ups.

Buford, a mystery solving hound, and The Galloping Ghost, a comical spirit, were the remaining elements. This umbrella split apart quickly leaving three separate series which were quickly canceled as well. However, it did give Yogi the distinction of having two different starring series on during the same season.

YOGI BECOMES A HOLIDAY BEAR ON THE AIR

Yogi once again appeared in syndication, and once again in the early evening as the star of a two hour TV special in 1980. Advertised as "more colorful than FANTASIA," YOGI'S FIRST CHRISTMAS got back to Yogi's roots. Yogi, Boo Boo, Cindy and Ranger Smith were back in Jellystone. However, they still had their nostalgic friends in tow as Snagglepuss, Huckleberry Hound, Augie Doggie and Doggy Daddy helped convince Mrs. Throckmorton not to tear down Jellystone Lodge. Even Herman the hermit who is causing trouble gets Christmas spirit in the end.

1982 saw Yogi invade prime time with a network special, YOGI BEAR'S ALL-STAR COMEDY CHRISTMAS CAPER. A plot-heavy half-hour, the story concerned Yogi and Boo Boo going to the city to spend the holidays with the old buddies, Huckleberry, Quick Draw McGraw, Snagglepuss, and the usual group. However, that gang has gone to Jellystone to meet the bear pair. Once in the city, Yogi and Boo Boo team up with a little rich girl who only wants to spend time with her father. The father thinks his daughter has been kidnapped and a chase ensues. Needless to say, at the end the father sees the error of his ways and all have a happy holiday. *Variety* called the special a "half-hour of animated boredom," and it does not pop up with the other TV Christmas specials rerun each year.

In 1983, Yogi began to change from just being a cartoon star to being an animated spokesbear for important topics. His first venture was to assist Southern California residents in getting ready for the big quake. Starring in a special comic book and promotional material, Yogi warned, "An earthquake is no picnic, so be ready and don't panic." His likeness even appeared in the Los Angeles Museum of Science and Industry.

Yogi went back to the syndicated market with new animation in 1985. THE FUNTASTIC WORLD OF HANNA-BARBERA tried the umbrella concept of three different cartoon segments in a 90 minute slot. One of those segments was YOGI'S TREASURE HUNT which again featured Yogi leading some classic Hanna-Barbera characters. This time they used clues to locate hidden treasures. Yogi, as a costumed character, was one of several costumed characters that bridged the show with a series of live action bits featuring them working a TV studio control panel.

> **"At first Yogi was just another pen and ink cartoon creation doing the conventional antics common to cartoons. Gradually, however, Yogi's character projected itself so strongly that we found ourselves recording the doings of a real bear in a real Jellystone Park."**
>
> **— Joe Barbera**

In the Fall of 1987, "Hanna-Barbera's Superstars 10" debuted. Hanna-Barbera announced that they would produce ten two-hour movies for syndication featuring their classic characters. Yogi appeared in three of these efforts. YOGI'S GREAT ESCAPE (1987) sent Yogi and Boo Boo along with three abandoned cubs on a cross-country escape in the mistaken belief that Jellystone would close and they would all be sent to the zoo. YOGI AND THE MAGICAL FLIGHT OF THE SPRUCE GOOSE (1987) had Yogi and his friends touring the famous plane when it magically takes off. The little remembered YOGI AND THE INVASION OF THE SPACE BEARS aired in 1988.

Yogi truly returned to his roots in 1988 when THE YOGI BEAR SHOW debuted as a daily syndicated series. This new series incorporated the classic Yogi shorts with newly animated shorts in the early style. Yogi, Boo Boo, Cindy and Ranger Smith were once again roaming Jellystone and beyond. These new shorts had Yogi voiced by Greg Burson because Daws Butler had died in the Spring of 1988.

As the decade ended, Yogi once again stepped into the spotlight to aid a cause. Yogi became the national symbol of the Drug Abuse Resistance Education (D.A.R.E.) campaign. He starred, along with other H-B characters, in a series of comic books directed at young people. August 16, 1989 saw the debut of a five-minute rap video featuring the famed bruin. The tape was distributed to schools.

Fall of 1990 will find Yogi, again, returning to syndication in Hanna-Barbera's WAKE, RATTLE AND ROLL. This daily mix of live action comedy, music and cartoons is planned to include "Fender Bender 500," featuring Yogi and other classic H-B characters in 4x4 races around the world.

SUPPORTING CAST

Boo Boo was a bear who was much smaller than Yogi. Despite his childlike appearance, he was obviously meant to be older, perhaps more of a teenager. He certainly spoke more like an adult. Although he was often an unwilling participant in Yogi's many schemes, he acted as a voice of reason. He felt the rules should be followed not bent nor broken. His nasal, slow voice almost seemed to predict doom for Yogi's adventures. Still, his affection and respect for Yogi was unquestioned. Despite his own fears and standards, he stood by Yogi even on the wildest of escapades. He shared the cave with Yogi and wore a bow tie that varied in color. He was usually a lighter brown than Yogi.

Cindy Bear was a female bear about Yogi's size who wore a little skirt and a flower in her hair. She spoke in a Southern accent and cared about Yogi. She was classified as Yogi's girlfriend. It was clear that while Yogi cared for Cindy, he was having too much fun as a bachelor to settle down.

Ranger Smith was a black-haired, thin park ranger. Originally the Ranger was only identified as "Mr. Ranger, sir," but by 1962 he had acquired a last name. He took his job seriously including enforcing the rules. Despite the many problems Yogi gave him, Ranger Smith liked Yogi. When the ranger said, "I'm sorry, Yogi," he really meant it. In some ways he was a father to Yogi in that he established and enforced discipline. In one episode, he even forsakes a life of wealth because Yogi seems to be in trouble and needs his help.

OTHER MEDIA

Along with Huckleberry Hound, Yogi was one of the early merchandising gold mines for the new Hanna-Barbera studio. Thanks in particular to the characters' connection with Kellogg's cereals, many toys and related promotional items appeared.

A Yogi costumed character appeared at many retail promotions and traveling shows, such as the Ice Capades. For a while he also appeared at amusement parks owned and operated by Taft including Kings Island, Kings Dominion and Carowinds. He also appeared in Southern California's Marineland. The costume still appears in Northern California's Great America park. Yogi has also appeared in parades and TV commercials. Starting in 1990, Yogi and the Hanna-Barbera characters began appearing at Universal Studios Florida (even in a "thrill" ride) where they help guests rescue a kidnapped Elroy Jetson.

For many years, there have been Jellystone Camp Sites, with Yogi's image, where campers could spend some time. Recently New Zealand introduced a line of Yogi dairy products including Yogi Yogurt.

As an educational tool, Yogi has been used to promote earthquake awareness and bike safety among other issues.

Beginning in 1959, Yogi has appeared in dozens of comic books published by Dell, Gold Key, Charlton and Marvel. Besides these appearances, he has appeared in related Hanna-Barbera comic books and his own comic strip.

SUPERSTAR QUALITY

Yogi Bear remains one of the few animated superstars to come exclusively from TV. His free spirit and con-man ways won the hearts of millions. Even when his material in later years didn't always support him, Yogi could come off like a millionaire. As he would often say to someone being kind to him, Yogi was "one of the good ones, sir."

"He's the joy of the jet set, the hero of the hipsters, the sweetheart of sophisticates."

— Ad copy for HEY THERE, IT'S YOGI BEAR

YOGI BEAR

Top: Souvenirs of Jellystone Park.

Bottom Left: Rare Dell Comics give-away.

Bottom Right: Yogi mugs. The one on the left is from a Sixties Kellog's cereal promotion, the one on the right right from Jellystone Park in 1990.

© Hanna-Barbera

Boring, But Necessary Ordering Information!

Payment:

All orders must be prepaid by check or money order. Do not send cash. All payments must be made in US funds only.

Shipping:

We offer several methods of shipment for our product. Sometimes a book can be delayed if we are temporarily out of stock. You should note on your order whether you prefer us to ship the book as soon as available or send you a merchandise credit good for other goodies or send you your money back immediately.

Postage is as follows:

Normal Post Office: For books priced under $10.00—for the first book add $2.50. For each additional book under $10.00 add $1.00. (This is per indidividual book priced under $10.00. Not the order total.) For books priced over $10.00—for the first book add $3.25. For each additional book over $10.00 add $2.00.(This is per individual book priced over $10.00, not the order total.) These orders are filled as quickly as possible. Shipments normally take 2 or 3 weeks, but allow up to 12 weeks for delivery.

Special UPS 2 Day Blue Label Rush Service or Priority Mail(Our Choice). Special service is available for desperate Couch Potatoes. These books are shipped within 24 hours of when we receive the order and should normally take 2 to 3 days to get from us to you.

For the first RUSH SERVICE book under $10.00 add $5.00. For each additional 1 book under $10.00 add $1.75. (This is per individual book priced under $10.00, not the order total.) For the first RUSH SERVICE book over $10.00 add $7.00 For each additional book over $10.00 add $4.00 per book.(This is per individual book priced over $10.00, not the order total.)

Canadian shipping rates add 20% to the postage total.
Foreign shipping rates add 50% to the postage total.

All Canadian and foreign orders are shipped either book or printed matter.
Rush Service is not available.

DISCOUNTS!DISCOUNTS!

Because your orders keep us in business we offer a discount to people that buy a lot of our books as our way of saying thanks. On orders over $25,00 we give a 5% discount. On orders over $50.00 we give a 10% discount. On orders over $100.00 we give a 15% discount. On orders over over $150.00 we giver a 20 % discount.

Please list alternates when possible.

Please state if you wish a refund or for us to backorder an item if it is not in stock.

100% satisfaction guaranteed.

We value your support. You will receive a full refund as long as the copy of the book you are not happy with is received back by us in reasonable condition. No questions asked, except we would like to know how we failed you. Refunds and credits are given as soon as we receive back the item you do not want.

Please have mercy on Phyllis and carefully fill out this form in the neatest way you can. Remember, she has to read a lot of them every day and she wants to get it right and keep you happy! You may use a duplicate of this order blank as long as it is clear. Please don't forget to include payment! And remember, we love repeat friends.

COUPON PAGE

_____Secret File: The Unofficial Making Of A Wiseguy $14.95 ISBN # 1-55698-256-9

_____Number Six: The Prisoner Book $14.95   ISBN# 1-55698-158-9

_____Gerry Anderson: Supermarionation $14.95

_____Calling Tracy $14.95 ISBN# 1-55698-241-0

_____How To Draw Art For Comicbooks: Lessons From The Masters
ISBN# 1-55698-254-2

_____The 25th Anniversary Odd Couple Companion $12.95   ISBN# 1-55698-224-0

_____Growing up in The Sixties: The wonder Years $14.95   ISBN #1-55698-258-5

_____Batmania $14.95   ISBN# 1-55698-252-6

_____The Year Of The Bat $14.95

_____The King Comic Heroes $14.95

_____Its A Bird, Its A Plane $14.95   ISBN# 1-55698-201-1

_____The Green Hornet Book $14.95

_____The Green Hornet Book $16.95 Edition

_____The Unofficial Tale Of Beauty And The Beast $14.95   ISBN# 1-55698-261-5

_____Monsterland Fear Book $14.95

_____Nightmare On Elm Street: The Freddy Krueger Story $14.95

_____Robocop $16.95

_____The Aliens Story $14.95

_____The Dark Shadows Tribute Book $14.95   ISBN#1-55698-234-8

_____Stephen King & Clive Barker: An Illustrated Guide $14.95 ISBN#1-55698-253-4

_____Drug Wars: America fights Back $9.95 ISBN#1-55698-259-3

_____The Films Of Elvis: The Magic Lives On $14.95   ISBN#1-55698-223-2

_____Paul McCartney: 20 Years On His Own $9.95   ISBN#1-55698-263-1

_____Fists Of Fury: The Films Of Bruce Lee $14.95   ISBN# 1-55698-233-X

_____The Secret Of Michael F Fox $14.95   ISBN# 1-55698-232-1

_____The Films Of Eddie Murphy $14.95   ISBN# 1-55698-230-5

_____The Lost In Space Tribute Book $14.95   ISBN# 1-55698-226-7

_____The Lost In Space Technical Manual $14.95

_____Doctor Who: The Pertwee Years $19.95   ISBN#1-55698-212-7

_____Doctor Who: The Baker Years $19.95   ISBN# 1-55698-147-3

_____The Doctor Who Encyclopedia: The Baker Years $19.95   ISBN# 1-55698-160-0

_____The Doctor And The Enterprise $9.95   ISBN# 1-55698-218-6

_____The Phantom Serials $16.95

_____Batman Serials $16.95

MORE COUPON PAGE

_____Batman And Robin Serials $16.95

_____The Complete Batman And Robin Serials $19.95

_____The Green Hornet Serials $16.95

_____The Flash Gordon Serials Part 1 $16.95

_____The Flash Gordon Serials Part 2 $16.95

_____The Shadow Serials $16.95

_____Blackhawk Serials $16.95

_____Serial Adventures $14.95   ISBN#1-55698-236-4

_____Trek: The Lost Years $12.95   ISBN#1-55698-220-8

_____The Trek Encyclopedia $19.95   ISBN#1-55698-205-4

_____The Trek Crew Book $9.95   ISBN#1-55698-257-7

_____The Making Of The Next Generation $14.95   ISBN# 1-55698-219-4

_____The Complete Guide To The Next Generation $19.95

_____The Best Of Enterprise Incidents: The Magazine For Star Trek Fans $9.95
                                    ISBN# 1-55698-231-3

_____The Gunsmoke Years $14.95   ISBN# 1-55698-221-6

_____The Wild Wild West Book $14.95   ISBN# 1-55698-162-7

_____Who Was That Masked Man $14.95   ISBN#1-55698-227-5

NAME:_____

STREET:_____

CITY:_____

STATE:_____

ZIP:_____

TOTAL:_____ SHIPPING_____

SEND TO: Couch Potato, Inc. 5715 N. Balsam Rd., Las Vegas, NV 89130